never fly over an eagle's nest

never fly over

an eagle's nest

For :: Denny Bowen
joe garner Aug 12 - 1990
Best Wishes - Joe Garner

Cinnabar Press

Nanaimo, British Columbia

1982

First edition December 1980
Sixth printing November 1981
Seventh printing, revised, August 1982
Eighth printing September 1982
Ninth printing February 1983
Tenth printing November 1983
Eleventh printing April 1984
Twelfth printing November 1984
Thirteenth printing April 1985
Fourteenth printing August 1985
Fifteenth printing July 1986
Sixteenth printing July 1987
Seventeenth printing November 1987
Eighteenth printing September 1988
Nineteenth printing January 1989
Twentieth printing May 1989
Twenty-first printing October 1989

Available at most book outlets or order direct from:
Cinnabar Press
P.O. Box 392
Nanaimo, B.C., Canada V9R 5L3

Cover painting and frontispiece illustration by Pat Wright.

Printed in Canada by
Morriss Printing Company Ltd.

Published by
Cinnabar Press
P.O. Box 392, Nanaimo, B.C. V9R 5L3

Contents

Preface

Never Fly Over An Eagle's Nest was written to record a series of events that happened to one family from the early nineteenth century to the present. The episodes and events recounted are true and told as the author remembers and lived them. It covers a period of time from the oxcart to the float-equipped aircraft of the 1940's.

The story is written with a desire to leave a true picture of pioneering and the problems that faced the settlers of this era. It is hoped that the reader will better understand the people of North America who were born before the twentieth century began. This book was also written with the hope that one of the Garner grandchildren will pick up where I have left off and continue the family's story.

I owe sincere thanks and gratitude to the following people:

Paul St.Pierre for his encouragement and criticism, which helped me to get started in a meaningful way.

Gloria Hobson and her daughter Cathy for helping with

the research in the Carolinas and with typing and the general arrangement.

Pat Wright for the illustrations.

Dick Toynbee and his mother for helping with my research into the early days on Saltspring Island, and to all the other Islanders who tolerated my constant insistence on ferreting out the things of the past.

Vange Brossard for constant encouragement and inspiration.

Joyce Baker, with my special thanks for rescuing the manuscript from the fire in the old wood stove on various occasions.

A special Thank You to Mary Purdy, Colin Mouat, and all who attended the first class in the Chicken House School at Ganges.

Also, my sincere appreciation to Peggy St.Louis and Debby Baker for their patience and diligence in reducing my long hand scribble to a readable typed manuscript.

And finally, to Ron Smith and associates, thanks for the most important thing of all: the editing and publishing.

J.G.

Foreword

In the history books the building of this province is associated with the Hudson's Bay company, the Canadian Pacific Railway, the British Colonial Office and an endless progression of governmental negotiations and contracts. What may be overlooked is that British Columbia was built by people.

What is talked about even less is that a great many of these people were runaways. Most of them came from what we call Back East, the name for any region beyond the Rockies. They ran from the sheriff, they ran from wives and other relatives, from the police, from bad debts, from uncongenial memories and, sometimes, from habit. Some of them stopped at the shores of the Pacific only because they couldn't swim or speak Japanese.

The first of the British Columbia Garner family was of this tradition. He was running from the Ku Klux Klan, clutching a bride whom he had kidnapped at the point of a pistol. Not at all the sort of thing one expects to find in

C.P.R. boardrooms or Confederation conferences. Yet his many children and children's children helped shape this land into what we know today. They helped shape it physically, cutting the trees, raising the houses, building dams and factories, and they helped shape it temperamentally, as this book recounts in the chapter about the honorable sport of gambling.

Joe, the author, is a second generation Garner. He has been more or less retired for some years now and has time to shoot grouse in Scotland once a year, reminisce and do a few other worthwhile but non-productive things. We may be grateful that he has put his family history in print. Joe would be the first to agree that he is a better wingshot than a writer, but the story is a great one, a real one and it needed telling.

Joe has written his story plainly and the ring of simple truth is in it. His tone is like the tone of his spoken voice, soft and betraying no notes of surprise. If Grandfather Wash walked here from North Carolina, pushing a half a buggy, well, that was because Wash was a man who enjoyed walking so why shouldn't he cross the continent that way?

Joe is aware, we may judge, that during this century not many children went to work at the age of seven and turned over all their earnings to their father until they reached the age of eighteen. And he must have noticed, even as a very small boy, that most of the Gulf Island children wore shoes and lived in houses with plank floors. Of course, to any child, what his family does is the normal way of life, the other families are the different people. In Joe, much of this uncritical acceptance of an extraordinary childhood seems to have persisted in his later years.

All, it seems, took life as they found it and made good of it, losing neither their dignity, their will to work, nor their sense of humour. None, it seems, wasted an hour of their lives in navel-gazing. The obsessive self-interest of the Me Me Me Generation of the 1960's and 70's must puzzle them all.

They are strong people born to strong family ties. It is good that one of them is telling their story.

Paul St. Pierre

The Wedding

It was three o'clock in the morning of late July, 1903. Dawn was breaking over the little mill town of Whitney, South Carolina. Clouds and humid fog hung low over the landscape. A young man stepped out of the woods and headed down a wagon road that led from the mill towards a boarding-house. He was agile and good-looking. He moved with the assurance of someone used to having his own way. He carried a six-gun.

Tom Edwards was sitting in the kitchen of his father's boarding-house after a long shift at the cotton mill. He was snacking on cornbread, honey and coffee when the man with the gun knocked loudly on the kitchen door and barged in. The only light came from a coal-oil lamp hanging over the table, but Tom immediately recognized Oland Garner and was startled to see the six-gun in his right hand. He frantically searched his mind for some reason why this man would be after him. He had seen his unexpected visitor at dances, playing the banjo and having fun. Oland Garner was wild, he knew, but he wasn't crazy.

"Hello, Oland. What in the world brings you here at this hour?" he said, eyeing the six-gun and trying to sound nonchalant.

"Come to see Lona," Oland answered abruptly. "Would you call her down here?"

"Sure will," Tom said, his brain spinning, and thought, "My God! What's he got to do with her?-- My little sister?"

He eased himself out of his chair, started for the stairs and began to climb them.

"Hold it right there, Tom," Oland snapped, pointing the gun at his chest. "You just stay where you are 'til Lona's down here-- you don't try nothing! If all goes well there'll be no shooting."

"Lo-ona, Lo-o-ona," Tom called softly. There was no response from above.

"Y'all can do better than that!" Oland barked.

"Lona!!" Tom bellowed, his voice startling them both as it filled the house.

"What y'all wantin', Tom?" was the reply.

"Get on your clothes and come down here. Man by the name of Oland Garner wants to see you."

"Well, Lawsie sakes, I'se a-comin'," her dreamy voice floated down.

In a few minutes Tom's sleepy-eyed 19-year old sister appeared at the bottom of the stairs. Her dark hair was brushed off her face and fell almost to her waist. She had donned her best-- a pale yellow polka-dot blouse with a tight high neck, full sleeves and tightly buttoned cuffs, and a long sweeping grey skirt-- but she had neglected to put on shoes. Lona was indeed a very shapely and beautiful southern belle.

Seeing the gun in Oland's hand, she smiled her most appealing smile and said, "Why Olan' Gawna'! What y'all a-doin' here at this unholy hour in the mawnin'?"

Oland fixed his steely-blue eyes on the brother and sister and, without moving his gun from the direction of Tom's heart, said, as much to Tom as to Lona, "Y'all move over to that table and sit down. I have something to say to Lona."

The pair moved nervously to the table and sat. Oland followed, still holding the gun in his right hand.

"Lona, I want you to marry me, and if you don't, I'm going to shoot the both of us right here and now!"

This strange proposal was spoken in a hoarse whisper and, in the tense silence, sounded like a prayer. Lona paled and looked at her older brother. After a lengthy pause, which seemed an eternity to her, Tom said, "Lona, it seems that you could do a lot worse than to marry a Garner in this here town."

Lona looked steadily into Oland's eyes, then asked, "When?"

"Now!" he replied.

"Lawsie sakes! I'se never heard of such a thing!" she exclaimed, "Y'all wait right here and I'll go and put on my good hat and we'll just do that."

Without another word or backward glance, Lona rose from her chair and glided up the stairs to make herself ready for her wedding. A few minutes later they heard her calling, "I can't find no fit shoes to be married in!"

"Woman, you don't have no time to hunt your shoes. Just come as you are. Now hurry, y'hear?" Oland shouted back.

In less than twenty minutes she was back, looking radiant. She was wearing the same outfit, but had braided her hair and twisted it into a bun. She had put on her wide-brimmed grey hat, crowned with a great black ostrich feather wrapped around the brim. She still wore no shoes.

It was past four in the morning and almost daylight when Oland and Lona started walking up the three-mile trail to the Catholic church in Spartanburg, South Carolina. They had walked about half a mile when a young man stepped out of the woods and, without a word, joined them. Lona knew him only as a friend of her brother Tom. His name was Ed and he was a Lawman.

It was five o'clock by the time they arrived at the

15

church. Lona looked up at the building she was to be married in. It stood in a grove of huge Oak trees that cast strange-looking shadows in the morning light. She had never been in a Catholic church before and stood there wondering what weird rites went on inside. She wondered if all the things her Baptist family had told her about it were true.

They walked around to the back of the church. Oland told them to wait by the door.

"I'll just go and see if the priest can't be persuaded to do this little job for us," he said, with just the faintest glimmer of a smile.

In a few minutes he was back, preceeded by a disgruntled-looking man in long night attire. With them was a bright-eyed woman wearing a night-cap and a flannel dressing-gown. The man was Monsignor A.K.Gwynn. The woman was Miss Ella Dillard. She was the housekeeper and was brought along as a witness.

The priest looked too ordinary to do anything weird, Lona thought, so she relaxed somewhat about having to go into the church. The priest gestured to the two ladies to enter and then followed them. Oland brought up the rear, much like a border collie bringing in his cows. Once everyone was inside, Oland swung the door shut, then locked and barred it to prevent any interruptions from the outside.

The priest told them where to stand, then began asking the necessary questions for his records. When he learned that Lona was a Baptist, he froze momentarily. He explained to Oland that he couldn't possibly marry them until he received a special dispensation from the Bishop. "Without it, this marriage cannot be sanctified by the Catholic Church!" Great emphasis was placed on this last sentence.

Lona and the others were startled by the terrible rage that shook Oland Garner. His face turned red and his fierce look cut through them. His eyes filled with anger.

"There are none of us going to leave this room alive

16

unless we get married now! I don't have no time to wait, y'hear? I got six bullets in this here gun, so there's one extra if its needed."

"Now, son, just wait before you commit any sins. I'm sure there is some way out of our problem. Just let me think a moment." The priest was visibly shaken.

They all stood in the sticky silence while the priest had his "think." Finally, he told them the wedding could proceed-- that he would send for the special dispensation.

"I will date this wedding when it arrives," he said. A sigh of relief escaped the lips of all present, the most audible from Oland himself.

Thus, before six on that July morning of 1903, Oland Joseph Garner and Lona Beatrice Edwards-- my father and mother-- became man and wife.

The witness, Ella Dillard, retreated to her quarters wondering if she would ever be the same.

Monsignor A.K.Gwynn returned to his, to pray and worry about the possible repercussions of this, the most unorthodox marriage ceremony he had ever performed. He was unable to rest until he sent for the special dispensation, yet, when he did receive it, he neglected to enter the date in the register.

Their marriage remains the only one in the long history of St. Paul's Catholic church in Spartanburg, South Carolina, which bears no date.

Relaxed and laughing, Mr. and Mrs. O.J.Garner headed up the trail towards home. Ed Glover, their other witness, was ahead, acting as a scout. They hadn't gone far when Oland holstered his gun and, gathering his wife into his arms, said, "Well, Honeychile, the best is yet to come!"

Lona felt excited and pleased, never guessing what else was in store for her that day.

As they turned off the trail to take a back road to the house, she began to wonder why there was such a need for secrecy. A hundred yards along the road another young man joined them.

17

"Y'all got married fine?" he asked.

"We sure did!" Oland exclaimed, patting his six-gun. "You have no trouble here?"

"No sir. There's been no stirring in the woods, and I don't see no trouble for y'all today."

Lona wondered what on earth could be the matter. She was about to tell Oland not to worry about her father when his younger brother, Frank, appeared out of nowhere.

"They've been setting things up since you left and they're packing the wagon now. We'll be ready to roll afore dark!" he said.

"The wagon? Ready to roll? Where's we gonna roll to, Olan'?" Lona asked, panic rising in her voice.

Oland looked at her a long time before answering.

"Honeychile, you and me and our brothers all are leaving for Canadi today-- to the land where milk and honey flows!"

Without another word he turned and walked on up the trail.

In a daze, Lona followed him through the heavy trees along the riverbank, across a log bridge and into the lower fields of the Garner place.

Up at the house she could see a lot of commotion. Her brother Tom and sister Cecil were there, along with Oland's brothers and their younger sister, Josie. A few other friends and relatives from both families had been hastily gathered together, making a party of about twenty people. Everyone was carrying things from the house to the wagon, to which a team of greys was hitched.

Oland's mother made a great fuss over Lona when she arrived. They had a little cry together.

Being a woman of the south, she offered no resistance when given the news of her sons' imminent departure.

The previous evening, Oland had told her that he would be bringing home a bride in the morning and he wanted a party lunch for them before they went away. During the night, Mrs. Garner went alone to the chicken-house and wrung the necks of five of her precious

18

chickens that had survived the flood about six weeks earlier. As she plucked and cleaned them, she thought of the hard times she would have to face after her boys had gone. She would have to find some way to finish rebuilding the corn mill that had been washed away.

"Surely they won't be gone long," she kept telling herself. She was glad when people began to arrive. She kept everyone busy until the meal was set out under the big Oaks.

Oland's friend, Ed, had gathered enough Lawmen to guard the roads and protect the guests assembled at the newlyweds' reception. He told Oland that they would be able to do this for only about four more hours-- then the party would have to break up.

Lona couldn't help but wonder why they were in such a big rush to leave for Canada, but "why" was something only the Garners, the Law, and the Ku Klux Klan knew.

The festivities proceeded without incident. Oland remained secretive about which part of Canada they were going to and how they were going to get there.

It was a day of mixed feelings for Lona. The excitement of marrying the mysterious and romantic figure of Oland Garner was marred by the loss she felt as she contemplated leaving her family and everything familiar behind her.

As they were finishing their lunch, Ed called Oland aside and told him that he and three of his best friends had decided to ride with the wagon until they were safely out of the danger area.

After a tearful farewell, the five young people piled into the democrat. Lona, Oland and Frank were perched on the high front seat, with Earl and Ed riding on the back. If it had not been for the side-arms worn by all four boys, they could easily have been mistaken for young people on their way to church. Two young deputies rode about a hundred feet ahead of the wagon and two followed a short distance behind. The team started out at a brisk walk and soon broke into a steady trot that would cover about six miles in an

19

hour. It was a long, gruelling trip to a cousin's farm, some sixty miles to the north.

The only ones who enjoyed it were Lona and perhaps Frank, who tried hard to maintain a serious manner about the expedition. The others never relaxed-- every turn in the road could be a possible ambush, every passing cart could be someone who was after them.

Before daylight the following morning, the group was safely at the cousin's place. Ed and his cohorts said their goodbyes, wheeled their horses around and started their long journey home. The Garners and their team bedded down for some much-needed rest.

For years, the vanishing of the Garner boys and the young bride remained a mystery.

The Flood

On the night of June 5, 1903, about a month and a half before his wedding, Oland Garner went to bed earlier than usual.

For the past two weeks it had been raining steadily and this day was no exception. The roads were impassable. The creeks had swollen so much that many of the bridges were washed away.

His two-room cabin stood on a piece of high ground across the Lawson River from the family home. Two dams built on a level above the cabin had filled to overflowing. He could hear the roar of water above the pounding of the rain on the roof.

Just as he was drifting off to sleep, Oland noticed that the rain had stopped. Heaving a sigh of relief, he soon sank into a deep sleep, to the familiar roar of water sweeping over the dams.

Suddenly wide awake, he bolted upright in bed and, ever alert for intruders, automatically reached for his long-barrelled squirrel gun which he kept loaded and handy on pegs above his bed.

It was black dark in the little cabin. His hearing, long attuned to the sound of nature in this rural environment, told him that something was desperately wrong-- but what?

Then it hit him-- the ominous, absolute silence!

He leaped out of bed into two feet of icy-cold water. When the initial shock passed, Oland realized that it was a flood and rising fast. It had already washed out both dams. He grabbed his trousers from the end of the bed, pulled them on, and then sloshed through the bone-chilling water to the opposite side of the room, groping in the darkness until he located his banjo and yanked it from its place on the wall. He felt the water rising above his knees. With his free hand he felt for the handle of an old suitcase which sat on a trunk against the wall.

All his prized belongings-- six-gun and shells, two fighting tops, rooster spurs, long blacksnake whip, Ku Klux Klan shroud and baseball mitt, were in that suitcase. He jerked it from its resting place and, holding both arms high, floundered across the room to the door, which was jammed tightly shut by the weight of the fast-moving water. With superhuman effort he managed to worm his way through and onto the porch. Oland almost fell with the force of the current that surged against him as he lurched outside. He fought his way to the end of the porch and then stepped into water above his waist. Carried downstream by the muddy water, Oland worked his way towards higher ground in back of his cabin.

As the dawn broke on that morning of June 6, 1903, Oland Garner witnessed an incredible sight. Wet and shivering, he watched the churning flood rise steadily to the very eaves of his cabin. Before his unbelieving eyes the water lifted the little building off its foundation, pulled it into the current and swept it out of sight around a bend. In a daze he watched the panorama of nature gone berserk-- huge trees, horses and cattle swept by, some still alive and struggling to free themselves from the wreckage-filled water. Walls of houses and barns disintegrated, lonely rooftops separated from their bodies and floated in the wake of the flood.

Added to his misery was the sight of a family of six being swept by, clinging to the roof ridge of their own home, their terrified faces leaving an indelible mark on his mind. He knew this family as neighbours, their names, likes and dislikes, almost as brothers and sisters. Helpless, he watched them being swept out of sight, not knowing if they would ever reach safety.

Oland worked his way up the hillside to a point where he could see the sloping fields of the Garner farm on the far side of the river, now being slowly swallowed by the rising water.

Unable to warn his family of the approaching danger, he sat helplessly and watched as the water crept up around his mother's house. By this time it had reached the floor of the porch and Oland desperately wished that one of the fools inside would wake up.

"Couldn't they hear the water sloshing around the sides of the house," he thought, "and the banging of the uprooted trees and logs?"

The water was well above the porch before he saw his brother Ed appear in the doorway. A few minutes later his three brothers, wearing just their pants, and his sister and mother in long nightgowns, spilled onto the porch. His sister Josie clutched something. It was her doll.

They splashed their way to the end of the porch. Earl jumped into waist-deep water and held up his arms for Josie, then carried her through to higher ground. She stood shivering while Ed rescued their mother, whose nightdress floated above her waist. Earl then returned for young Frank and together they worked their way back to safety.

It was cold, but soon they all stood around a fire.

The water stopped rising about two feet above the floor of the porch.

As he sat waiting for the flood to subside, Oland thought about the damage it had brought to his family. The corn mill and dam were gone, water had ruined most of the hay and probably swept all the topsoil from the crop-producing meadows. The timber was gone. He wondered how much damage had been done to the family home. His 'still', carefully hidden in the hillside back of his cabin was destroyed. His fighting cocks, penned downstream, were most likely drowned.

He was least concerned about the livestock. The horses were in the barn and the cattle free to seek high ground. But all in all, the scene that presented itself to Oland's eyes was a horrific mess. He speculated on the amount of time involved to restore the family place to some semblance of its former condition.

"Maybe I really should join Dad in his wanderings-- see the country-- go up to Canada and never worry about all the things settled people worry about," he thought.

Later, a man told of how he had stood, along with many others, on the riverbank and watched helplessly as a woman and a small boy drowned before their eyes.

Most victims of the flood were left with only the few possessions they had had time to grab before fleeing from their homes. Many drowned inside their houses because the flood descended in the form of a tidal wave: high, swift and deadly.

In the aftermath of the flood, Oland found one small consolation. Up in some bushes he spotted two of his fighting cocks who had miraculously escaped. He decided to leave them there until he found some way of getting them back to the farm.

Later that morning he searched for a place to cross the river and found a skiff that had lodged in some bushes. He saw two other men heading towards Spartanburg. He hailed them and all three hauled the boat upstream to the road crossing opposite the Edwards' boarding-house. Using long poles, they were able to cross the river in safety. Oland then hiked to the farm.

Meanwhile, Ed had waded out to the water-logged house and found food and clothing. After the family was fed, they decided the best thing to do was to walk down to the Edwards' boarding-house, stay there and do what they could to help.

Arriving, they found scores of people milling about. Some were sleeping on the floor, others huddled in bunches talking excitedly, some were crying. Clothes were drying everywhere. Lona and Cecil Edwards were comforting the crying women and bustling around the kitchen making coffee and biscuits for everyone.

The Edwards' boarding-house, perched on a high knoll about forty feet above the normal river level, was spared the ravages of the flood. The family had stood at their windows watching the water inch its way up the hill until it was barely two feet below the floor of their back porch. The tension was horrible. They had no way of knowing where the water would stop.

The wagon road skirted the boarding-house, then dipped into the river bed (which was now covered with thirty feet of water), crossed the bridge and rose again to continue into Spartanburg. The road had formed a sheltered bay and people with rowboats could pull in from the main stream at this spot and get safely ashore.

Years later, Mother would talk about the many people, stranded and homeless, she and her sister fed and provided for.

"Lawsie sakes," she would say, "there musta' been over a thousand biscuits ate."

Their supplies lasted for two days. By that time the water had receeded to the point where folks could get across the river and into Spartanburg, where food and lodging were available.

The Spartanburg newspaper reported the flood as being the worst calamity to hit the area, bar none, including the Civil War.

The Garner boys saw the desperate need for some kind of transportation, so the flat-bottomed skiff Oland had found was used as a small ferry. They strung a long rope across the river and, spelling each other off, two at a time, around the clock, they pulled the boat, loaded with people

25

and supplies, to safety. Frank, the youngest, had the time of his life working with Oland.

The Edwards' boarding-house was near the east terminal of their makeshift ferry. The boys were welcomed in at all hours for coffee and goodies.

It may be that, during this crisis, Oland saw for the first time how capable and efficient the pretty Lona Edwards was. Something may have clicked in his ever-active mind. Who knows? Maybe plans were being made? A conventional courtship? A marriage? Dad often said he drank too much coffee and ate more good hot biscuits than he should have during the ferry-boat operation.

"They sure knew how to make a fella' feel welcome!"

After the flood subsided, local workmen built a temporary bridge which did away with the necessity for the little ferry. The Garner boys hauled the skiff high up on the bank by the boarding-house and, turning it upside down, painted a sign and nailed it to the boat. The sign read:

GARNER'S EMERGENCY FERRYBOAT
READY FOR THE NEXT CRISIS

The flood had a lifelong effect on Lona and Oland. Years later, Dad explained to us "younguns," (when we complained about packing buckets of water up the steep hills), "Those creeks are sure nice to hear and look at. It's when you can't hear them that they're dangerous. Only safe place to be is high up on a knoll."

Going back to look at the place where I was born made me realize just how strong this flood fear was in the minds of my parents. The little log shed stood at least 100 feet directly above a small creek, on a knoll. When I say small, I mean SMALL! It dried up in summer except for a few clear pools and one could jump across it in the floods of winter!

Three Pumpkin Seeds

Ever since the flood, the Garner boys had been jumpy and running wild, especially Oland and Earl, the two oldest.

Instead of making their own, the boys were hauling in a couple of loads of white lightning every week from their contacts in the hills of North Carolina. The round trip was over thirty miles. They had a democrat and a fast team of greys.

To ensure their horses would be fresh, Oland would go up in the afternoon of one day and leave the next morning, getting back to Whitney before noon.

Most of this whiskey was kept in gallon jugs. The jugs, or demijohns, had a finger handle on each side of the neck. These handles were used to tie the cork so it couldn't blow off in transit. To sample the contents, you had only to untie the cork, give a little shake, and pow!-- the jug was ready. The accepted method of sampling was to put the jug over your right shoulder and, using your left hand, pull the neck around. This way a good mouthful could be taken without spilling a drop, leaving your right hand free in case you had to shoot a snake or something. Most men carried side-arms in those days.

These mountain stills were located where they could be guarded day and night, usually in a box canyon. No one went in or out without being challenged. Making or selling moonshine was illegal. All transactions were strictly cash whether buying or selling.

By now the boys had reconstructed their rooster fighting pit and put together a grandstand of sorts. A good supply of white lightning was laid in. The first rooster fight since the flood was planned for the month of July.

A big crowd gathered for this special occasion. Competitions started about ten o'clock, with the poorer birds being fought off first. There were both black and white competitors. It was a rule of the game that blacks competed against blacks and whites against whites. To have allowed mixed competition would certainly have led to bad feelings, economic hardship, and perhaps bloodshed.

By noon most of the negroes had finished their fights. The winners were beginning to celebrate and bet on the white contenders.

There was one big white lad by the name of Oswald who had some pretty good fighting roosters. He had won quite a bit of money. His first two fights had been easy victories so he was hitting the jug and getting loud.

By now Oland and Earl had a fair amount of cash in their pockets. They were making sure that everyone had plenty to drink. Up to this time the betting had not been heavy. A two-dollar bet, substantial in those days, was about as high as things had gone.

Oswald won his third fight, collected his bets and was bragging.

"My birds can whup anything here that's got feathers."

Oland's reputation as a rooster fighter was well-known and respected. He had for competition only the two roosters which had survived the flood. These were among the best of his former flock of over twenty birds. During the month before the fight he had brought them to the peak of condition. He fed them cooked whole corn as a main diet, supplemented by raw meat and apples cut into small pieces.

Oswald challenged Oland. "Y'all a-goin' to eat your roosters or fight them? Look more like eating birds to me."

"Y'all don't have enough money to see my birds fight!" Oland snapped back.

This exchange and challenge got the attention of everyone. It was common knowledge that bad blood existed between these two young men.

Oswald took another long pull on his jug and walked over to where Oland was now inspecting and massaging his two fighters.

"I've got twenty dollars that says my bird can whup yours," Oswald declared, in a voice loud enough for everyone to hear. A bet of this size jolted the crowd to silence. Oland stood up and faced Oswald. In tense, even tones, he said, "Boy! My birds don't even come outta the cage for less than thirty dollars."

Oswald shouted, "That's a bet, boy! Let's get at it!"

The judges called. "Get your birds here and weigh in for the next fight."

Oland's bird was lighter than Oswald's but appeared in better condition. Both birds weighed over five pounds apiece.

"Places!" the judge called.

Oland and Oswald took their positions on opposite sides of the ring, facing its center. Each held his rooster in such a way that the feet didn't quite touch the ground. The contenders watched the judge carefully, ready to release the fighters the instant the word "Pit!" was barked.

Oland always told us that by watching the judge's lips closely, a split-second advantage could be gained in the release of the bird. That fraction of a second was all-important. If a contender was slow on the release, his rooster could be killed because of it.

Oland's release was a split-second before Oswald's.

His bird caught its opponent before it was a quarter of the way to the center of the ring, driving it back against the side and sinking a steel spur in the base of its neck. Blood spurted from the gash and the fight was over. This brought loud shouts and cheers from a, by now, well-oiled crowd. Everyone was busy for the next few minutes collecting and paying bets.

After returning his rooster to its cage, Oland walked over to Oswald and held out his hand for the thirty dollars. All eyes were upon them. "I'll just take my money now, Mr. Loudmouth," Oland said, with a grin.

"Just hold on there for a minute!" Oswald yelled. "Y'all got another rooster. I'm willing to double the bet for the next fight!"

Oland gave Oswald his cold stare for a long minute before he answered. "Y'all know what you're saying? You got that much money here?"

"Y'all worry about your money and I'll look out for mine. Is you gonna bet or not?"

"Y'all got yourself a bet, mister, and you better have money enough to pay up."

The judge called for the birds to be weighed. Bets were being made by everyone, but none as big as those made by the competitors.

This time Garner's bird had a slight advantage. Both birds looked in perfect fighting condition.

After the steel gaffs were fitted, each took his position at ringside. The judge yelled, "Get ready!"-- and then-- "Pit!"

Both came out evenly and met in the center of the ring. They flew into the air, slashing at each other with beaks, spurs and wings. Oswald's fighter got a spur into the other rooster's breast and drew blood. A cheer went up from the Oswald backers. As they met again in mid-air, Oland's rooster sunk a spur under the wing of his opponent, drawing more blood.

The two gladiators fought head to head for almost a full minute-- loss of blood was sapping the strength of both gamecocks. The next rush put the Garner bird off balance and it looked as though it was all over. Somehow, this game rooster regained its feet, though badly gaffed in the neck. When the next charge came he leaped into the air, sinking a lucky spur into the head of his opponent. This was instant death. It was all over.

Oland picked up his bird, licked the gashes with his tongue to stop the bleeding, placed the exhausted rooster in its cage and walked over to collect his winnings.

Oswald was having another big slug of white lightning when Oland held out his hand for the cash. Someone picked up the dead rooster and put it into an old sack.

"I'm not going to pay you that bet and you can't make me! My daddy's head of this here Ku Klux Klan and I'll get him to handle you if you don't like it!"

The crowd was silent. Oland's backers gathered behind him. Oswalds friends took the opposite side and it was plain there was going to be a showdown.

Oland placed his hand near his six-gun and told Oswald, "You'll pay your bet now or you won't be walking outta here."

"I'm not paying and I'm walking out." He turned to go.

"Hold it!" Oland snapped.

"Hold it yourself!" was the reply, and Oswald went for his gun.

Oland beat him to the draw, shooting him in the right leg below the knee. Oswald fired as he collapsed, the bullet whistling harmlessly over Oland's head. As he was falling, there was a second shot from somewhere. The second bullet struck Oswald in the right shoulder. He went down and lay very still. No one knew if he was dead or alive-- there was a lot of blood. Some of Oswald's friends got him into a buggy and headed for the Spartanburg hospital.

The shooting split the gathering into two factions, the Ku Klux Klan and Oswald's gang against the Garners and their backers. There were over fifty men facing each other across the rooster pit. Many of Oswald's friends were following his lead and not paying their bets. Blacks and whites stood shoulder to shoulder.

In less than a minute the battle was raging-- clubs, knives, razor blades, fists and feet flying. There was cursing and blood everywhere. The noise of the fight had attracted the attention of the law. Some young officers rode in on horseback and fired a few shots over the heads of the fighting mob. When they saw the law, everybody scattered for the woods.

From then on things happened fast, at least as far as the Garners were concerned.

Although Oland was a member of the Ku Klux Klan, before dark that evening a hooded man handed him an envelope which contained three pumpkin seeds. This meant he had three days to clear out or be killed. Earl, Ed and Frank were also handed envelopes containing five seeds; this meant they had five days to leave or be horsewhipped-- twenty lashes each. Any lash stroke that did not draw blood had to be repeated.

The brothers did not think 12-year old Frank could stand this much punishment. They decided not to sleep in their house that night. They stayed out in the woods because there was no way of knowing whether some trigger-happy Klansman would pay them a deadly visit before their time was up.

They now had to make decisions that would change their entire lives. They all knew enough about the Ku Klux Klan to fear its deadly threats. There was no doubt that the Klan's warnings would be implemented, and most likely ahead of time, because of Oswald and his father's authority.

As if in answer to a prayer, a young man rode into the yard. It was Ed Glover, Oland's lifelong friend.

Ed and Oland had ridden together on many of the Klan's missions. These missions were night rides, when men and horses were completely covered by shrouds. Only the ears and eyes of the horses were visible. The riders wore high peaked hoods with holes cut in for vision. A black veil hung over the rest of the face. Oland said later you could be riding next to your own brother and not recognize him. Few words were spoken on these missions.

The overall ruler of the Ku Klux Klan in the United States was known as the Grand Wizard. Second in command was the Grand Dragon, while third in line was the Exalted Cyclops, and fourth was the Grand Giant, followed by the Grand Titans. Finally came the regular members who were known as Ghouls.

The Grand Titans ruled over the dens. Each den had its own regulations and usually represented a town or complete district. Oswald's father was the Grand Titan of a local den.

The name Ku Klux Klan was derived from the Greek word *kuklos,* meaning 'circle'. This is why all Klan hoods and shrouds show a black circle with a cross inside, plainly displayed front and back. These symbols are also worn on both sides of the horses' shrouds. The cross was supposed to symbolize the religious aspect of the Klan.

The 'firey cross' was always burned on some high place just before a mission. The cross-burning struck terror into all in the community.

With the mix-up after the rooster fight it was like a civil war around Spartanburg and Whitney. The law was siding with the Garners against the Ku Klux Klan.

Oland and Ed held a meeting with Mrs. Garner and the three younger brothers. It was decided that the boys should clear out the next day and head for Canada. Then Oland made his announcement.

"I'm not going to leave here unless I marry Lona Edwards and take her along as my wife."

Mrs. Garner was the first to speak. "Oland," she said hesitantly, "What about your engagement to Ethel, that rich Catholic girl?"

"Can't do it now. I've decided Lona's the only one in this whole world for me." Oland replied.

"How are you going to do that afore noon tomorrow?" Ed asked, and added, "That's about as long as y'all can

33

count on being safe round here.''

It was now that Oland took complete charge. He outlined how he would go to the Edwards house, see Lona, and ask her to be his wife. He told Ed, ''I'll be on the trail to the church by five o'clock in the morning or not at all. I don't intend to leave her for nobody else.''

It was these events that lead to Lona and Oland's marriage, and to their subsequent escape to Canada.

The Journey North

In Knoxville, Tennessee, the Garners boarded a train heading for San Francisco. They transferred their belongings to a rail car and then sold the democrat and the team of greys. This gave them some much-needed extra cash. A few uncles, aunts and cousins were on hand to bid them goodbye when the train headed northwest in August, 1903.

There was concern in the minds of the three older boys. They realized they were facing a new life in a strange country, among strangers, including Indians. To Frank and Lona it was an exciting adventure.

From San Francisco they travelled up the coast by steamship to Vancouver, British Columbia. Accommodation they could afford was scarce, so they bought a tent and camped on the beach at what is now known as Coal Harbour in Stanley Park.

On the first Sunday they all got dressed in their best to attend morning Mass at the Catholic church. This young group, with their southern drawls, attracted too much notice for Oland's liking. The young men paid so much attention to Lona that she and Oland had a big row about it.

That same afternoon they were packed and on a boat headed for the city of Victoria. Here they rented a house on Lawrence Street.

There were plenty of jobs to be had if one was willing to take whatever came along. The three older boys worked on the docks that fall and winter, unloading cargo from the ships and helping with deliveries around town. Oland worked in the Carrs' warehouse and store. (The owner of this store was the father of Emily Carr, the well-known Canadian artist.) Frank got a job as a delivery boy for a butcher shop just up the street from where the Empress Hotel now stands.

There was money enough coming in-- wages were double what they were in the southern states-- and their house was comfortable.

The boys adapted well to their new environment. They participated in the local sports, especially baseball, and Oland sometimes played his banjo for dances and socials. They all enjoyed the hunting and fishing.

Deer and grouse were close by and plentiful, cod and salmon almost at the back door. An old Indian taught them how to dig clams and catch large crabs. One of Frank's favourite sayings was, "When the tide's out, the table's set." No one ever went hungry. No license of any sort was required to fish and hunt for the open market. Blue grouse sold for fifty cents per brace and a good buck deer fetched two or three dollars. All were happy with their new life even if homesickness did rear its head during the first winter.

In the fall, Earl, Ed and Frank rented their own house and started batching; although Lona always seemed to find time to bake a few hot biscuits and extra goodies for them.

In the spring of 1904, the three younger Garner boys got itchy feet and just had to go back to Vancouver and up the Fraser Valley. This was the area their father had described as the real "land of milk and honey." They bought a small farm near New Westminster and farmed for about two years. Eventually, homesickness and their mother's pleas to come back to the south got to Earl and

Ed. They sold their farm, and then visited with Lona and Oland on Saltspring Island.

On the day of their departure for Greenville, South Carolina, in 1906, Ed's parting words to his older brother were brief. "Oland," he said, "you know all that milk and honey Dad told us so much about?"

"Yes," Oland answered.

"Well sir, most of it turned out to be big stumps and lots of rocks." He turned up his calloused palms. Then they were on the boat and away.

Though they suspected that memories of the chicken fight and shooting had dimmed, they never went back to Spartanburg. Greenville and Spartanburg are some sixty miles apart and that was close enough. There they set up their own businesses and prospered, married southern girls, and raised their families.

With Frank it was different. He was 16 and the hunting and fishing had become a way of life. He moved back in with Lona and Oland for a while; then he got his own place and stayed on for some ten years. Then, he too returned to Greenville, married, started a grocery business and raised a family. Like brothers Earl and Ed, he avoided Spartanburg. There were people in that town they neither trusted nor cared to be near, partcularly after dark.

In the spring of 1904, Oland was able to get a good job on the construction of the Empress Hotel. He worked on the foundation and right on through to the finish of the framing. He explained to us, after we were old enough to see the hotel and appreciate the beautiful grounds, how the site had orginally been a smelly mud bay.

During the construction, Oland became friendly with the Beddis brothers: Jack, Harry, Charlie and Lionel. They invited him and Lona to visit them on Saltspring Island. Harry was a first-class finishing carpenter. Jack, who was known as Captain Beddis, was the eldest, and skippered a sailing ship some sixty feet long and heavy enough to carry many tons of cargo. The Beddis family had built this boat completely. The boat was almost finished when Samuel, the father, died of pneumonia in 1893. The ship was named *Wideawake*, and plied the waters from Victoria and Sidney, through the Gulf Islands. Saltspring Island, being the largest and most populated, demanded most of the ship's time, taking mail and produce to Victoria and bringing back groceries and other cargo.

Emily, or 'Granny Beddis' as she was known, lived in a big log cabin right near the beach where the outlet of Cusheon Lake runs into the sea. Oland and Lona visited this beautiful beach during the early spring of 1905, travelling both ways on the *Wideawake* and helping with the cargo to pay their fares. To them this was paradise-- then and there they decided that Saltspring would be their future home.

They moved into an empty log cabin known as the Robertson Place at the south end of Cusheon Lake. This cabin was about two miles from the Beddis farm. Here they stayed for a couple of weeks, looking over the general area for a piece of land they could pre-empt. They found a 160-acre block high on a hillside near a small lake that was full of trout. A good stream ran through the property. They decided to return the following year to start their homestead and build a new life.

Upon inquiring in Victoria, they found that the property would cost one dollar per acre to have it surveyed and obtain title. The full payment of $160.00 was a small problem compared to that of finding a qualified surveyor to stake out the property for registration. It took from 1905 to 1912 to get the final papers and clear title issued.

In 1978, I went to the Land Registry Office in Victoria to check on this transaction. To the lady in this office I gave the only description I knew for the property: *The North half of the North half of Section 79, Central Saltspring Island, British Columbia,* and the approximate date of the pre-emption. She gave me a strange look and said, "You know, I have worked here for many years and have never heard of a similar land description." I produced a tax receipt for the year 1918. She looked at it with a puzzled expression and said, "You just wait a few minutes and I'll see what can be found." About twenty minutes later she returned with the complete history of the property. When I thanked her, she remarked, with a faraway look in her eyes, "They did things much more simply in those days."

After buying their land, Lona and Oland went back to Victoria-- Oland to his job on the construction of the Empress and Lona to prepare for the arrival of her first baby. Ethel Mary Garner was born on the evening of July 12, 1905. She was blonde and beautiful.

My parents were so enthused about the prospect of a new life on their own land that in late September of 1905 they vacated their house, bought a large, flat-bottomed rowboat, piled in all their belongings and, with their two-month old baby, proceeded to row the twelve miles to the 'Wilderness', which was then the name of the Beddis property. It took over ten hours to row the heavy boat and its precious cargo to their destination.

Off the southern tip of Saltspring Island they ran into heavy seas whipped up by a strong north wind and had to spend the night in Cusheon Cove. It was cool, but the weather turned good at daylight and they arrived at the Beddis place just before noon.

Mother always told us Granny Beddis had the warmest cook-stove and could make the best grouse stew in the world.

The Garners stayed at the Beddis cabin while they were packing their household goods, on their backs, up the trail to the log cabin where they had stayed earlier in the year. It was a rough two miles of uphill slogging. The young baby was left with Granny Beddis, but mother took time out to breast feed her every second trip. They lived in this cabin until the end of April of the following year.

During their seven month stay at the Cusheon Lake cabin, my dad helped Charlie Beddis build his new house. It was a large home for those times, built not of logs, but of lumber freighted in on the *Wideawake* from Sidney. The big flat-bottomed rowboat came in very handy, hauling the lumber to shore from the anchored sailboat. Dad would accept no pay for his labour, but it was agreed that Charlie Beddis would help Dad when he was ready to build his own cabin. Mother visited the Beddis home almost every day while Dad was helping with the building, learning more and more about living with nature.

By this time, their young daughter was toddling around and needed lots of attention. Again they moved, some three miles nearer to their future homestead, carrying their belongings mostly by packboard.

A rough wagon road led part way to a log cabin known as the Dukes property. Dukes, who was a batchelor and stone deaf, had moved to Saltspring in 1887, built his cabin and planted a small orchard. He decided to move back to Vancouver when Dad and Mother rented his place. The rent was four dollars a month. About this time my mother became pregnant for the second time.

My parents were excited about moving to this new place. It had two rooms and a wood floor, while the former cabin had consisted of one room and boasted only a dirt floor. They lived here through one winter and spring. Both Mom and Dad told us some years later that moving to the Dukes cabin was like going on a second honeymoon.

Tom was born there January 1, 1907, delivered by a local midwife, Mrs. Rogers. Mother always said she was never exactly sure of the date, but thought New Year's Day was an appropriate day to celebrate the birthday of one's first son, and so this date was recorded on his birth certificate.

An unusual amount of snow fell that winter and the young Garner family was pinned down from early January to March. When the snow melted sufficiently, Dad hiked the five miles to Mouat's store at Ganges to stock up on much-needed food and other supplies. Shortly after, a trail was hacked to their new homesight. In spite of the fact that they did not yet have clear title to the land, they began clearing and building.

In late summer of 1907, my Granddad, George Washington Garner, came to Canada to visit his sons and spend some time with his new grandson, Tom, and granddaughter, Ethel. He stayed about two months, helping my parents cut logs to build a shed for tools and supplies. They also put up a frame for the big tent Dad had bought in Vancouver and proceeded to live in it. Again, the only floor was Mother Earth.

With the coming of September and fall frosts, Mother was having such a difficult time keeping herself and two small children warm in these crude shelters that Granddad offered to take the whole family down to Whitney, South Carolina, for the winter and pay the fares out of his own pocket. Granddad was not one to spend money without good reason. Dad refused, stating, "It will never be safe for me to go back to the United States." He would stay and work on their new house. They agreed that this solution was best, especially for the children. The four travelled by train via Chicago and arrived at their destination in plenty of time for Christmas.

Mother and the two children stayed part of the time with Dad's mother, Alice, and part of the time with Mother's older brother, Tom Edwards. She received no money from Dad, so took in sewing to pay their way.

Ancestors: *The Edwards And Garners*

Mother's forebears, the Edwards, landed in the U.S.A. in 1750, after a seven-month voyage. The original ancestral name was Beam. The Beam line has been traced back to German aristocracy.

Cousin Virginia Green, a Carolinian, traced the family's history and found some royalty related to the Edwards clan. The family crest indicates origins as ancient as the Knights of Malta. The Garners came from England but the family history is not clear.

Less illustrious, but perhaps more interesting, relations include John Nance Garner, second-term Vice-President with Roosevelt, and Jesse James, the outlaw. The connection with the James family resulted when Mother's great-aunt married a Robert James, who was Jesse's uncle. This would make her a kind of "kissing cousin." The legends of the James boys are too well-known to recount. Dad would often tell us how they lived wild lives and sang to us the songs describing their exploits and the death of Jesse at the hands of one of his own gang.

John Nance Garner IV was Dad's cousin. His parents

moved from the Carolinas to Texas, where they lived in a log cabin. He, like Abe Lincoln, rose to prominence from a humble beginning. He was admitted to the bar at the age of 21 and went on to become a county judge before getting involved in politics.

In his early twenties, John contracted tuberculosis and was advised by his doctor, "Get to a drier climate if you wish to live." Taking this advice, he moved further west to Uvalde, Texas in 1893. This proved to be one of the wisest decisions he ever made. Here he lived to the ripe old age of ninety-eight.

He served two terms as Vice-President under Franklin D. Roosevelt, who usually referred to him as "Mr. Commonsense." John was Roosevelt's running mate for two presidential elections, but opposed him for the presidential nomination when Roosevelt sought a third term. John felt Roosevelt's ambitions were unconstitutional. After the nominating convention, he said, "I would have opposed my own brother had he been seeking a third term. Hell, I didn't want the bloody job, but danged if I was going to stand by and watch our traditions being upset by one selfish man."

After thirty-eight years in politics he retired. He was offered a $100,000 a year job to appear on some radio program, but he declined, saying, "As John Garner, I am not worth that much. Any value I have attained as Vice-President of the United States is not for sale."

Garner continued to invest in land, amassing a fortune reputed to be equal to, or greater than, that of his presidential running mate. Roosevelt's wealth was inherited. Garner, through foresight and planning, built his total fortune from $151.60-- this was all he had when he moved west.

As "Cactus Jack," he had a reputation for big poker games and a love of good whiskey, which persisted into his ninety-seventh year. A typical story of his prudence involved one of his poker games. He was caught bluffing and lost a ten-dollar bet. The winner asked if he would

43

autograph the bill so he could hang it in his study. Garner asked if this meant the ten dollars would never be spent. When he found this to be the case, he offered his personal cheque for the amount and asked that the ten-dollar bill be returned.

John L. Lewis, the powerful labour leader, described Garner as "a whiskey-drinking, poker-playing, evil old man." This tickled Garner, so he continued to needle the big labour boss whenever an opportunity presented itself. There was great respect between these two men.

Another anecdote which reveals the individualistic nature of this man concerns his trip to Japan in 1935. It was the Japanese custom that shoes be removed in the Emperor's presence and Garner was advised to comply. He sent word that he was American and would meet the Emperor in the American custom. Later, word came back that the removal of shoes would not be mandatory during their meeting.

In his ninety-seventh year, while being interviewed, he was asked what had been the most important thing he had learned in his lifetime. Without hesitation he replied, "I have learned to forgive all the bad things people have done against me. I hate no man, but I do like some a little better than others."

According to Garner's wishes, the family home in Uvalde is now a museum, operated for the needy people of the community.

Mother's second cousin was Ralph A. Edwards, the "Crusoe of Lonesome Lake." He emigrated from a three cents an hour job in North Carolina. Dad met him in Vancouver in 1912, when Ralph arrived to pre-empt land in the Bella Coola valley of British Columbia. Edwards gained worldwide recognition in the 1920's for his work to save the Trumpeter swans from extinction.

Great-Aunt Eliza was another character who certainly left her mark in the south. She was the first leader of the Suffragettes. She taught senior school and wrote music and was the first person to advocate free books for all school children. She was also the first woman to run for public office in Union County, in an era when women were regarded as chattels, had no say in the shaping of things and had virtually no rights and no vote. Outspoken in her opinion of right and wrong, she was labelled by her male contemporaries as "a witch only fit for burning." Whenever Dad and Mother spoke to us about her, they commented that she was "a hundred years ahead of her time."

There were many stories of her so-called eccentricities, but to pursue her own lifestyle and interests and to challenge the social and political system of her era required a tremendous amount of courage and personal dignity. Today she would be respected as "Ms. Garner" and admired.

Aunt Eliza owned and ran her own farm. She had a special kinship with her honeybees. It was a well-known fact that she could move amongst them without a mask or any kind of protection, take out the honey and move the bees around as she wished without getting stung.

Eliza's brother, George Washington Garner III, was my grandfather. Dad and I met him when he arrived in Vancouver in 1918, after walking the entire distance from South Carolina in 152 days. His clothes were tattered and patched. His beard was white and came way down his chest. With him he had his meagre belongings and camping utensils. All this had been transported in what he called his "Georgia buggy," a contraption consisting of a two-wheeled cart made by cutting and shortening the front axle of an old buggy. A three-foot square by one-foot high wooden box was mounted on the axle and covered with a piece of old canvas. A handlebar attached to the top of the box was used to push or pull the cart. Two legs were braced and fastened to the underside so it could be left to stand and remain level. The hippies of the 1960's could never hope to be in his class.

Dad shook his hand and, after introducing me as his grandson, inquired about the trip from the south.

"Walked every step of the way. Don't hurt anybody to walk a bit," was his reply, in a soft southern drawl.

"Better we unload your cart here. You won't need it where we live on Saltspring Island," Dad was quick to explain.

Now past 60, Granddad had perfect teeth. He carried a short hardwood stick, frayed at one one by chewing on it. This he used after every meal as a toothbrush. He would sometimes put a little salt on the bristly end before brushing. There was no toothpaste in those days.

Like a gypsy, Wash was always on the move. His wife never knew when he would get a yen and just disappear. By 1902 he had travelled to the west coast of Canada, returning to give his sons glowing reports about this new land of "milk and honey," as he called it. I've been told that what finally pushed him from his home for good was the following incident.

Granny Garner had headed out to do some shopping in Whitney but had forgotten her handbag. When she returned a few minutes later to get it, she was stunned to find her husband in bed with their hired girl. She picked up her purse, walked quietly to the kitchen, grabbed a kettle of boiling water, returned to the bedroom, and poured the contents over the two lovers. While they thrashed around in pain, she shrieked from the doorway, "Y'all better be gone before I get back, you hear?" Both had packed their belongings and were gone by the time she got back from the store.

Wash never did come back to stay. Occasionally, he would come back, but only to spend a day with his sons. He and his wife were never reconciled.

Wash usually rested between his travels at his sister's house near Union, South Carolina. When he arrived from his trips he was never too clean, so Eliza did what she thought best, under the circumstances. Her roomy, two-storey farmhouse had a fireplace at each end and a long central hall that divided it into two sections. She would cut down some small bushy pines and lash them across the middle of the hall, confining Wash to one end of the house and herself to the other. When he left, down would come the pines. When he returned, new ones would be put back in place.

Granddad was never concerned about his appearance. He seemed to have money to do whatever he wanted. He told us, by way of explanation, "If you don't look rich no one will try to rob you." He was hit and killed by a truck in North Carolina and buried there as an unclaimed pauper.

With this bit of background it will be easier for the reader to understand some of the unusual things that happened to this family of "New Canadians."

Birth In A Log Tool Shed

February 11, 1909, dawned clear and very cold, one of several such days in an unusual winter cold snap. I've been told by both parents that the ice on Blackburn's Lake was making such noises it could be heard from their little log shelter, over a mile away. Thick ice on lakes always crunches and groans-- sometimes it cracks like a rifle shot. This year it was so thick that Bud Conery had been driving his team and wagon across the lake to feed his cattle. The snow was eighteen inches deep outside the door of the little tool shed. There was no road, as such, closer than a mile away. A pack trail-- yes.

Mother had started her labour in the morning. Because of the extreme cold and the severity of the pains, she had begged Dad to leave some dry wood and go for Dr. Beech. Dad ran the five miles and luckily Dr. Lionel Beech, the only doctor on the island, was at home. They threw a harness on his horse and drove back in his open buggy as fast as the road conditions would permit.

Tying the horse to a tree where the road ended, they threw a blanket over it and gave it some hay; then the doctor and Dad ran the last mile over the snowbound trail. They arrived to find Mother lying on her pole bed with a straw tick for a mattress. (A "straw tick" is a few sacks sewn together and filled with hay or straw.) The fire had gone out because the pains were so bad she was unable to stand. Ethel was three and positively blue with cold. Tom, who had just turned two, was in bed with Mother, fully clothed, including shoes.

The log tool shed, which measured eight by ten feet outside, had open spaces between the logs. A week earlier Dad and Mother had cut up the big tent, hung the canvas inside against the logs and made it fairly tight. This kept them from freezing to death. The log roof was covered with six inches of dirt and straw. The floor was clay and frozen solid, even under the bed.

Ethel and Tom usually slept together in a homemade hammock that hung from the roof logs. Under normal conditions it was put away in the daytime. This day it still hung in the corner, leaving just enough clear space for three people to stand upright if they kept very close together.

The doctor took a quick look and backed out of the only door. "Oland," he said, "get that stove going and heat some water fast." Then to himself, aloud, "May the Good Lord lend us a helping hand on this frosty afternoon."

In no time a pot and big kettle were boiling on the tiny stove, which stood on a pole stand covered with a piece of metal. Two inches of sand over the metal kept the wood in the stand from catching fire.

After some two and a half hours I was delivered-- perfectly healthy in every way, but weighing only three pounds. I was always considered small for my age until I was past ten. (I am now just over six feet and weigh 220 pounds.)

When we were old enough to remember things, Mother would get her big milk jug off the shelf, take a rag doll that wasn't a foot long and put it into this pitcher.

"Now, y'all see that?"

"Yes," we three kids would answer together. Then she would point at me and, with a laugh, explain.

"For the first two months after you were born, I used to put you in that pitcher filled with nice warm water to keep you from freezing to death."

At the age of four I couldn't imagine how a live baby could fit into that pitcher.

Recently, my brother Oliver and I made a special trip to look over the site where I was born. The only remains were some broken pieces of old china buried in the dirt. The place where the clay bank had been dug away was still visible. Most of the bark from the foundation logs was there, covered with moss and pine needles. This gave an outline and location of my birth cabin. The trees we had known as saplings had grown to three feet in diameter and some were over 100 feet tall.

We spent a couple of hours at this "upper house," as we used to call it. We tried to understand why our parents with two young children and one on the way, would live in such isolation.

"Dad had to be hiding out," Ollie said. "You notice how the cabin, sitting on this knoll, overlooks the only trail leading to the place? He would be able to see intruders coming for half a mile."

"It doesn't make sense to me," was my reply. "That creek down there is where they had to get their water."

Part of the old trail down to the creek had dirt steps, dug out of the clay bank. It is so steep that without the steps no one could have packed water up. I could visualize Mother, seven or eight months pregnant, carrying pails of water up that hill. It's little wonder she had a three-pound child.

Later in that spring of 1909, a building bee was organized. Some twenty people were there, including the Beddis family. The wives brought cakes, cookies, fried chicken and roast venison. John Rogers brought a good supply of wine and apple cider. That Rogers brew was reputed to be very good indeed. Mother told me I was the

50

center of attention because no one had ever seen such a small baby. Dad took a lot of good-natured ribbing from the men. John Rogers teased, "Oland, you just about got your seed back with that one!"

It cost one dollar to get a birth certificate in those days. Mine was issued some six years later-- Dad could see no reason for wasting a dollar if I didn't make it. He was always a frugal man.

I've been told the work bee lasted two days. With the logs and shakes already cut, the roof was on by dark of the second day. The bee was like a big outdoor picnic, with lots of good food and drink. It was a great day for the Garners. They moved into this brand new two-room cabin complete with plank floor. They had packed in another stove, piece by piece. It was cast iron and had a goodsized oven and four lids. Mother said things went along much better for the next year.

By the summer of 1910 she was pregnant again with sister Margaret. My parents realized that here was no place to have another baby. Together they located a new homesite a mile nearer the road and started to build again. With picks and shovels they cleared a rough wagon road to the site. A log bridge had to be built over the creek. Dad hired a team and wagon to bring in lumber and other necessary building materials, another big tent and another stove. The stove that they had packed in on their backs piece by piece finally rusted away in that upper house

Uncle Frank was now 18 and very capable. Harry Beddis came over and stayed to help with the building. Wilfred Seymour and other neighbours helped when they had time.

Mother cooked for us three children and all the men, doing the washing and mending in her spare time. How she managed will always be a mystery to me. The family slept and cooked in the tent. Uncle Frank and Harry Beddis had a makeshift roof to sleep under. It consisted of five panels of shakes nailed to poles and put up between four fir trees that stood about ten feet apart in a square. Four logs cut into seven-foot lengths and halved together at the corners formed a smaller square under the roof-- this kept their bedding dry. The square was then filled with moss and some balsam boughs and a canvas was stretched over it. They put their blankets on top and here they slept for some six weeks. Workmen certainly didn't demand as much then as they do today. Until it was torn down, we children used this shelter for a playhouse.

By working seven days a week, daylight till dark, the men put up the frame of our big four-room log house, complete with roof and stone fireplace. It was floored with rough-sawn fir lumber. Windows and doors were cut in and made to work perfectly. There were two good-sized bedrooms upstairs, each of which had a big window in the gable end. A wide verandah was built around three sides. A rough staircase led up from the main room. The stairs had a landing halfway up that made a right angle turn and came out into the largest bedroom. There was a door to the smaller room. In late August, the family moved in.

Mother was now just over four months pregnant with Margaret. She often told us, "Once we were moved in and had a road connection to outside, I had me some peace of mind at last. What a blessing!" she would sigh.

The creek was much closer than at the upper house, and there was a level trail to it. By now Ethel and Tom were old enough to help carry water.

Margaret Maude Garner was born January 11, 1911, weighing eleven pounds. Even now that would be a big baby. She was brought into this world perfectly healthy and with only Mrs. Rogers attending as midwife. There would be no hospital on Saltspring for another three years.

Dr. Lionel Beech had come to Saltspring Island from Victoria in May, 1904, to take over the practice of the famous Dr. Gerald Baker, who was leaving for the Cariboo District. Dr. Baker was the first doctor to live and practice on Saltspring. He came in 1897 and left in 1904. He was an ardent sportsman and had heard the deer and trout were larger and more plentiful in the Interior.

Dr. Baker spearheaded the building of the first hospital in Quesnel, B.C., while Dr. Beech donated land for the Lady Minto Hospital at Ganges.

The Oxen

It was the spring of 1913. Dad bought a team of oxen with yoke and harness. They were reported to be trained to work. The first time he tried to pull stumps they broke the wooden 'U', or 'Ox-bow', that goes up under the neck and through the oak neck yoke. Without this there was no way to hook the team to the speaders for pulling heavy loads. You couldn't just walk to a store and buy an ox-bow. First, they cost money, and second, stores did not keep them in stock. Dad and Frank had a couple of long discussions on how to replace these necessary contraptions. These talks usually took place after dark in front of a roaring fire in the big fireplace. Tom, Ethel and I were keen listeners and suggested things that were impossible. We were anxious to get the oxen back on the job so we could hear Dad yelling, "Gee! Haw! Woo!" or, "Geddi-up!"

Frank always used a lot of swear words and had a hefty chew of tobacco in his mouth whenever he tried to work these critters. Dad would send us children away when Uncle Frank was driving, because Frank could really swear and used a lot of words we had never heard before. We would get out of sight but try to stay close enough to learn the swearing. I was convinced that unless one could swear, there was little or no hope of becoming a professional "ox-skinner." I had already imagined myself as being one of the best "skinners" in the country. A young boy's memory is especially tuned to remember cussing. I recollect one hell of a licking when Dad caught me practicing some of this oxen jargon as I swung his big blacksnake whip and pretended to drive an old charred stump at the back of the barn.

To get back to the broken parts: these U's were made of round cedar limbs. They had to be heated in a steam box and then bent into shape. From somewhere, Dad and Uncle Frank got a piece of six-inch steel pipe about ten feet long and blocked up part of each end with clay and rocks. They filled it about half full of water and set it up level. A hot bark fire was built under the pipe. This was to be their steam box. After the fire was burning well, they left Tom, Ethel and me putting more bark on to keep the heat up. They went into the woods to get the special cedar limbs for bending.

They put three of these peeled limbs in the hot water inside the pipe for about two hours. Then the fun started. Using old sacks to protect their hands, they would pull one out of the hot water and try to bend it around a stump that was about the size of an ox's neck. They had driven two stout stakes in the ground to hold the hot wood in the proper shape. Two of the first three broke because they were not steamed enough. The third one held. After two full days of this, they suceeded in bending five of these cedar limbs into usable U's, or ox-bows. When one broke in the bending process, Uncle Frank would let fly, first with a stream of tobacco juice, then with a string of choice cuss words. I was so impressed by all this that I begged Uncle Frank to let me chew some of his tobacco.

"I got to learn someday," I would coax. At first he refused, saying Dad would not approve. I must have pestered him so much he finally agreed.

He put it this way-- "Next time your Daddy goes to the store all day, I'll teach you." Two days later I was taught.

Dad left for the store early. He had asked Frank to take us over to build some more road. We had started a new road, through a mile of virgin timber, that would take us to the main highway. About ten o'clock we all stopped for a drink of water. Frank needed a "chaw," as he called it. He took a plug of Big Ben from his shirt pocket and bit off what he needed. I was coaxing again, so he took out his pocket knife and cut off a small piece and passed it to me. "There, now try it, but don't tell your Daddy, you hear?" He gave Tom and Ethel a small piece but they didn't like the taste and spat it out. I didn't like the taste either, but if I was going to be an ox skinner there was no other way.

I must have chewed on that tobacco for about half an hour when things started spinning around and I couldn't walk anymore. I spat it out. I was sure the trees were floating up and around, then falling almost on top of me. Everything was moving in a haze. Even Tom and Ethel seemed to float away. Then I got sick. I vomited until it was time to go for lunch.

Uncle Frank must have been very concerned. When I wouldn't or couldn't go to the house, he said he would bring something back for me. I don't know what he told Mother. I drank a lot of water and vomited it out almost as soon as it was down. Eating was out of the question. I lay behind a big log and just suffered. After two or three more big drinks of water going down and then up, by about four in the afternoon I could stand and see things as they really were.

I could not eat a bite of supper that evening. When Frank took out his plug for a chaw later on, I had to run out of the house, because the smell upset me. Once outside I retched and retched, until there was nothing left to bring up. I was put to bed early that night. Both Mother and Dad thought I had eaten something that didn't agree with me.

Frank, Tom and Ethel never mentioned it to anyone. I'm quite sure Dad never knew. Some twenty years later I told Mother what had happened. She thought about it for a while, then said in her knowing way, "You know, son, it might have been the best thing ever happen to you. You'll never touch the stuff all your life." She patted my shoulder and we both had a good laugh. I have never taken a chew of tobacco from that day to this.

The team of oxen worked well and the road progressed slowly but surely down towards the main highway. We used pick and shovel and an old hand scraper, pulled by the oxen, for grading.

Uncle Frank was the powderman, blowing rock and stumps with black blasting powder. This powder was bought in 50-pound green metal kegs. The fuse and cap system was crude but effective. In those days, the fuses were not even waterproof. Caps were made of powder ground very fine and tied on the end of the fuse in a piece of silk cloth. If there was water in the blasting hole, Mica Axle Grease was used to waterproof the charge.

Before we leave the oxen, there is one incident that will never be forgotten and should be told.

Dad had raised a big black and white steer from a calf. Uncle Frank decided he could work him for harrowing the fields. The harrows were homemade, consisting of a forked tree with drifts driven through the two forks. The harrow looked like a big 'Y' with spikes for teeth. A two-inch hole was bored through the main trunk that joined the forks together. A heavy chain was fastened securely through this two-inch hole.

Uncle Frank got this wild steer into a stall in the barn. First he put a heavy halter on him and tied him up tightly in one corner. He then proceeded to put an ordinary horse collar around its neck, complete with harness, traces and singletree. This horse harness was borrowed from a neighbour, Wilfred Seymour, who was there to help and watch the fun. He was a strong and rugged young man. Tom, Ethel and I had ringside seats. We had climbed up into the hayloft and could see everything without being seen. We had to laugh silently to avoid detection.

It took the better part of the morning to get the harness

57

on this jumpy critter. There was a violent bucking session and lots of colourful cussing when the harness and traces were tightened. Frank and Wilfred were actually kicked out the back end of the stall. After a long string of cuss words, Frank took a big chew of tobacco. They were waiting for "Spot" to settle down.

Spot had been named by Uncle Frank. He had one large white spot right between the eyes of his jet-black face. This gave the steer a strange appearance from the front end: at a quick glance he looked at lot like a unicorn.

"Let's go in and have a bite of lunch while he gets a little more used to that harness," Frank said to Wilfred.

"Sure wouldn't want to see him untied in the mood he's in," was Wilfred's reply.

When they went to the house we got down from the hayloft and went for lunch too, making sure all the hay was brushed from our clothes. We could hardly wait to see what happened when this steer was hitched to the harrows. We pretended not to be interested while at the table. Mother and Mrs. Seymour asked a lot of questions.

After lunch, Wilfred and Frank got a heavy rope through the halter ring, tying it so there was about eight feet of rope on each side. They proceeded to lead the steer out of the barn, each holding on to an end on opposite sides of his head. He jumped and bucked, dragging the two men around for a few minutes. They were finally able to manoeuver him near the harrows.

"If we get him hooked to that it should slow him down a bit," was Frank's terse remark.

We had climbed on the roof of the woodshed to watch. We felt pretty safe up there. The ox was finally hooked up to the chain. Things happened fast from then on.

When the harness finally tightened and the steer could feel his load move, he became all muscle. He gained speed with every lunge, dragging both the men and the harrow. When the speed was too much for Frank and Wilfred, they let go, falling flat on their faces. About the same time, the harrow went up over some small trees, flew high into the air, and came down on the rear end of old Spot. There was a loud bellow, a lot of dust, chains rattling, then silence. The men got to their feet cussing and brushing the dust and dirt out of their clothes and hair, still heading in the general direction the steer had travelled. When the dust cleared, we could see the steer between two big logs over at the far end of the field. The tops of the logs pointed towards the field and were about twenty feet apart. The butts of the logs were almost tight together forming a long 'V'. This proved to be a perfect trap for Spot. He was jammed in so tightly he could go neither forward nor backward. The logs were much too high for him to jump over.

Somehow, Frank and Wilfred were able to get the harness and harrows clear of the trapped animal. Dad arrived with his team of oxen. He took one look and went for a heavy rope. By putting this long rope around old Spot's body and across his chest, they were able to drag him backwards. It took all the strength of the oxen team to handle this pull. Spot went strange when he got clear of the logs. He headed for the barn in short, stiff-legged jumps and ran straight through the closed doors; then he stopped, shaking, in his stall. Dad put a gate across the end of the stall and went out to talk with Frank and Wilfred.

."Y'all still think he could do any work?" Dad asked.

They both spoke at once. "No sir, never!"

"Well, we will just leave him where he is. We'll feed him up a bit, then hang him up."

Two weeks later he made beef. The Seymours bought half and we kept the rest. It seems I remember hearing remarks like, "good flavour, but a bit tough maybe."

Tom, Ethol and I got the job of grinding the hamburger. There were several big pans of chunks of hamburger meat. Dad and Frank also butchered a fat pig the same day they did the steer. We used one piece of fat pork to every three pieces of lean beef. When I say lean, I mean *lean*-- the meat was sort of blue and shiny. With the added pork and spices Mother used, some very tasty hamburger was produced.

The manual meat-grinder was attached to the heavy table top. It was hard to turn the handle, which was about a foot long. When a really tough piece of old Spot got stuck in the worm, it took two of us to turn it on through. This was my first introduction to a water-blister. By the first evening of grinding, there was a dandy between my thumb and forefinger. It felt good just to rub it at first, but when it got too big and tight, Mother and Dad came to the rescue.

"No problem," Dad consoled. He also had a word of praise for me for working so hard. Mother produced a needle and heated the sharp end red-hot over some glowing coals from the fireplace. With her holding my hand tightly, Dad slid the needle-- which was cool by now-- under the thick skin of my hand and tapped the water out of the blister through this little canal. Although I winced, it didn't hurt at all.

"Now it will heal up without peeling off, or getting infected," Dad assured me. Mother pulled my hand to her lips and gave the blister a kiss. "Blisters always need that for good luck," she said.

This lesson is still remembered and used whenever a blister gets too big and tight.

Neighbours

From 1910 to 1918, the Seymours were our closest neighbours both in distance and association. This family lived in the old Dukes cabin until Wilfred, the oldest son, married. Dad and Uncle Frank then helped him to build a house. It was of lumber and had three rooms with a big fireplace. Their daughter, Vera, was born there in 1910.

Wilfred had two other brothers, Carl and Dudley. These two stayed with their mother until they went away to war. Dad and Wilfred hunted a lot together. It seemed they were always dividing deer and grouse. Whatever they got was always shared evenly-- it didn't matter who shot it.

Our families visited a lot, borrowing food, supplies and equipment from each other when needed. I can remember walking the half mile of bush trail between the two places many times, returning a can of sugar or flour, or maybe a wrench or froe. On the way home I usually carried something Mother needed. Arriving at the Seymours' when it was cold, I would be given hot cocoa and cookies, or, on a summer day, wild blackberry pie and cool lemonade. Clara

Seymour was a very good cook and housekeeper, and besides, I liked to stay around to tease Vera.

An event still clear in my mind is Canada's Declaration of World War One, on August 4, 1914. England had made her declaration some six days previously, but somehow the news got through to Saltspring the same day. Wilfred and Carl had been working at Ganges Harbour and had heard about the news during the morning. They both quit their jobs and were back home before noon, to pack their bags before leaving for Victoria, where they would sign up for the duration. Dudley was only fifteen, but stood some 6 feet 6 inches tall and weighed over 200 pounds. He had packed his bag, fully aware that he had to be eighteen years old before he could be accepted as a soldier. That day all the Seymours came to our house with a gallon of John Rogers' best wine to have a farewell drink with Oland and Frank before meeting the boat at Fulford Harbour.

Clara and both children came with the men. Donald, their son, was still in diapers. Clara had brought along a big roast of venison and some pies which were still warm from the oven. There were drinks all round for the grown-ups and milk for the kids. This is the one and only time I ever remember Mother or Clara taking a drink. They each had a small glass, then proceeded to make their men and children a real feast.

Our garden was at its best. We gathered new potatoes, peas, carrots, green beans and half a dozen heads of crisp lettuce. We picked a bucket of peach plums for dessert. While the women cooked, the men talked and drank. When the wine ran low, Dad produced a bottle of good brandy and a 40-ounce crock of overproof rum. Needless to say, the men were feeling pretty good by sundown. They decided to make a night of it-- they would leave at daylight to catch their boat.

Clara and the children would stay on at their house and our family pledged themselves to see that things were going okay while the menfolk were away at war. Later on in the day Frank decided to pack his bag and go along with the Seymour men.

By sunrise next morning, everyone was up, dressed and fed. The men left, Dad going along to help carry the heavy packs down as far as Fulford Harbour. It was a five-mile walk. A launch was waiting to take them on to Sidney. There they would board the train to Victoria. Clara was sobbing as she kissed her husband goodbye.

Dudley and Uncle Frank were back home in less than a week — Dudley turned down because of his age, and Frank because he was an American citizen. Carl and Wilfred were put into uniform and were overseas for more than four years. They were both discharged as sergeants. Carl was awarded the Distinguished Service Cross for bravery during the battle of Vimy Ridge. Wilfred was badly wounded and had a rough experience with mustard gas.

While Frank got himself into the American army, Dudley joined the forces in Vancouver in the summer of 1915. Dudley lied about his age-- he had learned his lesson in Victoria. He was, by this time, 6 feet 9 inches tall and weighed over 250 pounds. I guess he looked old enough. He was said to be the tallest man in the Canadian Army. He became a celebrated sniper and was known throughout Canada for his marksmanship. Badly wounded in 1917, he was discharged with a silver plate in his head and problems from shrapnel in his abdomen.

While the war was on, the Seymour home burned to the ground. Mrs. Seymour had left a fire burning in the fireplace when she came to visit Mother. Everything was lost except what they wore. Mother invited the family to stay with us. When word got around about the house burning, it seemed everyone on the island was ready to help.

Dad organized a building bee. There must have been over fifty people helping. There was lumber, nails, a stove complete with pipe and chimney, tarpaper, roofing, two beds with flannelette sheets, blankets, pillows, clothes, dishes, knives and forks, spoons, pots and pans, towels, soap and even a table and chairs complete with a handmade table cloth. All this arrived by horse and wagon. The cleared land was completely filled with horses, buggies and wagons.

The ladies put up a great lunch and an even better supper. By nightfall there was a two-room house ready to live in. The outside was only tarpapered, but the inside was quite finished and comfortable. Mrs. Seymour and her children slept there that night. Tom and I went over with Dad next morning to put some finishing touches to the house and cut some wood. The woodshed had burned but the outhouse was still there and usable. As I recall, Mouat Brothers store had donated most of the lumber and nails. Everything else was given by the other people of the island.

We were very fond of the Seymour family, yet, in the fall of 1917, a strange thing happened. We, as children, were completely involved.

Prices were high and money scarce. The families who received the monthly cheques from the War Department were the only ones with money to spend. For over two months, Mrs. Seymour and her children had come over to visit. They arrived before lunch and stayed till after supper, and were invited to share both meals. Clara never brought anything along that would help out as far as food was concerned. The Garners, now with six children, were short of money. Dad and Mother had many long discussions as to what they should do. Mother finally made the decision for all of us. She called us together and gave us our instructions.

"None of you are to say a word to Vera or Donald about staying for supper this evening. They got more money than we have so I'm not going to keep feeding them every day unless they're willing to chip in a bit."

We knew Mother was dead serious. She didn't want to offend her neighbour but she couldn't go on this way.

Next day the Seymours arrived half an hour before lunch. Places were set for them at the kitchen table. Ten people sat down for lunch as usual. When it came time for the evening meal, Ethel and Margaret set seven places only. Mrs. Seymour looked at the table and knew something was wrong. Everyone was unhappy about this awkward affair. Mother told us to start our supper. She then walked over to Mrs. Seymour, who stood by the kitchen door, waiting. In her nicest voice and with a smile, she said, "You know, Clara, we just can't afford to go on supplying meals unless everyone chips in a bit one way or another."

Mrs. Seymour left in a big huff with her two children. She even forgot to take along their coats and hats which hung in a closet behind the door. Mother had a cry after they had gone. This upset us all so much we couldn't eat a thing.

Next day there were no neighbours at mealtime. Dad and Mother were very upset. They thought they might have acted wrongly. We all missed our friends and wondered if they would ever come back.

The next morning we were going about things as usual when we heard a lot of commotion at the barn. This was where the trail between the two homes passed. We went up to see what was happening. It was the Seymours. Donald and Vera were pulling their loaded play wagon and Mrs. Seymour had her arms full of packages. They were all smiling happily. They had walked the four miles to Mouat's store in Ganges; this would have taken a long day. There was a box of chocolates for Mother and a big bag of candy for us 'younguns'. There was lard, canned fruit, flour, sugar, raisins, spices, all they could haul, and, believe it or not, two plugs of Big Ben were wrapped with the chocolates, for Mother. She and Clara hugged each other and wept a bit. The two families had never been closer. Needless to say, there was a real feast that evening.

From then on there never was the least bit of friction between the two families. All had learned a valuable lesson. I even stopped pulling Vera's pigtails.

A little later there was another episode that involved Dad, Dudley and Ethel. It was the summer of 1918 and

Dudley was back from the war. Ethel had just turned fifteen but looked mature and grown up for her age. Dudley had come over to the farm and invited her to go to some social at Ganges. They asked Dad's permission and he gave it. A few days later when Dudley came to pick up Ethel for their first date, Dad called him in and sat him down by the kitchen table.

"Young man," he said, "I hope your intentions are honourable."

"Sure are," Dudley replied.

Ethel and Dudley left arm in arm for the three-mile walk to the Mahon Hall at Ganges. It was a whist drive affair with supper afterwards. Anyway, Dad waited up for them. It must have been about midnight when they came in. Tom and I had a knothole in our bedroom where we could see, one at a time, what went on in the kitchen. We had noticed that Dad seemed edgy and worried. He had the family Bible laid out on the table.

Then he loaded his 45-70 rifle and stood it by the door. When the young couple arrived, Dad met them at the door and invited Dudley to "step inside and sit down at the table." He told Ethel, "It's time you were in bed some two hours ago, young lady."

She hurried up the stairs without a word.

Dad looked Dudley in the eye and handed him the Bible. "Now, young man, I want you to swear on this Bible that my daughter's in the same condition as when she left here."

Dudley was embarrassed, but took the Bible and said, "I swear what you said to be true." He kissed the Book, picked up his hat and was on his way.

He never asked Ethel for another date, though they seemed very fond of each other.

I never expect to understand some of the things Dad did. One thing is certain-- it did not pay to argue or cross him. His temper was unpredictable, always. I'm sure he would have used that 45-70 had he got a wrong answer. I'm also sure Dudley had no doubts as to what might happen

66

either. Dad could stand under Dudley's outstretched arm and was less than half his weight. Both men had great respect for each other. Neither pushed too far, but neither backed off.

Tom and I were very close to Dudley. He taught us to shoot both rifle and shotgun. In those days no plug was required in pump guns. You could fire six shots without reloading. When we hunted, I would always keep as close to him as safety would allow, so I could watch his every move when a covey of grouse exploded out of some fern or salal patch. If there were five grouse he would kill the five; if six, all would be down before the last one was out of range.

I would ask, "How in the world can you shoot birds so close and not blow them to pieces?"

"Easy," was his reply. "Just take a wing or head off while they are close up, then shoot the other two or three straight on." If he ever missed, I was not around to see it. He was the fastest and most accurate man with a 12-gauge pump gun I have ever seen. On straight-away shots he could tear off a wing either left or right.

We rarely had a dog along. My job was to pick up and carry the grouse. Needless to say, this man was my hero. If we camped out, as we often did, Tom and I would clean and cut up the birds. We always took two big cast-iron frying pans along. We two would have one grouse each for supper while Dudley ate at least three. About this time we started calling him 'Tiny', and the name stuck for the rest of his life. Especially in logging circles, he was always known as Tiny Seymour.

Dudley taught Tom and me how to play poker. He loved the game, especially stud.

"If you want to win, never drink booze."

"Cards have no eyes," he would explain, "so you have to bluff once in a while. All you need to win is lots of money and plenty of patience." He was rated as an above-average player.

To say this man was handsome would be a gross understatement. He was put together like a heavyweight boxer, with a dark complexion and jet-black curly hair. With his height he didn't look overweight at 300 pounds. He had learned how to dress in England. All his clothes were made to measure, especially designed to complement his unusual height and physique. He had been introduced to, and used, some of the best tailors in Europe.

"My ladies usually paid the bills," Tiny explained. "They made sure I had the best."

Even his shoes were a problem. He wore a size sixteen, and these had to be custom made. To me, Tiny will always be remembered as quite a man.

He was in France for his eighteenth birthday. On that day he was rummaging around in a church that had been hit by artillery. He found three full gallons of overproof rum. He proceeded to bury the jugs near some big trees. He marked the spot in his memory. In his sixty-fifth year he made a special trip back to France, dug up the rum and brought it back to Vancouver where he shared it with his war comrades at one of their annual get-togethers.

Dudley and his wife lived out their later years in the town of Courtenay on Vancouver Island. He died there, a very wealthy retired truck logger.

Soon after arriving home from the war, Wilfred and Carl moved to Ganges Harbour and built new homes with assistance from the Soldiers' Settlement Board. Wilfred and Clara spent their last years in Vancouver.

At this time our family left the old log house to move closer to Ganges where there were better schools and shopping facilities.

School Days

While we were living and growing up in our farmhouse, we felt we were a fortunate group of children. Things Dad didn't teach us, Uncle Frank did.

My first day of school was in early September, 1914, at the Divide school in the middle of Saltspring Island. The school overlooked Blackburn's Lake to the south and up to the Divide Mountains in the north. Ten pupils were needed to qualify for a teacher. That's why I started at the age of five and a half, being the only one available to make up the required number. Dad was a trustee on the appointed school board of three.

Miss Morris, our teacher, taught all grades from one to eight. She also taught us singing and dancing. We could all do the Highland Fling and the Sword Dance before her year was up. The Divide school had its own small organ which she played for songs, dancing and the Christmas concert.

Miss Morris boarded with us at the farm. Mother charged her ten dollars per month for board. This fee included her laundry. Her breakfast was served at seven each morning at a separate small table in the front room.

The teaching salary was sixty dollars a month, and I think a good portion of it probably went to buy shoes. The six-mile round trip to the school every day on gravel roads seemed to wear the leather soles off in about five or six weeks. She would leave for the school a good half hour before us, to walk the three miles. The young Garners usually ran most of the way. We didn't want to walk with the teacher anyway. There would be nothing to talk about and besides, it would seriously curtail our investigations of snakes, frogs, young deer, trout, birds' nests and so on. I had a fair collection of moths and butterflies and was always trying to catch some new species.

My first public embarrassment came that Christmas. I had memorized and rehearsed to perfection, " 'Twas the night before Christmas and all through the house, not a creature was stirring, not even a mouse." That was to be my contribution to the concert.

With all the parents and young brothers and sisters watching, I froze and could not utter a sound. I ran off the stage and out into the dark to hide in the woodshed. This practically ruined the concert. Everything came to a stand-still until I was hunted down and brought back inside. It took all the parents and children over half an hour to find me. There were no flashlights in those days, so lanterns and lamps had to be lit. I expected Dad to give me a licking so I sobbed with embarrassment and fear. Mother consoled me and I was allowed to stay at her side the rest of the evening. My embarrassment was so great that to this day it is almost impossible for me to face an audience or give a speech.

That year was not all bad. I caught my first trout on Easter Sunday. We had been told we could go fishing that day, providing we finished all our usual chores, such as getting in wood for the stove and fireplace, cleaning the barn and chicken-house, etc. Uncle Frank showed us how to cut long willows for fishing poles, and how to get wrapping string and bent pins all put together so that when an angleworm was put on the bent pin no hungry trout could

70

resist it. I was five years old then and almost grown, or so I thought.

We planned to fish in Wakelin's Creek. The creek that flowed through our farm joined it about a half mile below, then flowed on down into Ford Lake, which was full of pan-sized rainbow. We crossed Wakelim Creek on an old split cedar bridge, coming from and going to school. There were some broken places in the deck and we could look down through the holes and see the trout that stayed under the bridge. It seems to me there were a dozen little ones about three inches long and one "biggie" between five and six inches. From the day we knew we could go fishing, I planned how to catch this monster trout.

Every day I dug some worms out of the garden and put them in a pepper can with a bit of moss and black dirt. For a week I fed the trout that lived under the bridge. The small ones always came out first and usually gobbled up all the bait before the big one would show himself. This would never do if I was going to catch old "biggie."

The second day a plan hatched in my mind. The first worms were broken into small pieces and thrown in the south side of the creek. When all the three-inchers were on that side gobbling up the pieces, a couple of larger, livelier worms were dropped in the middle and deepest part. On the second try old "biggie" came out and took the bait without hesitation. I kept this up from Tuesday till Good Friday. This monster trout was sure going along with my plan.

We could hardly wait to finish our breakfast before heading out to the creek. We had barely finished our porridge and cream when Mother handed each of us a paper beg of hard-boiled coloured eggs and buttered biscuits, saying, "Now, y'all better be off if you are going to catch us a mess of nice, fat trout for supper."

We left the table on the run and snatched up our poles and bait cans that stood ready outside the kitchen door. On the way down, Tom and Ethel agreed to let me fish the bridge hole while they went farther downstream. I guess

71

they were glad to leave me there so I wouldn't slow them down in the rougher going.

I sneaked up on the bridge as quiet as a mouse and threw the small pieces of worms to the south side. The little ones came out in a rush. I baited the bent pin and dropped it in exactly the same spot I had been dropping the big worms for the past four days. In a minute the big trout came out, snatched the worm off the pin and dashed back under the bridge to swallow it. I barely felt any tug on the line. Keeping as quiet as I could and trying to stop trembling with excitement, I broke up more worms and fed them to the small ones. On the second try a good tug came on the line but the worm was in old "biggie's" mouth as he flashed to cover under the bridge. I just lay there, stunned at such bad luck. My plans were not working out.

I left to find some old horse manure to replenish the bait can-- I had already learned that fishing worms lived under horse manure and cow-pats. On the third try, when the big trout took the bait, I gave a wild heave on the pole and old "biggie" sailed over my head and landed in the long grass about ten feet away. I yelled, "Yeaaa, yeaaa!" and pounced on my prize. The fishing pole fell out of my hands into the creek and floated away. After things quieted down, with the fish strung on a forked stick, I lay in the grass for a long time admiring my catch. I guess I was the proudest and happiest kid in the world.

That afternoon, when we got home, Mother praised us all. Tom and Ethel had more than a dozen nice trout, ten inches and over. These were cleaned, rolled in flour, and then fried in butter to a nice crisp brown. Mine got special attention. It was cooked with the head, tail and fins on, and I was allowed to eat it all by myself. It tasted so good Mother just had to have a wee bite so she could agree. Margaret, who was just past three years old, let us all know she was going with us on our next fishing expedition. What a privilege to be able to share such a day with my family!

To give some idea of how plentiful trout were in those days, I'll just relate our fishing trip the following spring.

Trout season opened March 15. Tom, Ethel and I slept very little the night before. We had dug our worms and fixed up our poles and lines to be ready one hour before daylight. We had long willows for poles and ordinary white wrapping string for lines. We had been allowed to buy a card of six gut hooks from Mouat's store. I think the six hooks cost ten cents. They were certainly more effective than the bent pins.

We found some bottle corks and tied them on the lines about four feet from the hook. Then a rusty old nut on each line about six inches above the hook was used as a sinker.

We had received permission from the Blackburns to fish in their lake the day before. This lake is about ten acres in size and has a good fishing creek flowing in and out. These creeks have gravelly bottoms and make excellent spawning grounds. We walked the two miles in the dark. There was a skim of ice around the lake where it flooded back into the buck-brush and fields. We either had to wade almost to the waist through this cold water, or walk the top rails of an old split-rail snake fence that went out to a tiny floating island. Once we reached this point, the water was deep enough to fish in. Ethel and Tom both fell off the fence and decided to walk, carry their poles, and be wet. I managed to get to the fishing spot fairly dry. We all wore running shoes but our excitement was so great we hardly noticed the cold of the morning.

We baited up and each of us had a fish on the first cast. There was no playing these trout. When the cork float made its third bob under the water, we just gave a yank, lifted the fish up to where one of us caught it in his hands, took it off the hook and threaded it through the gills onto a forked stick. We had not even heard of a landing net or reel. About an hour and some seventy-five trout later, the lines cut through the corks, and they floated away out of reach. This slowed us down for a few minutes. Ethel pulled some reeds and folded them into a ball. We were able to tie the line around them. This was more cumbersome than the bottle corks but worked well enough.

By about nine o'clock we were starting to get hungry and very, very cold. We gathered up our strings of fish and, not even trying to walk the fence, waded the 200 feet to shore and dry land. The cold water came above my waist. We noticed for the first time how heavy the trout were to carry. By the time we walked home we were still wet but not cold. The last half mile was up a fairly steep hill and I swear those trout grew heavier at every step. Mother looked at us and then at the trout. "Lawsie sakes! Y'all must be the best fishermen in the whole world!" We smiled our pleasure.

"Just put them in this tub and get some dry clothes on while I fix y'all some hotcakes and bacon." In less than ten minutes we were devouring hotcakes smothered in fresh butter and honey, washed down with gulps of hot cocoa that was made from fresh milk. The kitchen was warm and we were very, very happy.

After breakfast we counted and helped clean the trout. Our young sister, Margaret, was allowed to help although she was still pouting because she had not been allowed to go with us. We had caught 123 fish, averaging better than half a pound each. Needless to say, we had fried trout for lunch, supper and breakfast the next morning. The remainder went into Mother's Mason jars for winter.

By 1916, I had passed up to Grade Three. Miss Mercer was our new teacher. During the Christmas holidays, there was a heavy fall of wet snow. Over four feet of the white stuff covered the ground. The school's roof caved in under the weight, pushing out the east wall. This was the wall with all the windows. Over half the glass and wall was smashed beyond repair. The rafters and roof were lying on top of the desks. This kept the desks and books from being completely destroyed. The trustees had a meeting and arranged a work bee.

Nearby was an old log shed about fifteen feet wide and eighteen feet long, with a hay shed attached to one end. It had a rough lumber door and one small window. The window was only about two feet square. It was so dark inside when the door was closed, that candles and lamps

74

were needed to see your hand in front of your face. It had been lived in some time in the past, but for at least five or six years it had been used as a sheep shed. The floor was planks laid on the dirt, and had rotted out in several places.

The trustees decided to carry all the books and desks down to this shed, which was a quarter of a mile from the collapsed school. Miss Mercer was there to help. Using shovels and brooms, the floor was cleaned enough so the planks could be seen. As the desks arrived, she placed them in rows. By late evening everything that could be salvaged was under the roof of this old log shed. The school stove, which was still usable, had been moved down and set up and a fire lit in it. We hoped this would keep things dry or at least prevent further damage and mould. Someone produced coffee and a pot. There were a few cups and spoons that had been in the school cupboard. A meeting was convened, and coffee was served in that little room everyone remembers as "the sheep shed." It smelled strongly of manure and musty hay. It was decided, with Miss Mercer's sanction, to try holding classes in this dilapidated room until the other school could be repaired. A piece of blackboard about two by four feet was salvaged and nailed to the logs at one end of the room. Two lighted coal-oil lamps were needed so the children could see the writing. Even with the door wide open, it was still pretty dark inside. This door let in plenty of cold air. The fire in the stove had to be well stoked and kept hot all day long.

There was a cold snap in February. Our hands got so numb we couldn't hold our pencils. During this spell, we wore our heavy coats and mitts when sitting at our desks. We did most of our studying standing up around the big wood heater. Miss Mercer was just past eighteen and this was her first teaching assignment. I often wonder how she coped against such odds.

The school inspector visited this temporary room in late February. His first remark to our teacher was, "You poor, poor dear. How in God's name do you teach in here? Please

75

let the children out so I can have a good look. I just can't believe what I am seeing."

We were all dismissed and went up to the old school yard to start a game of rounders. Rounders is much like baseball but is played with a soft rubber ball. That day we were allowed to stay out until it was time to leave for home. We thought this inspector was great and hoped he would come often.

Charlie Beddis and Dad were working every day repairing the old school. Tom and I worked on Saturdays, helping to shingle the roof. Everthing was moved back to the repaired building by mid-March. Miss Mercer and the trustees declared a school holiday and we had a picnic to celebrate the occasion. It was a gala day for everyone. All parents and their children came to enjoy the celebration. The inspector had arranged to be there and gave a short speech praising Miss Mercer to the skies. The Catholic priest often stayed with the Blackburns. He just happened to arrive in time to give the school his blessing and also found time for some fried chicken, potato salad, coffee and cake. This was Father Sheiland. He presided over the first morning Mass that Tom, Ethel and I ever attended. Mass was held in an upstairs room of the Blackburns' private home.

The Cranberry school was closed to be used for shelter for the Gardner family, whose home had been destroyed by fire. There was enough room at the Divide to take care of students from both districts. The war was on and many people had moved away.

When the Divide school opened in September 1917, some sixteen pupils attended. The amalgamation of the two schools created a romantic era. I was going on nine years old and got my first desperate crush on pretty Lorna Rogers from the Cranberry. It was pathetic! I would carry her books until our trails parted just below what is now the Webster property. We would stand close together for a short time, blushing and saying nothing. It was a year and a half later that I first kissed her at a valentine's party. We were sure this was going to lead to our marriage, so we started to think up names for our first children. After all, we were both ten years old!

In 1918, Dad bought some land at Ganges. That summer we moved the small house that Uncle Frank had lived in to this new lot. We just cut it into six sections, loaded it on our wagon, hauled it the four miles and set it up again on the back of the lot. There we lived, in two rooms, while we were building another new home. This would be the fifth house the Garners had lived in since coming to Saltspring some twelve years earlier. The seventh Garner child, Oliver, was born in this little house on May 3, 1918. Things got a bit crowded, to say the least.

This meant a change of schools. I was heartsick because Lorna was going to the Divide and I would be at the new Ganges school. I tried to coax Mother and Dad to let me walk the extra two miles each day so I could be at the Divide, explaining how it would be much better to keep on studying where I knew all the kids. No way. When September came along I was enrolled at Ganges.

"It would wear out too much shoe leather to go up there," Dad explained. Lorna wrote letters and we met occasionally when she came to Ganges to shop with her parents. Absence makes the heart grow fonder-- *of someone else*. She got a crush on another and I'm afraid I did the same. Puppy love was great, but did not survive the few miles that separated us.

We were privileged to attend the first public school class ever taught in the immediate Ganges area. This class was taught in the old Frank Scott home at the end of Church Road almost directly behind the Mahon Hall. Miss Stubbs was our teacher. She was a tall, husky lady and was strict and efficient. The "House School" as we called it had previously been rented by the Gilbert Mouat family. Colin Mouat tells me he was born there in the fall of 1911. He also remembers being bound up with ropes and tied on the mantel shelf over a fireplace in one of the empty rooms when he attended school there in 1918. Colin could not remember why he and his pal Charlie Nelson were trussed up and tied on this broad shelf or who did the tying. It was Desmond Crofton and Tom Garner who did the job. The reason was a marble game that was going on in the room because it was too wet that day to play outside. The two small boys kept grabbing the marbles that lay on the floor around the ring of a serious game of "keeps." The older boys eliminated this problem in short order, but when the noon hour ended everyone forgot to free the two young boys. Miss Stubbs found them there when she heard strange noises coming from this empty room about an hour later. Colin tells me he bought the property many years later and then tore the old house down. Surely he didn't have visions of being tied on the mantle shelf again.

The only other important things to happen that year were the end of World War One and the terrible fight I had with Harry Caldwell. The fight started during lunch hour one spring day. Harry was almost two years older and was known to be very stubborn and wirey. He thought he could boss me around because of his size and age. I took his guff for a while, then challenged him to do battle. The older boys formed a ring of sorts in amongst the trees where there was a reasonably level bit of ground. We stripped off our coats and rolled up our shirt-sleeves. The rules were announced by Desmond Crofton. No choking or gouging of eyes was allowed. The loser would be the first to say "Uncle."

We fought for over two hours. By the time the school bell rang to signal the end of lunch hour both our shirts and pants had been ripped and torn so badly that we didn't dare go where the girls were and certainly could not be seen by our teacher. Some of the older boys stayed to watch and referee while the others went back to class. Neither of us would give up. That Caldwell boy certainly was a stubborn one. When we tired of beating each other Harry headed for home. Tom brought me another shirt and a pair of pants so I could walk home decently.

The family moved back to live at the old farm house

and we attended the Divide school again until the big house at Ganges was roofed in and made livable after the war.

First year of high school was taught in the front room of Jimmy Rogers' home at Ganges. This was the old police building and had two lock-up cells in the back. Margaret and I both attended. Jimmy Rogers was in the provincial police force. He was a wonderful human being, teaching the young men of the island many things about sports, hunting, fishing and just being good citizens. The Rogers family kept living there without the use of their front room. That part of their furniture was stored in one of the cells.

Ivor Parfitt of Victoria was our first high school teacher. He was actually the first teacher who ever taught above Grade Eight on Saltspring Island. Being an aggressive young man, he used a bamboo pointer about two feet long. This was a dual purpose piece of equipment. It was used to point things out on the blackboard and also to sting a male student across the shoulders if he didn't pay enough attention to study and proper behaviour. Parfitt used this cane freely and there wasn't a boy in the class who did not feel its sting at least once a week. I do believe it helped. The boys got marks equal to, if not better than, the girls.

During the summer of 1924, Tom and I worked for the F.M.Singer Lumber Company in one of their tie mills. For getting rid of slabs and stacking the ties and lumber the pay was fourty-five cents an hour. This was heavy work for a 15-year old. Brother Tom was the head sawyer and got seventy-five cents an hour, plus a small bonus per 1000 board feet of lumber. That year the head faller was badly injured. His leg was broken by a rolling log. I was offered his job and accepted gladly. The pay was fifty cents an hour plus cleaner air and a bit of authority.

All our pay cheques were handed over to Dad. We would sometimes get five dollars for our own spending money. This had to buy gloves, socks, overalls or whatever. Tom was now eighteen and his earnings went the same way-- a bad deal. Our meals and lunches were great. We always had clean and mended clothes to start each new

79

week. I could tell that Mother resented Dad's taking most of our wages, especially in Tom's case. Although he was fully grown and accepting an adult's responsibilities, he was being deprived of the money that should go along with the workload he was carrying.

The F.M.Singer Company went broke that year and our family started to log the old Cotsford property at the north end of the island. Margaret helped Mother to cook for the crew while I went falling and bucking. We were kept out of school for the next year.

We used the good old cross-cut saws, known to the logging world as "Swede Fiddles." I learned to sharpen the saws and all the rest of the tricks of the trade-- to chop and saw left and right handed-- and I could cut a springboard hole with the best by the time the year was up. By now I had muscles like steel in my arms and across my chest and back.

I'm sure it was Mother's insistence that was responsible for Margaret's and my going back to high school. All through July and August of 1925, Mother pressured Dad to get us enrolled. His only argument against our having further education was the five dollars per month fee and the loss of wages. There were some bad rows in our home before we were signed in for the old chicken house. I will always be grateful to Mother for her foresight and persistence.

Our second year of high school was something else. There were now too many students for the existing schools and no high school building on the island. The school boards got together with the directors of the exhibition board. William Mouat acted on both boards and arranged everything. It was decided that the chicken house, where the poultry exhibits were held each year, could be used for a much-needed high school classroom. During the summer holidays the desks could be stacked so that the poultry exhibits could continue. The exhibition directors agreed to let the building be used, but with the definite understanding that the housing and feeding equipment for the poultry would not be taken out or disturbed in any way. The janitorial duties were my responsibility, for which I received ten dollars a month. This paid the tuition fees for Margaret and myself.

Mr. Archie Robertson was our teacher. He was strict but very capable. There were no options or choices of subjects. Everyone took Latin, French, Botany, Algebra, Math, English, and History, plus the usual school sports. We had a good basketball and a fair soccer team. I can't remember any of the students failing the government exams at the end of the term. Perhaps this is due to the fact that there were no school taxes, as such, in the 1920's. Things seem much different in our present school system. Progress? Maybe.

On a warm Friday afternoon in May, a bad problem developed in our schoolroom. Close inspection revealed thousands of chicken fleas cavorting around on the boards. The class was dismissed. After discussion with Mr. Robertson, it was decided to treat the room with flea powder. We were all back at class as usual the next Monday morning. There was a lot of sneezing for a few days but that was the only annoying effect I can remember, except for a bit of itching from flea bites.

This was the very first time Grade Ten was taught on Saltspring Island. There were twenty-three students starting grades nine and ten in the Chicken House that year.

Following is a list of those students as I remember them. If I make mistakes in spelling or forget someone, I hope they will forgive me:

> Tillie Akerman-- Fulford Harbour
> Jim Urquhart-- Fulford
> Loys and Shirley Wilson-- Central
> Dorothy Elliott-- Ganges
> Vera Seymour-- Ganges
> Charlie Nelson-- Central

81

Gladys Borridale-- Ganges-- Part Time only. (Gladys stopped attending when the teacher threw a piece of chalk and hit her in the face.)

Billy Mouat-- Ganges
Audley Gardner-- Cranberry
Lotus Frazer-- Fulford
Harry Caldwell-- North End
Enid Caldwell-- North End
Doreen Crofton-- Ganges
Lorna Rogers-- Cranberry
Eunice Curley-- Fulford
Norman Ruckle-- Fulford
Cree Shaw-- Fulford
Margaret Purdy-- Beddis Road. (Margaret became ill and attended only part time.)

Mary Purdy-- Beddis Road
Gladys Beech-- Ganges
Phyllis Taylor-- Ganges

Margaret and I attended this school and batched in our big house at Ganges. The rest of the family were at the north end living at the old Cotsford place. In the ensuing years, there were many others who attended this chicken house school before it was torn down to make way for the present high school building. This is where my formal schooling came to an end, in June of 1926.

Ganges, B.C. Feb. 27, 1926

Mr. O.J.Garner
Ganges, B.C.

In Account with
GANGES HARBOUR SCHOOL BOARD

To second year High School Fees for Joe Garner
Spring Term, 1926, January to June inclusive
at $5.00 per month.......................$30.00

Times have changed. We actually paid five dollars per month to attend this unusual school, as is evidenced by the above bill, sent to Dad at Ganges that year.

Students also bought all their books and were responsible for their own transportation, regardless of district or distance.

After we moved to Vancouver, I took two years of night school, studying drafting, estimating, general carpentry and a special course on the steel square. Its amazing what can be done with an ordinary carpenter's square.

Farewell To The Chicken House School

Old memories are fading while new ones arise
Delight is portrayed through students' happy cries!
The chicken house is gone, its passed through the years.
Yet not without spirit, our parents shed no tears!

by Elizabeth Riddell

Cougar Story

I had been down to the country store to pick up some groceries for Mother and was trekking home with them on my back, in an old tosack that had been made into a backpack by cutting the top into two strips for shoulder straps. It was just starting to get dusk as I came up the last half mile. The road was little more than a trail where it twisted its way along a gully between two steep hills.

Glancing up, I was jolted from my daydreams by the sight of a huge cougar stalking across the trail only fifty yards ahead of me. He looked about ten feet long. His head was turned and he was looking right at me. His great tail swooped almost to the ground, then curled up to a level with his back. The last six inches twitched about on a pivot all its own. He was in a crouching, stalking walk that suggested awesome power and deadly purpose. I froze in my tracks.

The hair on the back of my neck stood straight up. My eight year old brain panicked from the horror before my eyes. I searched frantically for my father's words about cougar: ''Never run. Never turn and run; stand if you have to. If the cougar doesn't leave, get two good-sized stones and bang them together, making as much noise as you can... then walk, heading for home if possible.''

The cougar crossed the road and stopped on the other hillside not more than twenty feet above the trail. I could plainly see his ears and whiskers flattened back against his head. His big fangs showed in an ugly half-snarl. Except for the twitching of his tail, he stayed perfectly still. This deadly cat had to be passed to get home.

Slowly sliding the straps of the backpack off my shoulders, I dropped it to the side of the road. This fifteen or twenty pounds off my back made me feel light and free. My desire to run was almost impossible to control. It was now evident the cougar was not moving on. To force myself to bend over and pick up two rounded rocks which lay near my feet and stand there without running needed one hell of a lot of self-control.

I began to walk towards what seemed certain death like a programmed robot powered by steel springs. The nearer I came to the big cat, the harder and louder I banged the stones. It was like being in a trance. I just did exactly what I had been told to do. I could see the end of the cougar's tail twitching back and forth as I passed. Except for the twitching he stayed perfectly still. I could feel his power and knew without the sound of those rocks banging, he would spring on me.

My legs stiffened up like pokers and every muscle was as tight as a fiddle string. An eternity passed-- ''never run...same speed...never run...''

After passing the cougar it again took all the self-control of my mind and body to keep from breaking into a run. I took one step, then another until I was twenty-five yards beyond him, then forty. I looked back over my shoulder: he was still there, staring!

Getting out of sight around the bend, I dropped the rocks and began to run. Though my feet were bare, they were as tough as shoe leather, as we went all summer without shoes.

I could hear noises in the brush across the creek and I knew the cougar was on the gallop, travelling in the same direction.

Running full out I crossed a little bridge. That left him on one side of the steep creek gully and me on the other. Farther up the hill I could still hear him coming through the salal brush-- *crash-- crash-- crash!* Looking to my left I saw him coming for me.

At that moment something snapped in my brain. My subconscious woke up and took over. Instantly, I felt as light as a feather and seemed to be flying; my feet barely touched the ground. It was like being part of a slow-motion film. The cougar was moving fast, but I could see him in every detail as he charged purposefully towards me: every spot his feet touched, every rock, every ripple of his muscles.

There were now only about twenty yard separating us. I felt myself spring into the air with each forward stride. Running was effortless-- I didn't even seem to be breathing. I felt no fear-- my body was flooded with a feeling of superhuman power as I raced in slow motion towards the gate and home.

Reaching the gate, I sprang smoothly over, seeing my bare feet, complete with toes and toenails, clear the top board by several inches. I felt like a bird sailing into the wind. As I hit the ground on the other side I heard the dog start to bark and his chain rattle as he surged against it. Some twenty yards into the field I collapsed. How I wished that dog would break his chain and charge down to chase the cougar to hell out of there!

I lay in the grass for several minutes before trying to get to my feet. My legs were so rubbery it was impossible to stand upright. I was finally able to half-crawl, half-stagger up to the house where the dog was. I was completely and absolutely exhausted. Brother Tom and Dad were there. I must have been white as a ghost. They looked at me and Tom said, "What's the matter with you?"

"Well, quite a bit's the matter with me! A big cougar

chased me all the way up the hill. He damned near caught me at the gate and he's down there right now!''

This was big excitement! They ran into the house. Dad got his old 45-70 and Tom got the 12-gauge shotgun. They let the dog loose. It was only minutes from the time they saw me until they were down to where the cougar should be-- and there he was, in the creek again, underneath a tangle of jumbled and piled-up windfall logs.

The cougar had apparently jumped the gate right behind me and lay in the field not more than fifty feet from where I was recuperating. The rattling of the dog's chain and the loud barking had been enough to stop him. He watched me staggering to the house, but headed for the creek when he saw Tom, Dad and the black dog coming for him.

In the field, the dog picked up the cougar's scent. He followed it into the logs, barking and snarling. Soon there was one hell of a commotion. The cougar came out and jumped the creek down below them. They both took a shot at it but missed. It was pretty dark by this time.

That big cat hung around for two or three days, killing a deer and two sheep within a quarter of a mile of our house. Dad and Tom tried to get him with our dog but the old cougar could not be treed. He just ran and kept out of sight, returning at night to feed on his kills.

You can be sure Mother never let us small children out of the house.

Finally, Ernest Collins brought his cougar hounds and killed the cougar within less than a mile of our house. He was a 5-year old tom, weighing 140 pounds and measuring over nine feet from nose to tip of tail.

Had he caught me, he may not have eaten me, but undoubtedly he would have mauled me to death.

Collins took the skin and headed home to his farm. It made a very nice rug. We cooked the meat in a big washtub and fed it to our chickens.

From that first brush with a cougar, I would never trust

one and still do everything possible to avoid an encounter, even with a good gun in my hands.

When Tom and Ethel had time to think about this episode, they teased me a lot, "You didn't jump that gate! Nobody can jump it coming uphill!"

I kept insisting, "I did so jump it-- I had to!"

We went down to the gate and took several runs at it, but we couldn't jump it. The three of us tried all one day in every way we knew. We sidestepped and tried every trick in the book, but there was no way. We even took a section of the old rail snake fence down to get a side run at it on the same level but with no more success. Ethel was twelve and Tom was ten; they were in good shape and could run and jump, as any country kid can, but there was no way they could jump that gate.

I have thought about this cougar event many times and tried to figure out what made him behave as he did. It is certainly not a normal thing for a cougar to chase every child that passes by.

The day we were trying to jump the gate, we went down to where the cougar had crossed the road. We could clearly see where he had sat, and where his back claws had dug into the dirt when he began to run up the trail on the opposite side of the creek gully. We backtracked and found the place under a little overhanging cliff where he had been lying. His kill was there, about twenty yards from his resting place. It was a full-grown sheep, partly eaten and covered with moss and sticks. This kill may have been what he was protecting.

I feel sure that, though I was out of sight, the cougar knew I had started to run and for whatever perverse reason, decided to have some fun and catch me at the top of the gully. There is no doubt in my mind that he knew the trail and road well and may have been watching us three children going to and coming from school. The fact that I was alone this day and that it was getting dark may have prompted this chase. My being small for an eight-year old could also have been a factor.

Cougars are very strange animals.

Years later, while I was hunting deer with a friend who was also an experienced cougar hunter, we came upon fresh cougar tracks in ten inches of new snow and decided to follow them, hoping to get a chance to kill him for the $25 bounty. The tracks of this cougar, which turned out to be a three-year old tom, led us to within fifty yards of a farmhouse. Signs showed us where the cougar had lain behind some brush and watched the house. We knew he had paused there but a short time, because the snow had only melted slightly from his body heat.

We tracked him to where he crossed a well-travelled road which led to an old abandoned copper mine on top of Mount Sicker. Several children walked this road on school days. Two of the smaller children left the road and travelled a quarter mile on a narrow trail, through thick, second-growth fir and cedar, that led to their home.

We carefully read the cougar's tracks, stunned and surprised at the story the fresh snow told us. He had crouched in some ferns and brush at the junction of the trail and the road, well-screened, but able to see everything that was going on. We could see where he had dug his back feet down to the ground through the snow in preparation for a spring, much like a house-cat stalking a bird. There was the imprint of his long body and the fan-shaped impression where his tail tip had twitched back and forth. The snow had melted where he had rested his head. From there he had watched the children as they parted from road to trail.

As the children hiked along the trail, the cougar moved parallel to them, crouched and ready to spring from behind some bush. From reading the signs, we deduced that he had watched and stalked those children four times and that four times he had prepared to spring. Fortunately, he never did.

We still wonder what would have happened to those small kids had they slipped and fallen, or in playing, had wrestled each other to the ground, or had started to run. The cougar probably would have attacked them instantly.

89

A cougar can stun a large deer with a single blow to the head from either of its front paws. I have seen where one struck hard enough to shatter a large dog's skull and scatter the brains over a ten-foot circle. Unlike some books, the stories in the snow are always true, if you know how to read them.

In September, 1916 there was another near-fatal accident involving a cougar and children in the Lake Cowichan area of Vancouver Island. This gory incident was what sparked Dad to give us such complete instructions about how to act if we ever met a cougar in the woods.

Two small children, Doreen Ashburnham, aged eleven, and Tony Farrer, aged eight, were walking through the woods with a bridle, going for their pony. They were heading for a meadow but, before they reached it, they came on a cougar. He was crouched up on a bank, ready to attack. When the children saw him, they turned and began to run for home. The cougar instantly sprang on Doreen's shoulders and dragged her to the ground. The little boy began beating on the cougar's head with the bridle and managed to direct its attention from Doreen to himself. Doreen fought the cougar and, although she was badly hurt, somehow managed to blind him.

By some miracle he gave up the fight and the children escaped. It was probably the Ashburnhams' small dog that saved the day by charging in. Both children were badly mauled but lived to tell the story. They were honoured by the Governor-General of Canada with the Royal Albert Medal for their bravery in fighting for one another. The cougar was tracked down and shot. He proved to be old and hungry and the children had made the mistake of running.

"Never turn and run... stand if you have to... never run."

Had Doreen and Tony had this sort of instruction they might have saved themselves a terrible mauling. Apart from other wounds, it took 36 stitches just to close the gashes in Tony's head. The little dog needed many stitches on his neck and shoulders. Doreen, now over 70, still

90

carries the scars on her arms and body. This attack at Lake Cowichan took place a few months before my experience on Saltspring Island.

Dad told us about a man he had worked with on the Empress Hotel, who, in 1904, had found a den of six cougar kittens during a hunting trip in the Campbell River area of Vancouver Island. Cougars were so numerous the elk and deer population had been severely depleted.

He contacted a doctor friend in Victoria, who apparently injected a house cat with syphilis serum. With the cat bundled in a sack, they travelled by boat to the valley, where the doctor injected the cougar kittens. This action helped to keep the panther population in check for a considerable time, as their numbers decreased noticeably over a twenty year period.

I discussed this information with Dr. Larry Giovando. He believed the syphilis could cause brain damage and a great many abortions. Could this brain damage have been responsible for some of the cougar attacks ten or fifteen years later?

Another incident occurred on Saltspring about 1860, when Mrs. Joe Akerman, near Fulford Harbour, was hoeing her garden on a warm day in June. She brought her young baby, who was the first white child born on Saltspring, out of the house and laid him on a blanket to play or snooze, or just to be in her sight while she worked. The baby lay between her and the house which was only a few yards away.

She had hoed the length of one row of vegetables and, as she turned to do the next, she glanced at the baby. She saw what at first she thought was a large dog standing over her child, rolling him over with its front paw. With a start, she suddenly realized it was not a dog but a great panther with its mouth only inches from the baby's face. Mrs. Akerman let out a shriek and without hesitation charged the cougar with her hoe, shouting, ''Get out of here! Get out of here, before I kill you!''

The cougar stalked off, looking back over its shoulder at the frenzied mother.

The Akerman men hunted down and killed the big cat before dark that same day. It still remains the largest cougar ever recorded shot on Saltspring, measuring ten feet from nose to tip of tail.

Mrs. Akerman was teased a lot by the men. They said that none of them would ever talk back to her if she had her hoe along. Even a cougar had more sense. She would just smile.

The second brush our family had with cougar was a year after my chase.

Normally, our cattle came home on their own, but this night Marg and Tom had to be sent to find them. They located the cows about half a mile from the farmhouse. To get there they followed a narrow, rocky trail that twisted through the timber. There were a couple of gullies and creeks to cross. Tom told Margaret to wait below while he went up to take a look. He couldn't understand why the cows were so interested in a willow bush. He sneaked around very quietly to get above them so he could see what was happening.

Then he saw a cougar sitting under the willow. It was perfectly still, its ears and whiskers flattened against its head. Under the chin was something like a little bubble moving in and out in much the same way a frog's throat does when it is croaking. Tom said he thought the cougar was purring to the cattle in an attempt to mesmerize them into coming closer.

He ran back to Margaret and they high-tailed for home.

Once again he and Dad got the old 45-70 and the 12-gauge shotgun. They were back to the willow tree with the black dog within half an hour. The cattle had started down the trail and the cougar was following them.

The men went around by another trail and as soon as they were behind the cattle, the dog went wild. The hair on his back stood up, and he barked and bared his teeth. As he leaped up on a log pile, the cougar flew out from under like a flash. For 200 yards the dog chased it up a gully until the cougar climbed a cedar tree. Some forty feet up the big cat crouched on a limb. The dog stayed under the tree, howling and barking, while Tom and Dad ran over. They spotted the cougar, which was looking straight at them with its teeth bared, its whiskers and ears laid back, and its tail twitching from side to side.

When they were within twenty-five yards, they stopped. Dad turned to Tom and said, "I'm going to count to three...one, two, three and BANG! That's how its going to be, Tom."

Then he said, "Make sure your gun's loaded right and get the hammers back."

I stood and watched with a heart that beat harder and faster than normal. The vision of that other big cougar crossing the creek towards me came back, very clear and terrifying.

Standing side by side, the man and boy put up their guns and Dad counted, "One...two...three!" They fired. The cougar folded, feet in the air, and landed on its back, stone dead. Dad had shot it through the heart. Five of the SSG slugs from Tom's shotgun had also found their mark. One had struck the cougar in the ear, two behind the shoulder and two a little farther back. The dog rushed in, tearing out fur as though the cougar were still alive. Luckily, it wasn't.

The cattle were already home when we packed the cougar into the barnyard, but would not go into the barn as they usually did. They were grouped in a field below, obviously smitten with a bad case of the spooks.

Dad and Tom put the cougar by the barn about fifteen feet from the door and we went to bring up the cattle. Three of them had to be milked, which was my job.

We drove the cows right up to the barn but when they got the smell and sight of the cougar lying there, their tails went straight up over their backs and they were gone, just GONE!-- in every direction. They ploughed through fences, crashed through woodpiles, scattered milk-pails and overturned everything else that stood in their way. They didn't get milked that night; we couldn't get them anywhere near the place.

The next morning we took water and washed down the area where the cougar had lain, removing enough of the smell to finally coax the cows inside. They were very nervous, kicking one pail out of my hands and giving little milk that day.

Most of the cougars on Saltspring got there by swimming Sansum Narrows, which separates Saltspring from Vancouver Island. Cougars don't normally like to swim, but once in the water they are fast and powerful. The distance between the two islands is less than a quarter of a mile in some places. I don't know why these big cats do it, I only know that they do swim from one island to another.

We skinned the cougar. Dad told us to bury the guts, but being kids, we had to cut them open to see what we could find. It didn't matter what we got in those days-- a trout, grouse, or deer-- we felt compelled to dissect it and see what it had been eating.

When we cut this cougar open we discovered tapeworms. We had heard about tapeworms! We thought if one little segment got on you, you would get them yourself. We had been told that if one of these was cut in half it would grow a new head and tail and become two worms instead of one.

We quickly got some forked sticks and began to wind those slimy parasites on them in much the same way one winds spaghetti on a fork. We ended up with balls the size of goose eggs on the end of each stick. We didn't dare touch them with our hands so we carefully burned everything.

Everyone in the area was sure that a mother cougar with two or three half-grown kittens had been killing many sheep, but here was just one scrawny, 3-year old female who had to feed that mess of tapeworms to stay alive. She had killed a sheep every day for ten days before being shot. This is twice or three times the amount a healthy cougar would normally eat.

A Pet Racoon

Shortly after Ernest Collins shot the cougar that had chased me, Tom and I wandered over to where the carcass of the sheep he had killed lay, stinking to high heaven. There were many racoon signs around it. I asked Tom, "Do you think we could tame a 'coon if we caught one?"

"Why sure," was his reply.

Back home I dug out one of our traps, carried it over, secured it to a log and set it near the dead sheep. Next morning the trap was sprung but no 'coon. I reset it differently and covered it with some sheep wool. There was a gob of hair in the jaws next morning. I was convinced we would catch him the next night. Again I set the trap and went home, and with Tom's help built a cage using four pieces of one by twelve inch lumber nailed together, with strong chicken wire stapled top and bottom. We cut a trap-door at one end.

The next morning I found our new pet caught fast in the trap, held by the sole of one back foot. There seemed to be no injury to the bones or skin of the leg. While I held the 'coon down with a forked stick, Tom loosened the chain from the log, then tied it to a stout four-foot pole.

We started for home, a half mile away, with our prize. It took over two hours to get there. The vicious little creature did everything but turn inside out trying to get close enough to bite us.

We tried carrying him with his feet off the ground. He'd do a somersault and start climbing the pole, snapping at our hands. We were about halfway home when, by accident, things got better. I began walking backwards along the trail just about a foot out of his reach. The little creature was so determined to sink his teeth into one of my feet, he was actually scrambling after me on his three free legs. I just kept on backing up and he kept following.

We pushed him through the trapdoor into the cage with stout sticks, then released him. He sat and licked his foot for a while, then walked around the cage, never taking his eyes off us. He didn't limp much, his foot was just numbed. For about half an hour he checked the chicken wire for strength by pulling it up with his front paws and trying to bite through it. Then he gave up, curled himself in a corner, and went fast asleep.

Though we offered him water and food, it was three days before he drank, and four before he ate a few pieces of meat. He seemed friendly enough, but tried to bite our hands when we gave him food. We fitted an old wooden nail keg in a corner of the cage, complete with moss and dry grass for bedding. This seemed to make "Coonie," as we called him, very, very happy. He slept in the barrel through most of the daylight hours.

Racoons are nocturnal by nature and seldom move about during the day. As darkness fell, out would come Coonie. He'd wander about the cage for a while and then sit over by his water and food. We would watch him until it was too dark to see. If there was a moon we stayed longer. This was pre-radio, pre-television, so our entertainment was what we made it. You could say this was our "live show."

96

With those beady little eyes never leaving us, he would feel around and pick up a plum or piece of meat, roll it around in his front paws for a while, put it in the water pan, roll it under water, then take it out and roll it some more. Then he would sample the food and, though we watched very closely, he never seemed to look at whatever he was eating. Everything was done by feel, smell or taste.

If we wanted a really good show, we gave him a raw egg. First, he'd roll the egg in his front paws, then came the underwater wash. He would walk on his hind legs, carrying the egg in his front paws to some corner, then roll on his back and, holding the egg with all four feet, bite a small hole through the shell and proceed to eat the contents. We were never quite sure whether he licked out the contents with his tongue or sucked it out. The whole operation was done in silence, his eyes staring into ours. When he left the empty shell, we'd fish it out through the wire to marvel at how cleanly he did this job.

The only time he made any noise was when we gave him a fresh trout. He would growl constantly until the last morsel was swallowed. We never did tame this wirey little creature with the ringed tail; he was too old when we caught him. We kept him about two months. One morning I went to feed him and the cage was empty. Close examination showed a broken wire near the edge of the pen and a small hole dug in the hard dirt to the outside. A lot of fur was left around the broken wire, giving clear evidence of his great struggle for freedom. Though we missed him, I was glad he had returned to his natural environment.

One of our neighbours caught a very young racoon some years later. This little animal became a real pet and was not at all vicious. It acted like a spoiled kitten, wanting attention and petting all the time. If we wanted a good laugh we would give him what he liked most, a big teaspoon of peanut butter. This would stick to the roof of his mouth. The antics he went through to try and get it free were hilarious. He would roll around with both front paws in his mouth, smack his lips and even try to stand on his head in

97

an effort to dislodge the sticky food. As soon as he was able to swallow it, he was begging for more. If you get tired of television, try watching a racoon!

In the winter months Dad was usually around home teaching the kids lessons about nature and pioneering. He taught us all about trapping and tracking racoon and mink. During the last years of the war, and for a short time afterwards, an average racoon skin would bring ten dollars. A premium pelt would be worth up to eighteen dollars. Mink ranged from eight to twenty dollars. This was big money in the teens and twenties.

Our trapping was never too successful, but we did well tracking when the snow was fresh. To a couple of young boys, this was great fun and excitement. We were always hoping for snow. If it began falling in the afternoon of any winter day, all work and chores had to be done by other members of the family. Tom and I had to get our hunting gear ready. Shoes had to be oiled with a mixture of hot seal oil and beef tallow, then hung behind the stove so the oil would slowly penetrate the leather. This made them waterproof *and* smelly. The longer they hung there, the stronger the stink.

We wore overalls over longjohns. From our shoes to our knees we wound strips torn from an old blanket, similar to the khaki puttees worn during the war. This kept the snow from going down into our boots and also kept our legs dry for a while.

We would try out the .22 rifle for accuracy. If we couldn't hit a circle the size of a fifty-cent piece at twenty-five yards, we adjusted the sights until we could. Dad would get his pearl-handled six-gun and a box of shells. "Try this out and see if it's okay," he would say, handing the gun to Tom. A milk can was an easy target at fifty feet or more. We were warned never to shoot either gun until we made sure no snow was stuck or frozen in the barrel. He drilled this into us at an early age.

"If the barrel is blocked, you can get your face blown off," he would warn. "Always treat a gun like it's loaded and ready to fire. Never point it at yourself or anyone else for any reason.''

We were hunting one day and I rested the muzzle of the .22 on top of my foot while we stood talking. Dad noticed this and moved over to where he could reach me. Next thing I knew I was knocked flat on my face in the salal. When I got to my feet, looking hurt and surprised, he explained, "What you got is not nearly as bad as a bullet through your foot."

When snow conditions were favourable, we got up an hour or so before daylight. Mother would be up before us and have a lunch packed and breakfast ready. Then we went out into the dawn to search for some fresh 'coon tracks. We always hunted and tracked together. If we happened to be following two sets of tracks and they separated, we split up until we got both 'coons. The arrangement was to come back to where we had separated and wait for each other.

We learned the habits of these furry creatures as only youngsters can, and we could guess how much farther they would travel before denning up for the day. If not disturbed they will sleep on until dark.

We also had a system of separating if the tracking was difficult and led into heavy brush. Always keeping in clear snow, we would circle both sides until one of us hit the track coming out. Three whistles meant to come over and follow the trail. If we found nothing, we knew Mr. 'Coon was inside the circle. We looked up every likely tree. Sometimes we found our quarry in a hollow stump or log. Usually we could fish him out with a forked stick. Other times, we had to build a fire and pile on green boughs to force smoke into the den. It took only a few minutes before he had to come out for some air. We dispatched the animal quickly with a club or a bullet. We were careful about this, because any damage meant a dollar or more off the price of the pelt. If the snow was good we could get four or five critters in a long day, but if it began to rain, we were lucky to get one or two.

When we first began skinning, we took the skin off flat, stretched it on a wall and tacked it out like a beaver or bear skin. We learned later that this was wrong.

During the first winter our take was twelve 'coons and four mink. In the spring Tom and I were sent to Vancouver with the pelts tucked into a couple of suitcases. There were eight fur buyers on Water Street between Main and Granville, and we tried all of them, dickering for the best price.

On our last call, we found a buyer who explained what we were doing wrong in preparing the skins for market. He showed us some prime pelts bought from other trappers. He also gave us a pair of skin-stretching boards. He explained the process of "case-skinning" and showed us how to turn the fur side out after they had been scraped and dried. In his younger years he had trapped, so he knew good fur and how to handle it.

"A trick not too many trappers know, I'll pass on to you two young fellows," he said. "Find a big hollow cedar tree that the ants have been working on. There is usually a bag or two of "ant dust" in the hollow. Take this home and keep it dry. When the skin is clean and almost dry, rub the ant dust over it before taking it off the stretching-board. Turn the fur side out and you will have a soft, dry pelt that will keep. Almost as good as tanning," he said, with a smile.

We were paid in cash: eight dollars for racoon and ten for mink. We had never seen so much money in our lives. He gave us six twenties, one ten, one five and a one dollar bill. He also rummaged around and came up with the two stretching-boards. He invited us to come back and do business the next year.

We were very proud boys.

"Matter of fact," I said to Tom, "we're almost grown men now." Tom was eleven and I had just turned nine.

Back home we turned the money over to Dad. He praised us for the job we had done and handed each of us a crisp one-dollar bill. That was the first dollar I earned. Dad never did believe in spoiling his children by over-paying them.

The next year our furs brought $308. We received $1.50 each for our winter's work. In the spring of 1920, I took the furs to Vancouver alone and handed Dad $710 on my return. Tom and I got two dollars each that year. I bought a good hunting knife and a pocket compass with my share.

The year I turned eleven, Tom was working in a sawmill, so I hunted alone most of the time. By now I had learned to set a trap that would catch Mr. 'Coon almost every time he passed. The system was to place it under water and cover it over with mud, except for the trigger. Instead of bait, I would use a piece of silver foil, which shone in the moonlight. The curious nature of the creatures led them to investigate. They usually ended up in the trap.

That winter, an incident happened that almost cost me my life. It was bitterly cold, with snow over ten inches deep. I had killed one 'coon and was tracking another on the west side of Cusheon Lake. For some reason, the critter decided to cross the lake. Before venturing out, I cut a hole to see how thick the ice was. It was over an inch, so it was strong enough to carry my weight in safety. I followed his trail to the opposite shore and then about one hundred yards along to where, for some reason, he had decided to go back across the lake. Following his trail was so easy I became careless. Forty feet out, his tracks led beneath a big overhanging cedar, under which, of course, the ice was thinner.

Without warning, I broke through and found myself in deep water. I threw the gun towards the shore and barely managed to grab an overhanging cedar limb to haul myself to where my feet touched bottom. A cold north wind was blowing and in less than two minutes my outer clothing was frozen stiff. My feet felt like blocks of ice.

It was a long three miles over a bush trail to home. I quickly pulled off my boots to wring the water out of my socks. The matches I carried were wet so a fire was out of

101

the question. The sun was disappearing behind the hills to the west. I started for home at a fast trot.

After a mile, the trail crossed an open slash. I spotted cougar tracks that looked as big as dinner plates. The cougar was travelling in the same direction I was going. A strange tingle went up and down my spine as I relived my previous experience. I pulled off my mitts and loaded the little gun. Taking four of the strongest shells from my frozen pants pocket, I carried them in my left hand in readiness. I went forward in the cougar's tracks, expecting to see him crouched and waiting at every turn in the trail. Any awareness of the cold was now forgotten. I didn't run, but moved towards home in a cautious walk. There was a distinct feeling of being stalked.

Ten minutes farther along, there was a large impression in the snow where the cougar had crouched. At this point, he left the trail to go into a jumble of logs and scrub timber.

After passing this point I kept glancing back over my shoulder to see if the big cat was after me. It was pitch dark before I saw the lights of our house in the distance.

Mother had sensed something was wrong and had been worrying about me. When she felt my clothes she pulled back.

"You is frozen up like a iceberg! What in the world happened?"

"Fell in the lake," I said.

"Get by that fire and get those icy clothes off while I make hot cocoa," she ordered.

Wrapped in a blanket, I related the incident between sips of hot chocolate. I was sent to bed early with a warning from Dad. "No more hunting alone unless you learn to be more careful about ice."

It was a day I will never forget.

Family Stories

On warm summer evenings our dinner was often cooked outside over an open fire. We children were taught how to cook our own pieces of venison, grouse or trout, on sticks or long metal forks, with just the right amount of salt and pepper. We toasted them to a mouth-watering dark brown. The smell was so good we could hardly wait to start eating. Potatoes were cooked by burying them under the campfire. There was no aluminum foil then to wrap them in, so we just buried them with their skins on. By the time the meat was done they were dug up, black and ready to eat.

Sometimes Mother made a pot of beans in the old cast-iron pot, then heated them slowly on some hot rocks by the side of the fire. Homemade biscuits were set on the lid of the pot to keep them warm enough to melt the freshly-churned butter. We had real feasts and we all realized how lucky we were.

While Ethel and Margaret helped Mother clear away the dishes, Dad would stoke up the fire. Tom and I would sit up close and ask for some stories. He seemed to have an everlasting supply, but the stories about "fighting chickens" intrigued me the most. Dad really liked to talk about this subject. He would go to the house and bring back a special package which was wrapped in oiled silk. In it was a pair of shiny steel spurs that looked like sharp, miniature ice-cream cones. Tiny buckskin ties were attached. He would tell us how many fights these spurs had helped his roosters win. They were among his most precious possessions, having survived the flood in Whitney.

He showed us how they fit over a rooster's natural spurs, which had to be shaped to fit inside the steel ones. Getting a stick about the size of a rooster's leg, with a small branch protruding from the stem, he would whittle the branch down to the size and shape of the silver spur. We were then shown how to tie the buckskin laces so they wouldn't slip off or be too tight. We were allowed to hold the stick and spur and feel the needle-sharp point.

These spurs had come from England and Dad was given them by his grandfather, George Washington Garner II. This man had been a renowned cockfighter from the 1850's to 1880, winning both money and fame. "Spurs," Dad explained, "are made either in Sweden or England."

Dad's grandfather had known a Mr. Arrington of Nashville, Tennessee, who had traded one of his best roosters to the President of Mexico for its weight in gold. Six pounds of gold was a small fortune in those days, about $3,000.

"That's what decided me in getting some fighting stock," Dad said. His grandfather had seen whole fortunes won and lost on the big cock fights. Dad started when he was just eight years old. He showed us scars on his hands and arms inflicted by these roosters. We wished there were rooster fights on Saltspring, and I'm sure Dad did too.

A few years later these stories produced results which caused real excitement in our family.

We kept chickens for eggs and meat. One day I decided I would teach our big Rhode Island Red rooster to fight. From the time that rooster could crow, I learned to imitate and answer him from some hiding place. He would get mad and frustrated and strut around looking for the trespasser on his domain. When I showed myself, answering his every cluck and crow, he would approach me in a fighting stance. I waited until he was close enough; then I'd push him around. He would fly at my arm and peck and beat it with his wings, at the same time striking with his spurs. I always wore a coat with long, heavy sleeves and an old winter glove that was at least two sizes too big. These protected me from his gaffs. He soon became pugnacious enough to fight almost anything that moved. He damned near killed the cat!

One day, Ethel was bent over a nest collecting eggs when Big Red sunk a spur in her cheek just below her right eye. Mother doctored the wound with Zambuck ointment, which was used for everything. Ethel was lucky the spur missed her eye. She carried the scar as long as she lived.

Mother developed a hatred for Big Red. I kept up the fighting to the point where he would fly up off the ground and try to spur me in the face. This was great fun for us both, but one day the fun was all over.

Mother was going to get eggs when the rooster made the mistake of flying up at her. With one hand she caught him by both legs in mid-air. Without stopping in her stride, she marched over to the chopping block and picked up the double-bitted axe. In one swift movement, she swung the rooster's head onto the block and, with her free hand, made the downward swing. Big Red's body lay on one side of the chopping block and his head on the other.

Mother moved on to the henhouse for the eggs. On her way back she picked up the dead rooster. There was chicken and dumplings for dinner that night.

I spotted my rooster's head as soon as I got home from school. It lay on its side facing me, one eye wide open in a shocked, frozen stare. His beak was open and the tongue stuck out. The beak looked exactly as it had so many times before, set and ready to take a good hard peck at the old glove.

105

For a full minute I stood there staring, tears of anger and remorse filling my eyes. Then I kicked the head as hard as I could. I followed it to where it came to rest, picked it up and tried hard not to look at it. Taking the thing behind the barn, I dug a grave and buried it, making a cross to mark the spot.

To make things worse, as I came nearer the house, the smell of cooking drifted from the kitchen. I knew who was in that big, black pot. I turned and went back to the grave and sat down to think, the worst thought being that Big Red was getting cooked for supper.

Didn't they realize that this was like eating one of the family? This was cannibalism! I wanted to puke! I could imagine them all sitting there, enjoying chicken and dumplings. I wondered where Mother had put the legs of the rooster. Thinking about pictures of Sinbad the Sailor in a heavy log cage and the cannibals standing around with large leg bones twisted in their hair, I thought that if I could take off most of my clothes and twist one of Big Red's leg bones in my hair, then parade around the table as they were starting to eat, it might spoil their appetites.

Then I began to worry about Big Red's head lying in its grave. Was this enough of him for a proper and dignified burial? I recalled what our Grade One teacher had explained to us about the head and brain; that the brain was the most important part of our bodies and not even a finger could move unless it got orders to do so. After considering this I decided the head was really very important and the burial was okay.

I stayed around the grave for about an hour, not wanting to see anyone, then headed for the house. Just as I entered supper was announced, but I would not even go into the kitchen. Pretending to be sick, I went around to the front door, slouched to the bedroom, and went to bed.

Later that same year, we had a rare experience with a nest of Mallards. We had been allowed to go fishing on the 24th of May and, on the way to Wakelin's Creek, a pair of Mallards gave us a start, flying out of the bushes almost at our feet. Tom went over to look and to his surprise there was a nest with ten speckled, greenish-coloured eggs. We decided to go on fishing and pick up the eggs on our return home. We thought they might hatch under our broody Leghorn hen.

When we got back some two hours later, two of the eggs had hatched, the fluffiest, cutest babies you could imagine. They were a beautiful yellow with light-green beaks and orange feet. We had a quick meeting for a plan of action.

Ethel took the fish and fishing-rods and hurried home to get things ready. Tom put the two newly-borns in his hat, using all the fluff and feathers from the nest to keep them warm and comfortable. Tightening out belts as much as we could, Margaret and I took four eggs each and put them inside our shirts right against our skin so they wouldn't get cold.

We couldn't travel too fast for fear of breaking the eggs. About halfway home I felt something wriggling and wet inside my shirt. I yelled for Tom to come and have a look; sure enough, another baby duck had hatched. We fished him out and put him into the hat with the others. I tried to clean out the mess in my shirt with some twigs and moss.

We barely got going again when Margaret had the same experience. We arrived home with five baby ducks and five eggs. Margaret and I didn't smell so good, so into a washtub with soap and water we went, after which we put on clean clothes.

Mother thought we should wait until dark before putting the eggs and babies under the Leghorn.

"She won't be able to see what y'all are doing," she explained.

To keep them warm, our prizes were placed behind the stove in a dishpan Ethel had lined with some old blanket cloth.

Mother was as excited as we were. "Be sure to take all

them chicken eggs out afore you give her the ducks,'' she advised.

At dusk, Tom and I took the pan and contents to the henhouse. We removed the chicken eggs, putting them under another hen, and then we put the ducklings and eggs under the Leghorn. There were the weirdest cluckings and peepings coming from that nest. Nature works in wondrous ways. I'm sure that hen knew something was not just as it should be; however, she stayed on the nest and covered the ducklings to keep them warm. During the night the remaining five eggs hatched.

At daylight the next morning, we headed for the henhouse. It was a funny sight. The Leghorn hen was clucking, scratching, and trying to feed the baby ducks, who paid little or no attention to her. They were much more interested in drinking water and trying to swim in the water trough. This went on for a couple of days. The hen was going crazy all day, but covering the ducklings at night. We all agreed that something had to be done to cool down this crazy hen. As it was, she ran around all day with her feathers stuck out, looking more like a turkey gobbler than a chicken.

We held another meeting. It was decided we would build a coop with a nest in it and put it down by our creek, inside a chicken-wire pen. We felt if the ducklings could swim, the Leghorn might relax and act a bit more normal. Two days later we made the big move to the creek. It took all four of us about an hour to catch the ducklings and pack them, along with the coop, to the new pen. The mother hen was so uptight she was put into an old sack to stop her pecking our hands. We released the mother first. Her feathers were almost back to normal and it was agreed by all that this was an improvement. When the ten little Mallards were let out, they first ran to the Leghorn, who was trying to find a bug for them, clucking as she searched.

Then the ducklings saw the water! They leapt off the bank and into the creek, playing, splashing and diving. I guess the hen thought they were drowning. She ran up and down the bank and along the creek, picking up sticks, stones and anything else she could hold in her beak, clucking and calling desperately. This performance went on for ten minutes or more, while we rolled with laughter in the grass, holding our sides. Finally, that crazy hen jumped into the water among the ducklings. By the time we stopped laughing enough to go over and fish her out, she was almost drowned. I've never seen a more bedraggled-looking chicken before or since. She died the very next day. Mother said, "The cold water probably caused pneumonia."

The four of us buried the hen where the ducklings could see the cross that marked the grave; then we held another of our short meetings. It was decided the cause of death was "lunacy, caused by a nervous breakdown." We all agreed that we didn't know enough about pneumonia to make a decision about such a dreaded disease.

Looking after and feeding the little ducks was an unforgettable pleasure for all of us. They huddled together, looking like one ball of fluff, to keep warm at night. During the day they ate, swam and grew. In two months they were getting feathers and trying to fly. By this time we had each picked and named a pair for our own. They were tamer than the chickens and would follow us from the creek up to the house. They were always hungry, so by coaxing them with food we taught them many tricks. One was to fly up, sit on our shoulders, and take bread from our mouths.

A racoon caught four of them one night. We shot the 'coon when he came back for his second duck dinner. When they could fly, the six would leave in the daytime, but for over a year, two of them came back every evening to be petted and fed. As we came home from school, these two would fly a quarter of a mile down the trail to meet us, then walk on home at our feet, quacking and pecking at our hands. We always managed to have some bread crumbs or other goodies they liked.

It was a real lesson for us all, to see how these wild ducks trusted us and became so friendly and tame. They were an influence that brought Tom, Margaret, Ethel and myself very close. Pearl, who was only three, almost fed her two ducks to death. No matter how we explained or scolded she just kept on feeding them. Her two never got sick, just grew. It was fun.

Another of our family's very first pets was a young buck deer. Dad and Uncle Frank had been out checking on the sheep. It was lambing season. They came upon fresh cougar tracks in the melting snow. They followed the tracks and found a recently-killed doe. It was partly eaten and had been crudely covered, in the manner of cougars. Close examination showed that the deer had already fawned and was nursing at least one.

Dad kept on the cougar trail, hoping to get a shot at the big cat. Though he trailed it for several hours, he never sighted the animal. Uncle Frank backtracked the doe and came upon fawn tracks. There, under a big windfall, lay our first wild pet. I can still remember when Dad carried it into the kitchen and laid it behind the stove to warm up. It was light-brown with yellowish spots and oh! so dainty. Frank named him "Rastus."

The fawn showed no fear, nor did it attempt to run away. Rather, it tried to follow anything that moved, including the cat. "Kitty," as we called her, promptly jumped up on the nearest window ledge, her tail bushed out to three times its normal size. She growled for a few minutes, then settled down to stare steadily at this new intruder.

Mother produced the bottle and nipple she kept handy for feeding young lambs that had lost their mothers. Half-filling the bottle with warm milk mixed with a bit of corn syrup, she first looked at the fawn, then at me. I was itching to pet this cuddly creature.

"Now son, if you can feed it you can call it yours and raise it for your own." If someone had given me the world the pleasure could not have been greater. The fawn was hungry so it was no problem to get him to drink. When he had taken what was in the bottle he just nuzzled my clothes and hands, looking for more.

Many happy hours were spent with our spotted playmate. He would follow us around like a puppy, and play, run and sleep at will. At four months he was not so dependent on his bottles of milk. He was beginning to eat grass and to chew at our clothes and anything else he could find. He was big enough to push me over with his head and smack me around with his front feet. He wasn't dangerous but it annoyed Mother when he started chewing at her apron and clothing. More than once he was found curled up on her bed. He could jump from the floor and land on top of the kitchen table with one bound. After he cleaned out the sugar bowl a few times and knocked everything else to the floor, Mother laid down the law.

"If y'all want to keep that thing around here, either tie it up or make a pen for it. He's not going to be allowed to eat anymore sugar or mess the house up again."

We tried a leather collar and dog chain, without success. He just pined and fretted until we let him loose. We tried building a pen and finally had to put up pickets some six feet high to keep him from jumping out. It was comical to try to get his feed through the gate and keep him inside. It took both Tom and I to do this. One of us guarded the gate while the other wrestled Rastus to the ground. When all were safe inside he would get his bottle and the grass we had gathered. He would eat bread or cake, but in the fall months apples were his favourite dish.

In late autumn a drastic change came over Rastus. He had lost all his spots and the velvet from his three-inch horns. They were now hard and sharp and he became quite belligerent. Though he weighed only about sixty pounds, he was strong and quick. I was not allowed to go into his pen with him after he just about ripped my sweater to shreds.

Uncle Frank and Dad knew that the problem was that it was the rutting season for deer, the time of the year when the bucks sparred and fought each other to show who was boss. They would fight almost to the death when a doe decided she was ready to reproduce her kind. It is a well-

111

known fact that most does are bred by the year-old bucks. Usually, there are two or more bucks around when a doe is in season. The older bucks can get into such a battle for her favour that they pay little or no attention to the ''spikes'' or one-year olds. While the fight is on, the young buck sneaks in and does the job willingly. In fact, he usually does so two or three times in quick succession. When he is noticed by the winner you can bet he is run to hell out of there, sometimes on the horns of the larger bucks.

Wild deer could be seen in our fields almost every evening. Dad and Frank waited for the right time. One late afternoon two bucks and a doe were not more than 100 yards from the pen where Rastus was kept. He had seen the other deer and when the gate was opened he bounded in their direction. One of the bigger bucks saw him coming and made a wild dash for him. Somehow, Rastus dodged and stood looking on from a distance. He was no different from young deer raised in the wild. It was getting dusk when the two old bucks began their battle. Some minutes later, Rastus moved in on the doe. Completely unnoticed by the fighting bucks, he did his job three times and then just stood there with his head down. The old bucks either saw or smelled him, for suddenly they stopped fighting and charged our pet. Rastus saw them coming in time to bound to the rail fence, jump it, then run into the woods. As he disappeared into the trees, the horns of the big bucks looked only inches from his rear end.

That was the last time we saw Rastus. Though we called and put feed out for several days he did not come back. He had found what he wanted and decided to stay with it.

Oland Garner c.1900

Lona Beatrice Garner 1902

Lona Garner and family 1923

Lona b.1884 d. 1961   Pearl b.1914
Ethel b.1905   Edie b.1916
Tom b.1907 d.1958   Ollie b.1918
Joe b.1909   Albert b.1920
Margaret b.1911   Lloyd b.1923

Dorothy (not present in photograph) b.1926

Oland Garner and son Tom with cougar 1918

Younger Garner children 1926: *l. to r.* Albert, Ollie, Edie, Lloyd and Pearl

Divide school, May 1, 1922:

Back row: Joe Garner, Decie Beddis, Mary Purdy, Phyllis Taylor, Margaret Garner

Center: Margaret Purdy

Front row: Edith Garner, Rob Ashby, Sheila Taylor, Sam Beddis, Pearl Garner, Jack Ashby, Kathleen Meyer

Chicken house school during a stock show in the early 1920's

Dorothy and Margaret in front of Vancouver house, 1930

The author on old trail to Maxwell's Peak

View from Maxwell Mountain,
Saltspring Island

Whale rub near Vesuvius, Saltspring Island. In the early part of this century, Grey whales still frequented the inland waters between Vancouver Island and the mainland. The whales would lie in the water and the waves would press them against this porous rock and help to loosen and remove barnacles from their bodies. The author remembers himself and the two older Garner children, Ethel and Tom, tying a rope around a tree to lower themselves onto the whales' backs to help kick off the barnacles. While one of the children climbed down, the other two would stand up top to warn of any sudden movement from the whales. This pastime was considered great excitement by all three children.

RECENT PHOTOGRAPHS OF SALTSPRING ISLAND BY ROBERT JOHNSON

Tom Garner on first logging truck on Saltspring Island, Vesuvius, 1922

Marble Island, 1942. *l. to r.* Tom Garner, Fred Robson, John Vonkerman, Ollie Garner, Earl Devlin, Jack Bursey, and prairie boy.

Sailboats being towed out to fishing grounds from Tallheo Cannery at Bella Coola, 1927

Bunkhouse at Tallheo, 1927. Tom and Joe ready to leave for home with their two barrels of salted humpback bellies.

Gravel loading by cat ramp near Duncan, 1940's

Gang from Duncan on hunting expedition at Churn Creek, 1947

First air tong shovel operating on salvage logging. Port Alberni, 1951. Built by Garner Bros. and Berger of Seattle.

Portable slack-line spar used at Alberni, 1951, for Bloedels on pulp salvage.

Garner Bros. store, Duncan, with mobile crane, 1950

Joe Garner and Ted Robson off west end of Chilco Lake, 1951

Moose shot in the Cariboo near Rosita Lake, c.1950.

back: Ted Robson, Donald Butt

front: Joe Garner, Tom Garner and Bill Auchinachie

Landing on snow with floatplane, Chilco Lake area, c.1953

Log hunting cabin, Rosita Lake, in the Chilcotin. Tom Garner with an evening's bag of geese and ducks.

Emily Carr And Growing Up

In the late spring of 1913, I was to go along with Dad on
a shopping and fishing trip, or so I thought. We walked the
four miles to Fulford Harbour where Dad kept our big skiff.
It had been on the beach above high tide and leaked like a
sieve when we first put it in the water. Dad did the rowing
while I bailed as hard as I could with a lard pail. The first
hour was exhausting. Finally the planking swelled to a
point where I could enjoy a brief rest and we could still keep
afloat. We headed for the Saanich peninsula about six miles
away. It seemed to take forever to get there. We caught
three nice salmon on the way.

Pulling our skiff up on the beach in a sheltered bay, we
walked over a rocky trail under a canopy of tall trees and
arrived at a little two-room shanty. It was a kitchen-living
room combination with one small bedroom. The roof was
rough boards and almost flat. There was a woodshed of
sorts and an outhouse. This outhouse was built of brush
with an old toilet seat set up on two logs. A three-foot hole
in the ground completed the structure.

I was warned by the lady who lived in this shanty,

"Don't get too close to that hole or you might fall in." So warned, I was sent out to play with her two big, shaggy sheep dogs. For the rest of the day I had a ball romping with these creatures. It was amazing that the dogs could see me or anything else, with all that hair over their eyes. When I parted the hair off their faces, we looked at each other, eye to eye. The dogs were a light-grey colour and loved to be petted.

We had poached salmon and brown bread for lunch. About four o'clock in the afternoon the wind started to blow. The big trees were swaying and making weird squeaking noises. I can remember Dad saying, "We will have to be leaving soon or it will be too rough to cross the water."

The lady threw her arms around Dad and became almost hysterical, pleading, "You mustn't leave me, you mustn't! You know I'm always terrified when the wind blows the trees."

Dad led her into the house and closed the door. They stayed inside for a long time while I played with the dogs. The sun was sinking below the mountains to the west of Cowichan Bay when they came to the door again. She carried a big pan of dog food and an old patchwork quilt.

After the dogs had eaten we all walked over to the woodshed. In one corner was a pile of straw held in place by some rough boards. The two dogs got in and curled up. Dad handed me the quilt, saying, "If you roll up in that you'll be warm for the night. Better sleep between them."

I crawled in with those wooly creatures and rolled up in the quilt. The lady and Dad went back to the cabin.

That night I'll remember as long as I live. I would just doze off when one of the dogs would lick my face with its wet tongue. The only way to stop the licking was to put the old quilt completely over my head. Somehow the quilt would slip off and then I would awaken again to another big, wet slurp. This went on till daylight.

When I got up the weather was great. The wind had slackened and the sun had warmed the morning air pleasantly. Dad was carrying some kindling and bark into the cabin. Dragging the old quilt, I went over and knocked on the door.

"Come in," the lady called.

Inside the cabin, salmon was frying on the sheet metal stove. A kettle of water boiled briskly. We had salmon steaks, brown bread and Eagle Brand condensed milk stirred into hot water for drinks. It seemed I was about starved, everything tasted so great.

I can still see that little cabin. It was the most messed-up place I have ever come across. On the make-shift shelves were dozens of clay bowls and pots of all shapes and sizes. Even the roof had some on it. There were so many paints and pots on the dresser there was no room for anything else. The table was piled with dishes and pans. There were clothes everywhere, on the floor, on the bed posts, on door knobs; a few things hung on nails driven in the walls. Outside there was a bucket of water by a wooden block, and on the block was a wash basin and soap. A stained old towel hung on a branch of a nearby tree.

The scrambled mess surrounding the cabin left an indelible impression on my mind. There were paintings on the walls and in the dresser drawers. The lady fished some out and she and Dad talked about them. Little did I know then that we were staying with the, later famous, Canadian artist and writer, Emily Carr. The cabin was one of her summer retreats.

Dad and Mother had lived at 64 St. Lawrence Street in 1904, only two blocks to the west of the Carr house. Dad would have been twenty-six and Emily thirty-three. This must have been the year those young people met. The Carr house, which now stands on a single city lot at 207 Government Street was, in 1904, on several acres of land, and the street was known then as Carr Street. Emily's dad had settled the family in Victoria in 1863. He was a merchant of considerable means. Dad worked in the Carr warehouse his first winter in Victoria.

When the old wooden trestle existed across the mud

115

slough just west of where the Empress Hotel now stands, Government Street ended there. South of the trestle was Carr Street. When the present concrete causeway was built in the early 1900's, Government Street was extended south and Carr Street was lost. The Carr home is now an active art center and has been designated a heritage building.

Rowing back to Saltspring we caught more salmon and shopped at the old R.P.Edwards store which was halfway between Fulford Harbour and Burgoyne Bay. In those days this was the only store and post office south of Ganges.

I was told to forget about having to stay overnight at the lady's house. This was our secret and no one else was to know about it, not even Tom or Ethel, and especially not Mother.

"If you mention it to anyone you'll feel that razor strap," Dad warned. I had already had several examples of how the strap felt on a bare bum.

I don't know how often Dad visited Emily Carr. I do know that he worked in Victoria helping to build Emily's "House of All Sorts," as she called her boarding-house and studio. He also worked on other construction jobs. This was in 1913 and 1914.

Dad was a skilled worker and could turn his hand to almost any type of building, including carpentry, bricklaying, painting or plumbing. His wages for four or five months in the summer would pay for all our groceries, shoes and clothes for a full year.

He always seemed to be away during the summers. During the later years of the war he was kept busy in the sawmills and logging camps. This work took priority over military service. The men with experience in this work were frozen in their jobs.

This left the haying and other farm work for us children and Mother to take care of. By this time Tom and I were both big enough to use a scythe. We did the cutting while Ethel and Margaret raked and piled the hay. Dad had sold the oxen and bought a horse and wagon. He built a hay-rack on the wagon and we learned to drive and haul

116

hay. This meant long days of hard work all during July and August. We would have our mid-day meal at the house during this first part of the work.

When we started to cut and make hay in the upper fields Mother would bring lunch out to us in a big basket. Pearl and Edie were now around and had to be taken care of. We had a homemade playwagon in which Mother would put Edie and the lunch basket. Pearl was almost three and big enough to help push or pull the little wagon on the steep grades.

Usually we lunched under a big spreading cedar tree near a spring of cool water. Mother would praise Pearl's efforts.

"Lawsie sakes, if Pearl hadn't helped so hard we'd have never got here at all."

Pearl would sparkle under this praise. She usually sat between Tom and me, believing this gave her more importance, being with the workers. She was always smiling and showing off. While Mother was praising our young sister so graciously, I would watch my chance to give a good hard pull to a strand of her hair, or a sharp pinch to an ear or elsewhere. This would result in an instant squeal and a fast retreat to Mother's lap where Edie usually slept. None of us older children could stand this younger sister playing the part of the big shot. It took all sorts of nasty little tricks to keep her in line.

It would take us the better part of two weeks to cut and stack the upper fields. The hauling to the barn took all of our skills and know-how. The road to the upper fields was so steep our horse had to rest halfway up the first climb. While I did the driving, Tom and Ethel had the chocks ready, and waited at a fairly level place part way up. These chocks were chunks split from a cedar block. When the horse stopped, a chock was jammed behind each rear wheel. Tom and Ethel would put their weight on a wheel spoke to prevent the wagon from rolling back. This allowed the horse to catch his wind enough to make it up the rest of the way. It was a real scramble for the horse to start the

117

wagon again and make that hill. When we reached the flat, we would stop and unhitch him from the hay wagon, go back down to the lower field, hook onto and drag our rough-lock contraption up to where the wagon was parked.

This rough-lock was made from a forked tree about eight inches in diameter, and looked like a big 'Y'. Through a hole bored in the stem of the Y, a stout chain was fastened. This chain was used to pull the thing up the hill and also to hold it securely to the wagon box so the back wheel would ride in the middle of the crotch. A sort of saddle was formed by a plank across the two prongs in a deep notch, just back of the wheel rim. We would leave this contraption on the side of the road until we came back with our load of hay. The rest of the road was rough and steep but not nearly as bad as this particular part.

Mother, Tom and Ethel pitched the hay up on the wagon, and Margaret and Pearl arranged it so it wouldn't slide off. I did the driving and supervised the loading.

The trip down to the barn was a hair-raising performance. We had an extra length of chain that we used to lock one back wheel on the steep places. When the load was down to more level ground, we unhooked the chain. To get the wagon wheel positioned on our rough-lock was a really tricky manoeuvre. First, we had to manhandle the damned thing under the wagon just in front of the rear wheel on the low side of the road. Tom and Ethel would handle the plank that had to go in the notches to hold the wheel forward in the crotch of the locking device. Then the wheel rode on the log like a sleighrunner, locking the wheel and helping to level the load. I would take the horse by the bit and ease him forward a foot or so, standing squarely in front of his head so he wouldn't go too far. He couldn't move forward unless he walked over the top of me, and he often tried to do exactly that. Once the wheel was in place and locked we fastened the forward end of the chain to a long shackle that was pinned to the heavy side board of the hayrack. This caused the wheel to ride exactly where we had blocked it.

118

The road was over solid rock and sloped to the low side so much that the wagon, when loaded, would tip over into a small, steep gully if the back wheel came off this rough-lock. This had happened when Dad and Uncle Frank were bringing in the hay the year before. The shafts broke and the wagon turned wheels up. This turnover scared the hell out of us. It had taken the best part of a week to upright the wagon and repair the broken parts.

To keep the load on the wagon, we tied a long piece of rope to the wagon box and passed it up over the hay, to the high side of the road. Mother, Tom and Ethel would hold back on this rope to keep the hay and wagon from separating or turning over. Big knots were tied in the rope for hand-grips.

I would take the reins and walk or run when necessary, along a trail just clear of the wagon wheels. If any one of us had tripped and fallen he would have gone under a wheel and been run over. This was as exciting as it was dangerous. Once the load was started and rolling down this steep hill, it continued to gain speed until it reached the lower field.

Our horse, named Dan Patch, was a wall-eyed cayuse. He had been caught out of a band of wild horses in the Chilcotin as a colt, broken to harness work, and sold to a horse trader in Vancouver. Dad paid $17.50 for him, wagon and harness, "as is, where is."

This horse wasn't big, but he was mean and wirey. For the start down this hill he would slide on all four feet. As the momentum increased he would start to trot and wind up at the lower field in a dead gallop. It was a bit chaotic with the four of us trying to keep up and hold the hay and horse in line. Once the wagon hit the level field everything stopped in a hurry. We would pry the plank out of its notch and from under the back wheel. I would then back the horse a couple of steps to clear the rough-lock. Once this was done, we would drive on to the barn and fork the hay into the haymow.

Mother and the two small ones would go on to the

119

house to get supper ready. By the time we unloaded and unhitched the horse it was late evening. We usually had fried, home-cured ham and scrambled eggs with lots of cold, fresh milk. By dark we would be in bed and asleep. After days like this, sleep was sound and easy to come by. We were up early every day and anxious to get the rest of the hay in the barn before it rained.

Dan Patch was something to reckon with. It was always my job to go out in the field to catch him and bring him into the barn. I would use a pan of oats to coax him up close enough to put a rope over his neck. Once this was accomplished he would stand still long enough to have the bridle slipped over his head. Getting a rope over his neck was like facing a mad lion. He would lay his ears back and charge straight at me with his mouth open and teeth bared. One could get bitten or struck with a front foot. After a couple of these wild charges the smell of oats usually quieted him down long enough to allow the rope to be slipped over his neck. Once the oats were gone, it became another fight to put on the collar and wagon harness without getting bitten. He could never be trusted as far as biting was concerned.

A horse's bite is a serious thing. He once grabbed Mother by her left arm and I had to smash him over the head with a club to make him let go. She actually fainted from the pain. Her upper arm was black and blue for over two months. That we were never seriously hurt was a miracle. I suspect our agility and conditioning were the major reasons for our staying alive around Dan Patch.

By the time haying was over it was almost time to get back to school. There was always a week or more for wild berry-picking. There were plenty of wild blackberries and black caps to be found in the old burned-over slashes. We would leave early in the morning so we could fill the pails before the day got too hot. The four oldest children would do the picking. Mother would give us each a three-pound lard pail and Ethel and Tom a waterbucket each, saying,

"Fill the small pails and dump them in the big buckets. If you fall down, that way you won't lose so many."

We would always ask, "How many do you want?"

"Fill them all up afore it gets too hot and come on home." She would then take our old .22 rifle off its pegs and hand it to me, saying, "Now, Joe, you hunt down and bring me four or five nice young grouse and I'll make us a feast fit for a king when y'all get home."

And indeed she did. There would be new potatoes and peas, fresh churned butter, fried grouse and gravy, and to top this off we had deep blackberry pie with whipped cream.

It was on one of these hot afternoons after a good dinner when we were all resting on the front porch, that Mother called us together and told us how she learned about tobacco and why she chewed it.

Where she had lived, almost all the young boys and girls from the age of ten up used tobacco. There were few, if any, smokers. Mother learned from some boys how to make her own chewing tobacco. Next to cotton it was a major crop in the south. The kids learned to pick the choicest tobacco leaves at just the right time, dry them a little, then soak them in blackstrap molasses. In a corner of an old rail fence, they would flatten two bottom rails to fit tightly together. With a long pole, one of them would pry up the top rails while the other placed the carefully folded tobacco between the flattened rails. Once all fingers were out of danger the top rails were eased down onto the tobacco leaves, squeezing them tightly together to form a sort of plug. The two who decided to work together on such projects were called "tobacco buddies" and were sworn to secrecy as to where their tobacco was being made. Mother teamed up with her brother Tom. They took great precautions to see that no one followed when they went to inspect their tobacco presses. Mother explained how they would walk backwards in the soft, dusty places. "People used to think we were going 'stead of coming." We would all laugh at this.

121

A couple could have up to a dozen or more plugs in the "make" at the same time and, after a month or so, the plugs would be retrieved and hidden some place in the barn or house to keep dry. The same fence corners were used year after year and it was a well-known fact that the longer a press was used, the stronger and better the tobacco came out.

Mother said that she was chewing tobacco regularly at the age of thirteen and she continued to do so for many, many years. She had started to work in the cotton mills at this age. About eight out of ten of the workers, both girls and boys, used tobacco, but few smoked it. Smoking was not allowed at any time in the mill. Mother breast-fed all of her ten children with no apparent bad effects.

In later years, plugs of chewing tobacco would be purchased at grocery stores, even up in Canada, but many in the south still preferred to make their own. They thought homemade was better. Mother warned us about using tobacco. "It's messy and does no good," she would say.

On school days, our routine would start about six in the morning. I fed and milked two or three cows before breakfast while Tom fed the pigs and chickens and filled the two wood boxes. Margaret and Ethel made our lunches for school and helped get breakfast. We usually had porridge, hot biscuits and home-cured bacon and eggs, jam and jelly. After a final inspection by Mother, we were ready to start the three-mile trek to the Divide school. We had to be on our way by 7:30 a.m. to get there by nine o'clock. In the spring and early fall we would leave the house with our shoes and socks on. A quarter of a mile down the trail we took off and cached these unnecessary items. The teacher would look at our bare feet but never made a big issue of it. Most of the school children did the same, just went barefoot. It was much easier to walk without shoes once our feet toughened up.

In the late fall and winter we did our chores by the light of a coal-oil lantern. It would be barely daylight both when we left and when we arrived home. Wearing shoes added at

122

least fifteen minutes to our travelling time both night and morning. If the snow got too deep we rode that horse, Dan Patch, to school. Three of us could sit on his back while the older ones took turns leading him. Two full sacks of hay were tied together and thrown over his back just forward of his shoulders. The horse was tied and fed while we played and studied. We didn't like the responsibility of the horse and only used him when absolutely necessary. He was always ready to bite anyone who came within reach. I preferred to walk rather than ride unless the snow was over eighteen inches deep. I wonder how the parents and children of today would relate to such conditions.

It was at the Divide school that I saw my first motor car. It was a black 1912 Model-T Ford with a brass radiator. This car was owned by the Blackburn family. Their son, Peter, had learned to drive the thing in Vancouver and had brought it to Saltspring in the summer of 1914. When the car came down the steep hill of the old Divide road, you could hear it backfiring a mile away. It sounded like gunfire and scared the hell out of any horses within hearing distance. The car had to be backed up this hill so that gas would flow by gravity from the tank under the front seat to the carburetor. Unless the front end of the car was level or below the back end, no gas could get to the engine. This was a problem with those early T-models.

As the car passed the school, after coming down this steep hill, there would be a trail of blue-black smoke pouring out of the exhaust pipe. To us it smelled terrible. When we heard the backfiring start, we'd all gather at the roadside, yelling, "Here comes Peter B and his stink-pot, here comes the stink-pot!"

Nevertheless, we watched this car with great excitement and interest and agreed riding was much better than walking. That spring, Peter came and took all the children for a ride in his "motor car" as he called it. We were all thrilled, especially the teacher.

Miss Morris gave a lecture about motor cars shortly after that first ride. I can still remember the point being stressed that cars would never become numerous because only the wealthiest people could afford to own one, and besides, they were dangerous; they scared the horses.

A Birth And A Baseball Game

Mother was forty-two and Dad forty-nine when the baby of the family came along. It was a sunny day, the 16th of May, 1926.

All that spring the young sports-minded men of the Ganges area had worked every weekend and on until dusk most weekday evenings. They were building a new baseball field. This field was north of Rainbow Road, opposite the old Oxenham private school. To celebrate the completion, Ganges had challenged the South Saltspring boys to a game.

The tie mills were operating full swing. Some of the men in the crews were pretty good amateur ball players.

We believed that with this new talent, Ganges could probably beat our old rivals, who, up to this time, usually humiliated the Ganges baseball team.

Well, this day the game was pretty even until the seventh inning. Ganges was ahead 5 to 4. Fulford came up to bat. Harry Jones was pitching and Tom Scott catching. Tom Garner was on first base, Ross Young, shortstop, Ed

125

Wakelin second base, and I was trying to handle third. The outfield was made up of our best hitters.

Harry Jones had been throwing many curves and his arm played out. Fulford had scored four runs and had the bases loaded with none out in the seventh inning. Harry called time out-- our team went into a huddle. Apart from Dad, Harry was the only pitcher Ganges had.

"Where's Oland Garner?" Tom Scott asked. Brother Tom and I explained how he had stayed with our mother because she was expecting a baby this afternoon.

"Good God!" Harry Jones shouted, "My arm's completely shot, surely someone else could stay with her." He looked straight at me.

"You go and get your dad, then stay on with your mother. I'll try third base, Oland can pitch."

"Hurry," Tom Scott urged.

I ran the block and a half to our house and explained the situation to Dad and told him to hurry over to the field as fast as he could. I would stay with Mother.

I believe Dad had been sitting outside listening, and had expected someone to come for him. He had his glove and spiked shoes hanging on the gatepost.

"You go and get Mrs. Harvey to help," he shouted back.

Without hesitation or a single word of explanation to Mother he headed for the ball game at a fast dogtrot.

Mrs. Harvey was experienced, having acted as midwife for many Saltspring Island mothers. Her home was only a block away so I ran down and got her to come as quickly as possible. I waited to walk back with her and carried her little bag that held the things she needed.

By the time we got back, Mother had started having severe pains.

"You get me some water and a bit of good wood for the stove," Mrs. Harvey ordered. This I did on the double. I filled the woodbox and put a big pot of water on the stove to boil. I could hear Mother let out a scream once in a while. She called me to the bedroom door.

126

"You go back to that ball game and tell your daddy he is needed here and be quick about it," she ordered.

I ran back to the ball park. It was the first of the ninth inning and Dad was pitching. While I was away he had struck out four batters in a row. Fulford had not scored a run since he went in to pitch. The score was now 8 to 7 in Fulford's favour.

I was put back in the game on arrival. Their side went out without a run being scored. Harry Jones' arm was now too sore to even swing a bat.

This was Ganges' big chance. It was the last half of the ninth inning, the end of the game. Ed Wakelin was first up and hit a fly ball out to their shortstop. I followed and hit a lucky double to right field. Dad followed me with a line drive into center field. I scored, tying the game on his hit. Ross Young flied out to their first baseman. Tom Scott was our best hitter and came up next. He slammed the first pitch out of the park for a homerun. It was all over.

Dad and Scott were the big heroes. Everyone was slapping them on the back and telling them what a great game they had played.

It was prearranged that the losers supplied the beer.

When I was able to get close enough to Dad, I told him what Mother had sent me back to tell him.

"You go back and tell your mother I'll come as soon as I can," he ordered. "You're too young for beer anyway."

I ran back to find things had worsened.

"You go and get Dr. Sutherland as fast as you can run," Mrs. Harvey shouted, as I came up the driveway. I didn't even stop, just kept on running. It was half a mile up the hill to the doctor's house. Luckily she and her husband were at home. They were just getting into their car for a Sunday evening drive. I explained why I was there. Dr. Sutherland rushed into the house to get her black bag. Her husband told me to get in the back seat. We arrived at our house not more than half an hour after the ballgame ended. I carried in the doctor's bag and set it by the door of

Mother's bedroom. Mrs. Harvey was very excited and ordered, "Go and get your father and be quick about it!"

I thought they just wanted me to hell out of the house because of the circumstances. Back at the ball field I let Dad know what was happening at home. He left as soon as he could.

It seems there were serious complications with this birth. Dr. Sutherland, Mrs. Harvey and Dad stayed up all night. Both Dorothy and Mother almost died. This was when Dr. Sutherland told Mother, "If you have another baby, there is less than one chance in ten of you living through it."

Mother was not strong enough to get out of bed for ten days. Mrs. Harvey came every morning and stayed all day. The doctor came twice a day for over a week. They were afraid of infection. On the third day I heard Dr. Sutherland telling Dad, "You should have your wife in the hospital. She is very weak and very sick. You could lose her and the baby too if things go wrong."

"Oh, she should be all right where she is for a few days. Those hospitals are too expensive for us," Dad argued.

"Mr. Garner, you are telling us you are gambling with your wife's life and the baby's for a few paltry dollars," Dr. Sutherland exclaimed with contempt. Mrs. Harvey was furious, but Dad stood firm on his decision.

Everyone knew Dad had considerable money in his bank account. He had sold logs and poles in the last three years for big sums. He certainly hadn't spent any of it on the family.

When she was able to sit up in an old easy chair with her new baby, Mother called Tom and me in one evening, just after we finished our supper. The other children had gone out to play or do chores.

"Y'all check the doors and make sure no one is listening," Mother ordered. Tom went and locked the front door while I checked and locked the inside one.

"Now I have to tell you my secret. No one else is to know until it happens," she explained.

"Now just what secret have you got?" Tom inquired with a laugh.

Mother told us what the doctor had said about her having more babies, and Dad's refusal to let the doctor put her in the hospital for better care and a possible operation.

"We are going to have to leave your daddy soon as I get strong enough so y'all better count on it. Say not a word to any of the others about this. I'll let you know when. That's all there is to it for now."

We left the room in silence. As soon as we were outside Tom and I went next door to the billiard hall and held our meeting. We could be alone there.

This was a great shock to both of us. I was seventeen and Tom was nineteen. The day before we had thought of ourselves as a complete family unit. Today we were planning for its disintegration.

We wrote out a list of things we wanted to take with us. Everything could be packed in the old train trunk Dad and Mother brought with them from the Carolinas some twenty-three years earlier.

Margaret's Story

"My fondest childhood memories are those centered about our home on the farm. We were surrounded by virgin forest. A beautiful stream ran near the house to supply 'good branch water,' as Dad described it. It also provided us children with an ever-present source of fun and amusement.

"Most of our household furniture was made from local materials of round poles and deer hides. We children slept on homemade beds with straw mattresses in two upstairs rooms, the boys in one, the girls in the other. The one I shared with my younger sisters, Pearl and Edie, had a nice window facing out over the orchard and fields. This room, with its privacy, was ideal for doing the things we chose to do. It was a lovely place to curl up with a book, and much of the reading I did there has remained vividly in my memory.

"*Little Women,* the Zane Grey books, *Black Beauty* and *Lonesome Pine,* opened vistas that one could only dream about. Though our parents forbade us to read late, we would stuff the crack around the door with paper so that light couldn't be seen as we read by coal-oil lamp far into the night, savouring every moment.

"There was a wide, covered verandah on three sides of the house, where moss roses and honeysuckle grew in profusion, covering the bannisters and providing shade. Here, during the summer, we ate both lunch and supper. Mealtimes were gay and full of laughter. Mother would usually have her meal before we arrived at the table so that she could eat in peace. She waited on the family during the meal, then would sit and drink her coffee with us. Dad was adamant that we children drank only milk or water. He lived strictly by this rule, not touching stimulants of any kind.

"There was no bathroom in the house. The big sink in the corner of the kitchen, with a cold water tap, was used by all the family to wash face and hands. Baths had to be taken in a large washtub in the kitchen with a blanket pulled across for privacy.

"Clothes were washed by hand, using a scrubbing board. This was an onerous task for such a large family. The white clothes had to be boiled in lye to keep them white. There was no bleach. Sad irons, heated on the stove, were used for pressing. Mother always set a full day aside for this chore.

"It was a great adventure when Mother would go off in the buggy to the store at Ganges. She would take one or two of the children with her, and the ones left at home would wait in great anticipation for the goodies she would bring them.

"In season, boxes of fresh vegetables were taken to partly pay for supplies not produced on the farm. Enough food was produced and preserved to help tide the family over the winters.

"As children, we picked big pails of wild blackberries and blackcaps, which were a delicacy when made into jam or warm berry pies. Picking berries took up a lot of our time during the summer holidays, and we knew all the good patches for miles around.

"Usually, there were large pots of peas and beans, or hominy corn, slowly cooking on the back of the woodstove. It was Joe's and my chore to carry our wheat to the neighbours, the Prices, to have it ground for use in bread and porridge. We enjoyed this task. It gave us contact with an adult family quite different from our own, and one which seemed interested in us. In summer they would let us pick some ripe grapes to take home.

"Before I was ten, Mother fully instructed me in the making of bread. The method was to take a hard Royal Yeast cake and soak it in potato water until dissolved, then mix it with salt and more warm water and flour, stir to soft dough stage, and then keep adding flour until it could be kneaded. This was the most enjoyable part, and one of the younger sisters always begged to help. It was great fun getting our hands into it and feeling the elasticity of the dough as it was punched down. We used brown and white flour, half and half, with no shortening, milk or eggs. The dough was put in a large, greased bowl, and covered, first with a white cloth, and then with several warmed woollen sweaters. This was set near the stove to rise overnight. Our cat found this a cozy place to sleep. The next morning we would punch it down and let it rise another couple of hours before putting it in loaf pans to rise again before baking. I have no memory of 'store boughten' bread in our house.

"We had a large earthenware churn. When it was full of cream, we children took turns lifting the dasher up and down until the butter came. When the buttermilk was drained off it was considered a great treat. The butter was salted and worked with the hands until the moisture was removed, then we put it in a square press to shape it for wrapping. This fresh butter was sweet and much enjoyed on the hot pan-breads and biscuits that Mother could turn out in a jiffy.

"Her cooking was naturally influenced by her Southern upbringing, and our regular fare was similar to that of the Carolinas. I remember especially her pan-fried chicken or grouse, with sweet milk gravy.

132

"Fruit, vegetables, salted meat and fish and sauer-
kraut were stored in our cellar. It was one of my evening
tasks to fetch a bowl of apples for the family. There were
numerous varieties, but our favourites were the golden
russets.

"Our parents felt that the best way to clean teeth
before retiring was to eat apples. None of us owned a toothbrush, or had any cavities until long after we had left the
farm. Dad was a prodigious apple eater, and had his own
teeth when he died at the age of eighty-three. He had never
visited a dentist.

"We were taught to dress and preserve the animals
raised on the farm without refrigeration. All the meat had
to be dealt with immediately. The whole family pitched in
on butchering days. I particularly remember when pork was
on the agenda.

"There was a fire with a big drum of boiling water at
one end of the scraping platform. The hogs were dunked
into this, then pulled back onto the platform. We were all
given knifes to scrape the hair from the skin.

"There was headcheese to make, bacon and hams to
smoke, sausage and pickled pig's feet to be preserved, as
well as some to be canned or salted. Nothing was left but
the squeal.

"Our meat supply was augmented by wild game, of
which there was no shortage. Venison was a staple food for
all residents. Dad, Tom and Joe were ardent hunters.

"Our meals were hearty and wholesome, and must
have included the ingredients for a well-balanced diet.
With our good appetites, it never occurred to us that some
children had to be coaxed to eat. There was never a thought
that there might be people in the world going hungry.

"Winter evenings were spent around the fireplace.
Mother would lie on the sofa while the school-age children
were doing their homework by coal-oil lamps. Often, Dad
would take his banjo from the wall to play and sing us
ballads of the South. He played by ear and could remember
verse after verse of many old songs. We were encouraged

133

to sing along with him, and if he was in an enthusiastic mood, he would teach us to do some tap-dancing. We were always proud when he was asked to sing and dance at the school concerts, or at other public functions. He recited the Uncle Remus stories. It was hard for us to understand them from the books, but hearing them in his southern drawl brought them to life.

"Mother's Baptist background had not encouraged stage play. She and Dad never danced together, yet I can remember her sweetly singing such old hymns as *Rock of Ages, Shall We Gather At The River,* and *In The Sweet Bye And Bye* while working about the house.

"Dad's religious background was Catholic, and he saw to it that we were baptized in a Catholic chapel. He insisted that we received catechism instruction from Father Sheiland, a priest who came to our house once a month, for this purpose. He usually spent the night with us. This was a most contentious issue with my parents, and in later years, Mother would not consent to having the younger children baptized in the Catholic faith. She felt that they should wait until they were old enough to make their own choices.

"Though there was no Baptist church on the Island, Mother had strong religious convictions. I remember her reading the Bible often. She had a very limited education, but a clear and keen mind. She made a study of the Bible, and was able to quote a fitting phrase to help us solve most of our problems.

"The realities and permanence of natural forces were acknowledged. Her instinctive goodness and common sense influenced all our lives. She instilled in each of us the necessity to cultivate independence. We were cautioned to take neither favours nor charity.

"Though our family may have appeared poor in material things, we never felt poor. She taught us to be neither envious nor self-conscious. The Golden Rule and 'What ye sow, so shall ye reap' were drilled into us as the basic guides of life.

"It was at grade school that we realized we spoke differently.

"Our parents had particularly broad Southern accents. The majority of the population on Saltspring was English, and their accents were rather exaggerated. It was natural that we were teased about our speech.

"As an example, my birth certificate showed my name as 'Moguet' instead of Margaret, so I had it legally changed later in life.

"The arrogance and pomposity of the English population irritated me for many years.

"Two outlets into fantasy worlds for me were the creek on one side of the farm and the trail which led through a forest to the Seymour place on the other. Vera Seymour and I were the same age and she was the only girlfriend I had as a child. We used this trail often and knew every curve along the way. Huge virgin trees, with limbs touching the ground, created a dark and foreboding atmosphere. 'Coons, deer, squirrels and other little animals abounded, but there was always the terrifying possibility of meeting a panther.

"The creek that ran near the house furnished us with never-ending interests. In spring we would follow it along through the woods, it seemed for miles, to where it ran into Price's Lake. Along its banks there were endless things to see. In the deep, dark pools, there were lots of speckled trout to catch. Fallen logs across the creek were a challenge to walk. Maidenhair fern grew in profusion. In spring we watched the tender, graceful shoots unfolding into umbrellas.

"I was nearly four when my sister Pearl was born, and then Edith less than two years later. As they grew out of babyhood, it was constantly pointed out to me by Mother that, as I was the older, I was responsible for their safety. They were super-active, making this quite a task. It was hard for Pearl to give way to another baby taking her place. Jealousy caused many a fracas. When the crying started, Edie had a habit of holding her breath until she turned blue

135

in the face. It would take a sharp smack on the back, or a cup of cold water in the face, to start her breathing again. Sometimes I was sure she wouldn't make it. Joe tells me he caught Pearl forcing Edith to eat round rocks from the creeks in an effort to eliminate her.

"Being the fourth member of the family, and coming along right behind my older brothers, it was natural that I should try to do the things they did. Ethel was seven years my senior and, as children, we did not share the same interests. When she was barely eighteen, she left home to train as a nurse in St. Joseph's Hospital. When she had completed a little over two years of her training, she was afflicted with osteomyelitis, which invalided her for years. She remained in the hospital, having several operations on her leg.

"Much of my childhood was spent trailing Tom and Joe. There was always great competition between them. I must have been more of a nuisance than a companion. I tagged along when they hunted deer and birds, never carrying a gun, though happy to help carry the game. They taught me to act as spotter and retriever. I was often the driver, generally through thick salal, in my bare feet. They would each take a stand in a position ahead of me. I had to thrash through the brush, driving the game towards them. This role was a pretty important one, I thought, and when we took in a good bag, I felt just as important as the hunters.

"My brothers loved to do acrobatic stunts, and prided themselves on their skills. They would practice by the hour on the high beams in the hay barn. I tried to do all the things they did. We could jump from the beams, turning double somersaults before hitting the hay. We would hang from the beams by our feet while one of us would swing from one pair of hands to another. We stretched a rope so that we could learn to walk a tight-rope in our bare feet.

"A favourite game was putting on a circus. We never seemed to get hurt, though I'm sure some of the things we did were dangerous.

136

"We all went barefoot during the summer and our feet got tough enough to bound over the gravel roads. We could always think of plenty of ways to pass the time without the company of other children. However, this lack of company made me very shy and self-conscious when strangers were around.

"Memories of our walk to school are still very clear to me. As a short-cut, we would walk over a log high above the fast-running water. As there was nothing to hang on to, it was a thrill each time we made it across.

"Students from the Divide school had to write the high school entrance exams at Ganges. I remember feeling terribly nervous and shy in these unfamiliar surroundings. Because of the tension and excitement, I did not do my best. My report showed that I had failed by nine marks. This was shattering news to me, and I felt devasted at letting the teacher and my family down.

"I was kept out of school the next term. I was thirteen. I stayed home that fall and winter, helping with the farm chores, feeling very worthless and depressed. Then, in the spring, Dad announced that I should go back to school, finish the term, and take the exam again. In June I passed and restored my faith in myself.

"During that summer, our family moved from the farm to a house in Ganges, primarily, I expect, so that Joe and I could attend high school there in the fall.

"The two years spent attending high school in Ganges were among the more impressionable ones of my life. Joe and I were warmly welcomed into all the school sports and the competition was just what we had longed for. Our groundwork at home was paying off, and we had no trouble making the top teams in baseball and basketball. This made us feel more accepted in society generally, and was a big step in helping me overcome my bashfulness.

"I applied for a job at a private school for boys near our home and got it. Waiting table for the evening meal for those schoolboys, most of whom were about my own age, was the most threatening task I ever faced. Serving the first time was an indescribable nightmare to me. However, noting their evening fare of skimpy portions of uninteresting-looking food did make me thankful for our own family meals. Slowly my embarrassment subsided and I was able to perform my duties with poise and some dignity. I never adjusted to this position, which I felt to be a servile one. I was glad when the job ended in June. The reward of this first job was that my shyness, which had been both a refuge and a torture, was gradually overcome.

"For the first time in my life, I became aware of my appearance. It was painfully distressing to me that I did not have bought dresses like most of the other girls. In the fall, Mother ordered some fine woollen material and a pattern from the catalogue, and painstakingly made me a school dress. I flatly refused to wear it because it was homemade. It hung in the closet all term. Since Mother had taken more than usual care in making the dress, she was naturally hurt, and stated emphatically that she would never make another thing for me, which she never did.

"Both Joe and I passed the government exams that year and were ready to go into Grade Ten. Our family moved again to the north end to commence logging there. This was about eight miles from the school, so it was decided that Joe and I would batch in our big house at Ganges. We had a one-ton Model-T Ford, which Joe drove. No licence was needed. It was assumed that if you thought you could drive, you could. We felt very proud and independent as we headed out on Monday mornings to spend the school week alone.

"Batching was a new experience, giving us freedom and responsibility. We were allowed to use the family credit account at Mouat's store for food, but were cautioned to practise some frugality. There was little advice from Mother about what we should eat. She knew we wouldn't heed her counsel. On Monday afternoon we would boil a big pot of potatoes with the skins on, enough to last five days. Some chickens had been left, so fried potatoes and scrambled eggs were our usual breakfast, lunch and supper. Little time was wasted on meal planning, though it seems we did keep healthy.

"Having lost most of my shyness, I felt self-assured enough to wear the dress Mother made for me. There were so many compliments on it, I rarely wore anything else that year. Though Mother noticed me wearing it, she never made any comment. She probably was well aware of the teen-age years when things that don't really matter, matter terribly.

"When I was fifteen, Dorothy was born. Apart from realizing that Mother had had some very bad days, and being completely involved with my own life, I gave little thought to her or the baby. I do remember being apologetic with my school friends about another child being added to our already large-enough family.

"Dad was acting like a free agent. The heavy burden of raising the family was falling more and more on Mother's shoulders.

"I was aware of friction in the house, but carried on with my own affairs. At the end of June I got a job at the Croftons' Harbour House, as a waitress. I was thrilled with the idea of making real money for the first time. The salary and tips were more than I ever expected. I was glad to give most of it to Mother.

"I swam a lot that summer with my new friends, once right across Ganges Harbour and back without an escort. We knew no fear and never told our parents of our escapades.

"One day near the end of August, Mother called me in and told me she was leaving for Vancouver. Tom and Joe were already over there, building a house. She instructed me to stay at my job until after Labour Day. Then I was to go over on a certain sailing.

"The prospect of going to Vancouver for the first time in my life was cause for great anticipation. When Mother left with Edie, Albert, Lloyd and Dorothy, I was at work. The fact that Pearl and Oliver were staying on with Dad did not register in my mind as being serious. It was some four years later that Pearl came to join us. She had grown into a young lady.

"At first, Tom, Joe and I were the only source of funds Mother had, and yet she kept their bargain and never asked for additional money or favours from Dad.

"This new challenge left us little time to dwell on minor problems. We all took it as a game to be enjoyed and won. Our spirits were high and gay and what should have seemed hardship turned into fun. Mother's outlook was always bright, and she remained the solid hub around which the family revolved. She convinced us of the need for unity as a way of survival. Her optimistic view showed the courage she had.

"As time passed, we each upgraded our working skills and were able to keep a satisfactory amount of pay for ourselves.

"Shortly after we were settled, Ethel came to live with us, and contributed in any way she could. We spent our single years in this house and it was always filled with young folks, happy times, and laughter.

"Both Ethel and I were courted and married while living there."

Pearl

Mom called Tom and me in one day. "Boys," she said, "I want you two to go to Vancouver and build me a house. Out in east Vancouver, towards Burnaby, there's a new subdivision. You can buy me a lot there. That is where I want to live. I'll be over in three weeks, so you boys go on over now and build us our new home."

She handed Tom thirty-five dollars, saying, "That should be enough to get us in and settled."

We took along this Swiss chap by the name of Frank, who had been working for us. He was a real hot-shot boxer and had fought Charlie Belanger, a top Canadian welterweight. For a couple of years before leaving Saltspring, he had taught Tom and me how to box and handle ourselves in a rough-and-tumble.

The first thing we did in Vancouver was to buy a corner lot on Second Avenue East, for a total price of $250. We put five dollars down and made arrangements to pay five dollars a month plus four percent interest. We took our list of materials to Excelsior Lumber at the foot of Victoria Drive, and ordered doors, windows, shiplap, some cement, shingles, everything we needed. We put $7.50 down on $180 worth of materials. By using our Agreement for Sale as collateral, we managed to make a deal to pay off the balance at seven dollars a month, which included three percent interest. We rode back to the lot on the lumber company truck with all the material.

There were no good roads. It was almost like a logging slash. We had to back the truck down Second Avenue from Renfrew Street to Windermere, over half a mile. We dumped the material right in the middle of the street. There were no sidewalks, not even board ones, at that time. We would be the only house within a radius of a quarter of a mile. The lots had not been selling although city water was available. We had to pay for a year in advance to have water for mixing the concrete. This depleted our funds by another $4.50.

When we left for Vancouver, we carried a suitcase, some blankets and our old phonograph with the big horn on it. We packed only one record, with *The Roses of Picardy* on one side and *The Prisoner's Song* on the other. We slept where the sidewalk should have been, right beside our pile of lumber. Our remaining capital now totalled $13.50. Our boat tickets had cost $1.50 each. We were there two days and had the concrete poured for the foundation, just little pads to keep the wood out of the dirt.

We were sleeping this particular night, after having played *The Roses of Picardy* until well after midnight. It must have been about three o'clock in the morning when a commotion startled us out of our sleep. There was a man standing over each of us and we could see two others by the lumber pile, rummaging through our clothes and suitcases. We knew they were there to rob us. They must have spotted us the day before and figured we had something worth stealing since we were building a house. Tom gave the signal. He just yelled, "FIGHT!" We all landed out of bed at the same time, swinging. Three of the burglars were down in about as many seconds and the others took off. When the three who were knocked down came to. they

142

headed towards Hastings Park. All five were intent on putting some distance between us as fast as possible. We chased them for several blocks. We had no trouble after that, we just went ahead and built the house.

Three weeks later, to the day, we met Mother on the five o'clock boat from Saltspring Island. The furniture shipped consisted of the trunk Tom and I had packed, an old stove, a couple of beds, a dresser or two, and some blankets, but very few dishes. She brought only the clothes she could carry. I don't think anybody helped her to the boat other than the children. Edie was ten years old, Albert was six, Lloyd three, and Mother carried three-month old Dorothy in her arms.

We had hired a one-ton Chevrolet truck with a flat deck. Tom drove with Mother, Dorothy and Lloyd crowded in the cab while the rest of us rode on the back to make sure our belongings stayed on.

We moved into our house that night. We had quite a time setting up the stove. The stove-pipe for the chimney went up through a square hole in the ceiling, out through a gable end window opening, and was tied to the peak of the roof with some wire to keep it from blowing away. We nailed a piece of galvanized tin against the wooden rafter to prevent it from catching fire. We had to use four elbows to get the pipe out and above the roof. Mother cooked supper there that evening.

After the meal she made a thorough inspection of her new home. She gave Tom, Frank and me a real compliment, saying, "It's just exactly what we need and it couldn't have been better if I'd have been here to help. Now let's put up the beds so we can get some sleep."

It was then we realized we had forgotten to put up or allow for a stairway to the two rooms upstairs. When Mother pointed this out, we just cut an opening in the ceiling and built a set of stairs as steep as a ladder. This proved to be a hazard for Lloyd and Albert. After a tumble or two they learned to get up and down without accidents. Mother handed Albert some shingles and nails to cover

143

some of the bigger knot holes in the walls. "Don't want people looking in where we're sleeping," she explained.

Eight-year old Ollie was left behind on Saltspring with Dad and Pearl. He remembers watching Mother walk down the road with Dorothy in her arms along with the rest of his brothers and sisters. He later told me, "I thought this was the end of my world! Mother was leaving!"

Several months before she left, Dad gave Mother $225 as a total settlement for their separation and divorce. They signed a letter to the effect that both agreed to get the divorce in seven years when it would be cheaper and easier. This letter also set out that the money paid by Dad was sufficient and Mother was never to try to get more. This was pretty shabby on Dad's part. Tom and I both knew that he had banked over $40,000 from our logging sales in the previous three years.

This is how Pearl remembered things after Mother left the Island...

"Well," she said, "Early that summer Dad had evidently cut off Mother's charge account at Mouat's store and she was having to buy all the groceries with some of her precious settlement money. For some reason I was always having to go to the store and get the groceries. Mom would give me the money. She was very cranky and unhappy, and I remember several times she would cook us porridge for supper. I had no clue, never gave it a thought, that she was going to leave Dad.

"The day before she was to leave, she called me out on the front verandah and said, 'You know, Pearl, what a hard time I had having Dorothy. You know how we almost let her die. Dr. Sutherland told me that I can't have any more babies or I will die. I am going to have to go away, because if I stay around your father I will get pregnant again and you won't have a mother anyway. I have got to go. Your dad has asked for you to stay to keep house for him. He wants Ollie to stay too. Margaret is going to work on at Harbour House for the Croftons, stay there, and come over to

Vancouver at the end of the summer. Ethel will come over from the hospital in Victoria when she feels better.

" 'Another reason I am leaving is because of the way your daddy treats Tom and Joe. He takes all their wages and never gives them one single cent. They have got to get away and make a life for themselves if they are ever going to amount to much. Tom's twenty now, so it's time for him to get away and make a life of his own. He's going to find a girl and marry her before long.'

"She told me then that one day I would start having my monthly periods, and I thought, 'There's no way; it can't be the way she's telling me.' But she had to tell me. She said that I mustn't let any boys near me because I could have a baby if I let that happen. That was my entire sexual education.

"When that was over she didn't cry and I didn't cry. She told me she was going on the boat to Vancouver the next day. Next morning everyone was up early and packing their things. Evidently Dad was afraid that I would make a scene. It was just about boat time. We were all standing around the front yard. Dad sent me up to the pasture on the pretext of getting the cow. I was not allowed to go to the boat even though I wasn't feeling bad.

"The next thing I knew I had to milk the cow. Evidently she hadn't got milked that morning and I didn't know a thing about milking. I had a terrible time.

"But there was one thing Dad did: he kept me busy, busy, busy. You know, the only thing that I really missed was not having someone to sleep with me. It hadn't hurt me to the quick. I was sort of stunned, in shock, I guess. Dad, Ollie and I walked up to Wilfred Seymour's that very afternoon so we wouldn't seem so alone. Mrs. Seymour said to me, 'So your mother finally left. I didn't think she would ever actually do it. She should have left your dad way back when you were up at the farm, when Margaret and Joe were little. No, I didn't think she would ever leave.'

"So, to try to make myself feel good I said, 'My Daddy chose me of all the kids to stay with him.' Mrs. Seymour

145

shut me up quick. She said, 'You always were that spoiled little brat.'

"I learned right quick... I never opened my mouth to anyone again! I never asked for advice and I never got it.

"At this point I didn't know how to cook a thing. When I looked in the pantry to see what there was, I found some junket tablets. The printing on the package said to put them in warm milk. I had no idea how to put the milk in a pot and warm it up or how warm to make it, so to use up those junket tablets I would dissolve them in water and put them in the milk when it was still warm from the cow. To my surprise it always set. So, Ollie and I ate junket. Then I got more.

"I don't know when Dad found out that a good way to keep us busy was to send us to the farm. That year he had started to build this three-storey building in Ganges and hired one of Captain Best's boys to come down and dig the footings. He was cranky about it because Mom had taken away those boys of his who always did his work for him.

"Ollie and I were too little to dig the foundation but we mixed the concrete. The rest of the summer was spent putting concrete into those footings.

"Just like Mom had told me, I had started to have my periods. I had a fellow that I liked, Audley Gardner. He used to like to kiss me and would stick his tongue in my mouth. So when I started menstruating, because I was at such an early age doing such heavy work, I menstruated for six months straight. I figured that this was just going to go on for the rest of my life. I thought it was because Audley had stuck his tongue in my mouth. It was quite an experience having to go through that alone. I imagined anything and everything.

"The next year Ollie and I would walk the four miles to the farm three or four times a week to pick the fruit, first the cherries and then the peach plums. We would go to the farm after school and pick two water pails full. We ate all the cherries we could and then we would start back to Ganges by way of the main road. Well, the pails were pretty heavy, and Ollie and I were pretty hungry, so we ate part of a pail of cherries each on the way back home. That, along with the junket and some peanut butter, pretty well took care of the cooking. Dad never once said to me, 'Cook this or cook that.'

"When he killed a sheep we would have the liver and tongue, the brains, and all the things he couldn't sell. I just fried everything in the big pan that was half full of bacon grease.

"Those cherries could make life a little embarrassing. They were more than a little windy. The kids would make fun of Ollie when he went to school. He wasn't in my room and they would pick on him, and you know? I wasn't very nice... I used to hurt for him but I wouldn't fight for him. I never beat up on any kids for picking on Ollie. He didn't seem to mind as much as I did.

"The next year Dad decided that he could trust us to do some extra work on the farm. After I had milked the cow, we would have breakfast at Ganges. Usually eggs, porridge and bread. Then Dad would send Ollie and I up to the farm with orders to cut down this tree, or do this, or clean out the barn. When we had our instructions we would walk up the Cranberry Road to the Jameskis' place. Mrs. Jameski always gave us cookies or some goodies. She didn't give us a full meal, but always had something for us. Then we would go on up to the Bennetts, who always asked us what we were going to do. They knew Dad would have laid out our work for the day. We just went ahead and did it... we never had any thought not to do what he said. If it took us to late evening to do whatever jobs he had given us, we did it, then walked back home in the dark

"We had food at both places, chickens at the farm and chickens at Ganges. This whole thing kept us busy, and it gave Ollie and me all this nice time together. We weren't really lonely, not after the initial shock. The only thing I remember that bothered me was that I didn't know how to cook or do anything, and I had to sleep by myself. I couldn't stand sleeping by myself, it governed my whole life.

147

Before, I could sleep with Margaret, Ethel, or Mother if I wished.

"We soon learned how to use a cross-cut saw and, for the first few years after Mother left, some of our chores included cutting fence posts, building brush fences and making shakes. We were forever working on that road, because there was a spring that was always washing it out. Through all this, Dad learned that we were completely reliable and could turn out a lot of work, so he got the notion of putting us to logging. We had already cut up winter wood with the cross-cut saw and we had a good axe, which we could sharpen on the grindstone ourselves. I had learned how to file that saw because the thing was so dull it was worth it to me to take time off to sharpen it. I don't know if I ever did a good job, but it used to cut better.

"We ate grouse because there were bunches of them, and I, being the big cheese, since my older brothers were gone, used to shout to Ollie, 'Bring the sledgehammer and some wedges!' This meant, of course, the gun and ammunition. Joe and Tom had always used this code when shooting grouse out of season. Ollie would go and light the fire while I picked off the grouse out of some cedar trees. They usually weren't any more than twenty-five feet away. I could shoot the head off a grouse at fifty feet, which saved me wringing its neck. I always aimed for the bird's neck. Its head would fall on one side of the limb and the body on the other. By the time I got to the house it was cleaned and ready to cook. We ate grouse and milk gravy and often the vegetables that were kept year round in the cellar. We had apples from the cellar too, but the one thing I will always remember is how good grouse tasted with that milk gravy.

"Some days we'd go out to the chicken house, find about a dozen eggs, fry them up and eat them. Nobody had ever told us that you were only supposed to eat two eggs at a time. Ollie was always hungry, so whatever eggs the chickens laid, that would be our afternoon snack. We sure didn't suffer.

"During these hard times, Dad always kept sheep for

his cash. It seemed we always had something to do with those foolish sheep. He would send us out to get them and we would have to go by Abe Wright's place. I was scared to death of old Abe Wright, always hoping that he wouldn't come out and see us as we tried to sneak by. His place seemed very far out in the woods and, because I had always had older brothers with me before, it took a long time to get over the fear of being lost in the forest. We had to go about two and a half miles through virgin timber to get to the top of Maxwell's Peak where the sheep usually grazed.

"After we passed Wright's place, we would turn off and head out for the peak, Ollie following along behind me like a puppy. There were no marked trails, so we followed the deer. As we got near the top, I always took time to have a good look at those giant ant-hills. The first time we went there they were about six feet high. The following summers they flattened out some. Tom had told me someone had tied an Indian up there by his feet and those ants had eaten his eyes out. This sure did stir my imagination! We would stay around the ant-hills for a while and I would tell Ollie these gruesome stories and try to insinuate that he had better do whatever I told him to do or he might get tied up by the heels! He never talked back, just took what I said for gospel, and hoped that I wouldn't tie him up near those ants.

"Then we'd go and sit out on the ledge at Maxwell's Peak, a beautiful place. That is where we usually had lunch, with a little candy to finish up. It was a great feeling to sit up there amongst the little blue flowers and look out over Fulford Harbour and Burgoyne Bay.

"We never fought when we sat there. I know that I must have talked then as much as I do now.

"After our rest on the ledge, we would listen for the bells and make our plan of attack on the sheep. Our strategy carefully planned, we'd head down into the salal in our bare feet. We would go down behind Tom Lee's place where there were some good trails and get the sheep started. Once we got them on the trail to home we only had to make sure that the leader kept going in the right direction and the rest would follow. We always had to think just a little ahead of the sheep. Ollie was better than a sheep dog, he could run up those rocks and head them off. Herding fifty or more sheep was nothing to us. It was over four miles through that rugged country. The drive would take us all day.

"You know, I often think, as I have seen Ollie go ahead and do so well for himself, that he learned his strategy of doing business from heading off those sheep. He never alarmed them, he was so quiet, but he always got them to do what he wanted.

"The winter I was fourteen and Ollie was ten, there was a two and a half foot snowfall. We were down at Ganges and we had watched the snow come down all day. It was around three o'clock in the afternoon when Dad said, 'Something has got to be done about those sheep on the farm! They've got to have some feed.' We knew that there was no hay in the barn, so he decided that, to feed the sheep, we would have to go up there and cut down some fir trees that had moss hanging from them. He gave us our instructions.

"We wrapped our legs in strips of blankets up to our knees and started out for the farm. There were some ruts in the main road so in some places it wasn't bad going. Turning from the road, we had to break trail all the way. When we got to the farm it was just before dark. We were soaked to the waist. We knew we had to go and cut those trees down before it got too dark. The sheep were all huddled together and there wasn't a thing for them to eat.

"We got our cross-cut saw and plowed through the snow to the end of the upper field. We cut down about five of these moss-covered trees. The sheep just got in there and started eating.

"We had planned on lighting the fireplace at the farmhouse before cutting the trees down, but it was so late we had to go to work without a fire. Originally, we planned to sleep in the old house for the night. However, I got a

150

brainwave and said to Ollie, 'You know Ollie, we are almost as close to the Bennetts' place as we are to the farmhouse. Why don't we go over there and stay instead of cutting wood and trying to keep warm here? I know it will be warm there and there'll be something good to eat.'

"All the way over to the Bennetts' place, I gave instructions to Ollie as to what he was going to say, and told him what I was going to say, so that they would invite us to stay for supper and spend the night. Sure enough, they had some hot food for us and a warm bed to sleep in. They had only two beds, so we were sleeping with their kids. Mrs. Bennett hung our clothes behind the big woodstove to dry. None of us had got to sleep yet. We were all a little excited. They weren't used to having company.

"I heard a knock on the door. I remember thinking, 'No one would be coming here at this time of night unless it is Dad.' 'Stay in the bedroom,' Mrs. Bennett ordered. Sure enough, I heard his voice. Mrs. Bennett didn't give him a very warm welcome. I heard him telling her, 'I got worried that they wouldn't make it, so have come to see where they are. I followed their tracks in the snow and have come to take them home.'

"I heard Mrs. Bennett say, 'You are not taking those kids out of here tonight.'

"She did not ask him to stay and she stood right at the bedroom door, and would not allow him to come in. I am sure she knew that we would get sick if we crawled back into those wet clothes and went out again into that cold, deep snow. It was some time before we were allowed to go back to the Bennetts'.

"Before we got hay for the sheep, we had to go back and cut trees several times. After that first time Dad always went with us and we left much earlier in the day. It was a hard way to feed sheep, but we did it.

"I think this was the incident that triggered the idea in Dad that Ollie and I were capable of cutting down trees. There was some beautiful first growth fir up there, tall, straight and good timber. We were given our instructions

151

and felled a lot of trees. He would give us a quota of trees to cut down and we didn't think not to do it. It didn't matter if we had to work until after dark, which we often did. You see, when we got tired, we would go over and have a swim, just in our pants, because I don't remember swimming naked. Or, if we were hungry, we would go over and have a feed of eggs, but we got the trees cut down.

"Dad would come up every week or ten days and would check over what we had done. I was always shaking in my shoes. Usually, he said words to the effect, 'You have done a good job,' but when I look back now, I think that he knew just how much work he could get out of us. He set up a plan to take out a boom of logs.

"Ollie was about eleven the year we logged, and he could pull the end of that cross-cut saw and carry his weight. I was certainly no expert and neither was he, but we sure could make that saw sing.

"The first tree I remember cutting was an old windfall cedar that was about four feet through. We had to cut it off at the stump and then into blocks for shakes. I can remember peeling out those shavings, six inches long. When we got enough trees felled and bucked, Dad brought up an old donkey. It had been sitting for several years and the cables were rusted and rotten. We didn't have gloves, and here we were, using this old, thorny, rusty cable that broke every time we got a log stuck. I tended hook mostly, because Ollie wasn't big enough. I was always afraid that the cable would break and hit him, that he wouldn't be able to get out of the way in time.

"It took Ollie and me together to start this old kerosene-burning, ten-horse, one-cylinder engine. If we had to get a big log out of the gully, we would just use a block on it. This gave us twice the pulling power of a straight line. In a way, it was very easy logging because it was fairly level. We could take all day if we had to, nobody was pushing us. We had a nice time. Ollie liked running the donkey and he was really good at it.

"Our biggest problem was that the cables always

broke. Then we had to splice that rusty, thorny cable bare-handed. The tools we had were the most primitive things. Sometimes I spent all morning splicing a cable. I could put a splice in that would never come out, but if I was asked to do it now I doubt that I could.

"We took out a whole boom of logs that summer. Dad hired a truck to come and haul the logs. They were dumped and boomed at Burgoyne Bay. After the logs were sold and paid for, Dad never even gave us a dollar to say, 'You can spend that as you like... this is for your work.' But we had a charge account at all the stores and we could buy whatever we liked. I guess we never bought anything we shouldn't because he never questioned our spending.

"That summer, we would get Woodwards' 95-cent day flyer by mail. We learned that for one sheep and some boxes of plums, we could get shredded wheat, pork and beans, sardines, corned beef from South America, and all kinds of other goodies in cans, including Eagle Brand milk! So, if I got tired of cooking, or the chickens weren't laying, we would decide that we better send a sheep to Woodwards.

"We would catch a sheep and tie its legs. Ollie would hold its feet and I would cut its throat. Then we would hang it up, skin it, wrap it in cheesecloth and pack it the half mile down to the main road. There we would wait for a truck to come along and take us into Ganges. Sometimes we waited two days before a truck came along. If we did have to stay over, we just pulled the sheep off into the bush overnight. If we had to, Ollie and I could pack the sheep to Ganges; we had lots of time and it was only four miles. Usually, the creamery truck or one of Mouat's trucks, or Ted Akerman, the Road Superintendent, would take it in for us.

"When we made out the order for the store, I always ordered a lot of stuff because we didn't know what the sheep would bring. Then all we could do was wait for boat day. This was great excitement! We would get the stuff and boy would we ever have a feast! On that day we felt we were living a good life.

153

"Back to logging. We got really interested in how to fall the trees so they would be easier to get out. We did our own thinking. After they started hauling logs, I always ran the donkey and piled them up on the landing because it took a little more precision than yarding. Dad would come up with the truck to make sure no one was going to gyp him. He always sent me off saying things like, 'When the truck is here you just make yourself scarce. There's a big log over there, go sit behind it.' I would just sit behind the log or stump until the truck was gone. Ollie could stay around, but not me. Dad did not like anyone to know I worked, that being child labour and all, and he also didn't like men looking at me!

"I didn't question Dad, but there was one man who put this bug in my mind to question the way Ollie and I were living. That was Jack Bennett. He used to ask me what we were supposed to do today. When we told him, he would say, 'That's just awful, you are much too young for such jobs.' This gave me to think that maybe this wasn't the common thing for twelve-year olds to be doing.

"Those trees could have fallen on us. Nobody else was there and we had no way of getting help. Luckily, we never got hurt. We knew we had to be really smart, especially with that old, rusty cable.

"When the fall came and the logs were gone, there was a lot of bark left on the landing. Dad hired a team and was going to pick up a load or two of this bark for the fireplace. He wasn't used to these horses and they weren't used to him either. He was standing up in the wagon which was full of bark and limbs. These horses started to rear up so I got quickly out of the way. I was standing up on one of the big logs about fifty feet away, just standing there watching. I was scared.

"Dad had been really cranky that summer because he was having trouble with his back and I guess his temper flew up at those horses and me. I think he thought I was laughing at him or something, because he picked up a limb about two feet long and two inches thick and threw it at me.

154

I turned my head to try and get out of the way, but it came like a bullet and hit me behind the ear. It knocked me cold. When I woke up I was a bit dizzy and I could see in Dad's eyes that he was sorry. We just carried on like nothing had happened. I held no grudges.

"After the logs were sold, Dad let me go to Vancouver for the exhibition or something, for a week. When I got back we had to do the cleaning up from the logging and he used to spend a lot of time with me up there at the farm. For some reason, Ollie never seemed to be around. He would just get lost somewhere.

"During this time Dad was always quizzing me to see what Mom was doing. He was trying to be so subtle about it, like asking if there were any men around and what Joe, my brother, was doing. That was when I started to get foxy. I wasn't going to be telling tales that would give away anybody's life to someone else. I didn't like Dad questioning me about what Mom was doing, what the family was eating, what the house was like, and what they were wearing!

"I got so I could talk about a lot of things, but I didn't have to answer those questions. I didn't have to tell lies, but I discovered that I had a power over Dad by outfoxing him. As soon as he knew I was on to his tricks, he quit and knew he had to take another line of attack on me. People underestimate kids: they quickly learn how to protect themselves and stay alive.

"When it was school time again, we went back to live at Ganges. That was my first year in high school, Grade Nine. I had bought some sort of cotton material and made my one and only dress for school. It was like the style they have now, loose-fitting. I washed that dress out every night, it was a sort of seersucker, and wore it all that fall. I had learned from Mom how to wash my hair in rainwater. I knew enough to keep myself looking nice.

"After school we worked on that building Dad was putting up. By that time we had got the windows in and were working on the partitions which were made with two

155

by twelve trimmings off the side of the logs from Palmer's tie mill. Not a one of those trimmings was square. Ollie and I had to put those things up and use shingles to shim them out so that they were even. We put two together so the walls were four inches thick. Birch plywood was to go over the top of this. Those big planks were heavy to lift, but we put all the second floor up that fall. This was a two-storey building with over 4000 square feet on each floor. There were about six rooms on each side and each room was a little different size. Dad and I put in the windows, the ones with pulleys and weights. This created about twenty rows a day!

"I used to get chewed out something fierce, because it was so hard to put those weights in the windows. It was a full-fledged carpenter's job, especially when we were working with lumber that wasn't square. I don't think Dad ever carried one of those big planks up to that floor. Ollie and I carried them all ourselves, one on one end and one on the other. Dad didn't mind doing the precision work, but he didn't like the heavy work. Well, this sure kept us out of mischief.

"By this time, I had learned to cook a few more things and one of them was a cobbler. I would cut up some apples or cherries or pears, and pour sugar on them. After I finished breakfast, I would mix a little flour and baking powder with salt and cream together like a pancake mixture. Then I would pour it over the fruit, place it in a baking dish, and put it in the oven of our old woodstove. If I made the fire right, then when we got home for lunch the cobbler would be ready and still warm. We didn't look for anything else; we didn't know that you were supposed to have more than one course and not eat a whole cobbler in one meal. Everything being ready, I could be back down at Elliots' in twenty minutes from the time I left my friend Sonny there on the way home.

"I can remember Mrs. Elliot quizzing me. 'Well, what did you have for lunch today?' I had caught on not to talk too much. I told her about how I had made this cobbler and

156

how good it was. She started making cobbler too, but I know it wasn't as good as mine because she didn't have fresh cream.

"You know, I didn't like people asking me what I did. I didn't like the way they asked it. If they were really concerned I would have known. I figured they were being nosey, so I wasn't about to tell them what I was up to.

"My love life on Saltspring during those years wasn't much. It was just a case of healthy country boys looking for girls' pussies and they sure were after mine! I remembered that six-months menstruation so I wasn't taking many chances! I remembered Mom telling me, 'You don't want those boys getting near you with that thing of theirs, or you'll get a baby!' I couldn't see myself with a baby and I was pretty strong. All they would say to me was, 'Just let me put my hand on your knee.' I liked them to hug me and sit up close but mainly I liked the ride. They drove those old trucks. Ollie never interfered with any of this: they would just put him in the back and there he stayed.

"There was one other thing that kept those boys from getting too tough with me; they knew that if anything ever happened to me, like a baby, Dad would kill them.

"I did have several married men after me, because I was unprotected most of the time. There was this one in particular, a man who had stayed after the tie mills left. He got a little bit pushy with me and decided he was going to make some time. His wife was stout. He was in his thirties and I don't think he knew much about Dad. Well, anyway, we had gone to this dance. He was a good dancer. I liked to dance and he liked to hold me close. At that time I was wearing a size forty brassiere. I used to buy them at Mrs. Turner's and they had about as much shape as a flour sack. I would get them just as tight as I could but it still didn't hide some of the curves that were developing.

"Well, this chap had liked to hold me pretty close and this is where he made his mistake. All during this evening he said that he would take me home. We lived just down the road. At the end of the dance Dad said, 'I'll walk you home

157

tonight.' I replied, 'Oh, I was going to get a ride with Roy.'
'Oh no,' Dad said, 'We'll just skip this Roy bit and I'll walk
home with you.' He had worked himself into a temper so I
knew I had better not open my mouth. All the way home,
Dad asked me questions about this chap. 'What had he
said?' 'What had he done?' 'How had he done it?' and
'How far had it gone?' I knew I was being quizzed so I was
cagey.

"In less than two weeks this chap had sold his house
and, with his wife and all his belongings, was catching the
boat to leave the Island. Dad must have given him fair
warning.

"My girlfriend, Ruth Stevens, and I had this wild crush
on Audley Gardner and Harry Nicols. They chummed
together. They had gone to harvest in the prairies. They
wrote us letters and sent us pictures. We just used to drool
over those long eyelashes of Harry's. We would look at
those snaps, they were the poorest little black and white
photos, but Ruth and I would look at them for hours. Audley
liked me but I sort of liked Harry. Then Audley moved to
Crofton and only Harry was left. He was in the Army
Reserves and had a car. He was a good dancer and I would
see him at dances. He started taking me for rides and picking me up a few times and was beginning to get serious
with me. I was almost of marrying age and Harry had
money and he wanted to settle down. He wasn't pushy with
me, but asked me what I thought about getting married and
letting him look after me. He didn't let any other boys take
over at dances, we were going steady.

"I finally said to him, 'Dad would never let me get
married, you know that, Harry.' He cooled completely.

"People were scared of Dad-- they knew instinctively
that he wasn't to be fooled with. Harry never did get
married. He passed away at Ganges in the fall of 1978. He
was over sixty.

158

Ollie

"I was born in 1918. In the summer of my fourth year I was old enough to remember the things that were happening in our family. That year we were moving from Ganges up to the farm to do the haying and other farm tasks. Mother, Dad and young Albert were on the front seat of the old democrat while I rode in the back with Pearl and Edie. We had been told to watch the Jersey cow that was tied to the back end of our wagon to see she didn't get fouled up in the wheels. We each had a short willow stick to prevent this cow from sticking her horns through the spokes. We must have looked like a bunch of gypsies.

"Under the seat were pots, pans, boxes of food, bed clothes, milk pails and whatever else was needed. I sat on a crate that held about a dozen laying hens. It seems we were always moving to or from the farm when I was small. We had to pick cherries, plums and berries so Mother could make jam for the next winter. Joe and I would shoot grouse and deer, which Mother preserved in jars or salt, in big, brown crocks.

"When school opened after the summer holidays, we

159

had to pack up and go back to our house in Ganges. It took several trips to get all our things moved back again. It seemed like fun but we were kept so busy we had little or no time to play. We all helped to haul in the hay and pile it high in the old barn.

"When I was only five, Dad and Tom were logging up past the Seymours' on Rainbow Road. With a four-horse team, they were skidding logs about half a mile on the skid-roads into the long inlet known as the canal. Joe would help after school. I would ride the pig and help grease the skids with heated whale oil. This stuff smelled awful! We must have smelled like an old dead whale when we got home. We scrubbed in a galvanized washtub full of hot water every night before going to bed.

"The next year we moved to the Cotsfords' place up at the north end. This time not only the horse and buggy but also two T-model trucks were used. One had solid rubber tires on the back. Everything was piled high because we had to take the stove, beds, tables and everything we needed, including our cow, chickens and our horse. Our stay up there lasted for almost two years. I was allowed to steer the solid-tired truck once we got through the gate.

"I learned to be a whistle punk and to operate the single drum donkey. Our horse pulled the line back to the woods. In one place the logs made such deep trenches that the horse would be right out of sight as he passed the big stump where I stood to give signals.

"I was seven when we moved back to Ganges, starting school that fall. The Drake boys were my age and going to the same school. Their mother apparently had cancer. I was at school the day their dad came to take them out. She had ended her suffering with a double-barrelled shotgun. Their house was only a block from the school. This was a terrible shock to everyone. It made me do some serious thinking.

"During the next summer's holidays, I got an even worse shock. Mother, with all my brothers and sisters, except Pearl, packed up and left for Vancouver. I was eight years old and can remember seeing them walk away from our big house, heading for the boat over by Mouat's store. I was standing in the middle of the road watching. Mother had a suitcase in one hand and was carrying baby Dorothy on her other arm. I thought this was the end of my world; I was being left alone! At the bend by the Trading Company store, Mother turned, set down her suitcase, blew me a kiss and waved goodbye! That was it for me! I ran and hid amongst some lumber under the house and sobbed for a couple of hours.

"When I came out in the late afternoon, Pearl and Dad were there talking. We all walked up Rainbow Road to the Seymours' house and ate supper. It eased the hurt to be near our old friends at a time like this. Mrs. Seymour tried to be as motherly as she could by giving me goodies. She planned a picnic for all of us and invited Pearl and me back for supper anytime we wanted to come.

"Dad gave us more work than we could possibly handle. All that fall, we worked on the foundations of the house he had started at Ganges. We helped dig trenches and pour concrete. We were so tired we hadn't time to think or do anything but work and sleep. This helped to ease the loneliness. We were soon going to school five days a week and had our own cooking and washing to do. This was quite a responsibility for a boy of eight and a girl just turned twelve. Our meals and appearance were exactly what we made them. Dad never helped us to cook or do our clothes, no matter what the circumstances. If either Pearl or I got sick we did our own doctoring and nursing. We must have done something right, as we are both still alive and pretty healthy.

"That winter we had to walk four miles to feed the sheep up at the farm. It would be after dark by the time we got back home.

"During the Christmas holidays that year, we stayed up at the old farmhouse. We did our cooking on the open fireplace. Pearl had baked a Christmas cake in the woodstove at Ganges. This is about all we carried with us.

"I have some bad memories of that Christmas. That

day was probably the most disappointing in all my life. Pearl and I hung our stockings up on the nails that were still in the wood mantelshelf. We chose the same nails that we had used when the family was together. I had great visions of presents and goodies like we had known in the past. When we got up and came down early Christmas morning, our stockings were as empty as when we hung them up. Dad had made a fire and then gone to the barn. We looked at each other and Pearl gave me a big hug, saying, 'Merry Christmas, my brother!' I returned the wish and Pearl started to cook breakfast, eggs and porridge. When Dad came in he ordered us to hurry and get ready to go out. 'We're going to dig and put all the turnips and mangels in the cellar today.' We dug and trimmed those vegetables while our hands froze and our backs ached. A cold rain was falling, which turned to snow before noon. We had boiled turnips for our Christmas dinner that night. The cake Pearl made tasted great. The spirit of Christmas had ended when we took down our empty stockings and put them on to dig mangels out of the muck. I still get a sick and lonely feeling when I think of Dad's unforgivable thoughtlessness. The hurt of this Christmas Day seemed even worse than Mother's leaving.

"The year after Mother left, I had been sent down from the farm to look after the house at Ganges. When I walked in there were thousands of fleas on the floor. By the time I walked across the room, my bare legs and feet were black with those little bloodsuckers. I hurried up the stairs hoping to get away from them. I got in one of the old beds. I was bitten so much, by three in the morning I got up and ran out of the house. A Mrs. Johnston owned an old barn across the road with some hay in it. I decided sleeping in there would be better than sleeping with the fleas. I'd been sleeping in the barn for about a week when I noticed Mr. Tweedhope, the policeman, nosing around. Mrs. Johnston had found my sleeping place and phoned him. Guess she was afraid of fire. Two nights later I woke up and all I could see in the half light was a pair of those big, brown police boots belting me in the backside. I flew out the door and hid in the woods. That was the end of that place as sleeping quarters.

"Next night I took some canvas and an old quilt and went down in the clump of trees in McAfee's field and made a new bed. I slept there for a few days and things were pretty good. I awoke at daylight the fifth morning to find a big, black garter snake coiled up on my chest. His beady little eyes were staring only a few inches from my chin. Guess he must have liked the warmth of my body. Even for a boy of ten, I can assure you this was a crawly, creepy shock. I touched him with a short stick and he slithered away in the grass. I grabbed up the old quilt and walked the four miles back to the farm. I explained to Dad about the fleas. I got a licking and was told, 'At your age you should have been able to figure out something so you could have stayed.'

"When Pearl was in her teens she would get a job for the summer months working as cook and housekeeper for a wealthy widow who lived across the bay from Ganges. This left Dad and me together a lot. We spent the best part of five years cooking on that open fireplace and sleeping on hay from the barn. We had blankets in pieces but I never had a whole blanket to sleep under until I was thirteen. That year I got a job working as a faller for Mike Lumovitch. Out of my very first pay, I bought a pair of Hudson's Bay blankets. This made life a bit more bearable as far as cold winter nights were concerned. This same pair of blankets is still in use in our guest room on Galiano Island. Best investment I ever made.

"I went to the Divide school for a couple of years while we lived there. I only stayed in school long enough to finish Grade Four. At twelve, I was expected to work and earn my keep. Dad put together a light cart made out of the front wheels and axle of an old buggy. Its box was about four feet square. The shafts were cut short. The contraption resembled a Chinese rickshaw. Our horses had been sold, so we just pulled it ourselves. We hauled the hay in and the

163

manure out. I did the pulling while Dad followed, using a fork to spread. I sometimes hauled as many as four dressed sheep to Ganges in this cart. I would either sell them to Mouat's butcher shop or ship them on to Woodwards' store in Vancouver. On the return trip, I'd bring back a month's supply of groceries.

"All the sacked feed was hauled this way from the main road; our road was much too steep and crooked for the feed trucks to handle. Sometimes a ton or more had to be moved. I could only manage two of the heavy sacks at a time on the cart. When I was twelve, I could pack one hundred pounds a mile, without stopping to rest. There must be an easier way I thought.

"We had a two-year old steer that looked pretty strong. One day I tied him in a stall and proceeded to put horse harness on him. The collar went upside down so he could breathe when he was pulling. I hooked up hames and traces, using rope for a backband to hold the traces out of the way of his feet. Leading him out into the field was a bit dicey. When he was in the clear I put seven heavy split rails in a chain and hooked it to the singletree. As he got the rails moving, he kept looking back. He must have thought this load was chasing him, so he began to run. He tore around that field for over half an hour. He stopped when he ran out of wind, then turned to stare at the rails, heaving and puffing so hard he could be heard a hundred yards away. I walked over and petted him. He was quiet enough so I led him back to the barn, dragging the rails. A few more days of this and he pulled the load around the field without getting too excited. This gave me courage enough to hook him to that cart and try to haul the feed from the main road. I made several trips with five sacks on each load, a big improvement over backpacking or pulling the cart myself.

"On the last trip there were seven sacks left. What the hell! I thought, and piled them all aboard. He managed to pull them up all the grades but when we got to the downhill part, I did not have the weight or strength to hold the cart back. One stubbed-off shaft poked him square in the rear

164

end. He jumped forward and it hit him again! That started a runaway. I was between his back feet and the cart. If I let go I would be dragged under the wheels. There was no choice but to run and keep up. This steer ran a record half mile, then turned around and looked right at me and that cart. I was weak in the knees and shaking all over. When I went back to look where the runaway had happened, I found that some of my footprints were twenty feet apart. I must have been flying more than running. That was one of my closest calls. You can be sure there was never more than four sacks of feed on a load after that.

"By now, I could outrun and outjump all the kids at the Divide school. When Pearl wasn't around, I had to drive our sheep from Burgoyne Bay all the way over the mountains to the farm. This was not easy to do by myself. I learned a system that worked. First thing was to get the sheep headed in the right direction, then run them until their tongues hung out like panting dogs. Once they were winded, I could walk right up among them. Then, if they moved at a good pace they could be kept under control. I was always barefooted and could outrun any sheep.

"In the years between twelve and fourteen, I got some terrible beatings from Dad, usually for no reason at all. I got fooling around with my buddies one afternoon. It was my last year at school. I got home about six in the evening when I should have been home by four-thirty. Dad was cutting grass out back of the barn with his scythe. The blade was razor sharp and about three feet long. When he saw me coming he stopped cutting and just stared at me. I watched his face turn almost beet-red. Without a word he ran at me, swinging the scythe in a cutting motion. I took off, knowing very well he could cut me if he caught me. He chased me for over one hundred yards before he threw the scythe away and grabbed a stick about three feet long and an inch or more thick. I ran for a bit more and slowed down so he could catch up. He gave me a terrible beating with this stick, saying over and over, 'You had better be home by four-thirty from now on.' I said nothing.

"After the beating he asked, 'Why'd you run away when I had the scythe?'

" 'Because you would have cut my legs off if I hadn't.'

"There is not the slightest doubt in my mind that Dad went a bit crazy when he got mad. There was no telling what he would do. He almost clubbed our horse to death in a fit of temper one day, beating him over the head with a pick handle until the animal fell to the ground, unconscious. Being the only one around I suffered the brunt of his tantrums.

"Turning thirteen, I began to think and do most things my own way. This bothered Dad; he was losing control. Several times he challenged me to fight him. Taking off his coat and rolling up his sleeves, he'd say, 'Now just let's see who's the best man around here.' I would not back off. I would reply with a shrug or say, 'It's not a very good way to find out.' Dad was in his late fifties by then.

"After my fifteenth birthday, I made up my mind to get away from the farm and Dad's bullying. I was working in a logging camp and most of my wages Dad took and kept. I had forgotten to do something about the cow one Sunday morning. She had been let out into the wrong pasture. He got me in a corner of the fence and beat me with a stick for a full twenty minutes. I took it, though strong enough by now to break him into pieces. I never made a sound or gave any indication of being hurt. It was during this twenty minutes that I made my final decision.

"Dad left me alone at the farm when he made his trips to town. Several times a year he would get all dressed up and head for Vancouver or Victoria. He would stay away for up to a month. The day after this beating, he was gone again. Wasting no time, I put a rope on our Jersey cow and led her down to Price's dairy farm, explained what I was doing and left her there. They would milk her until Dad came back. While walking the mile back home I planned how I would leave. I packed all my belongings, including the Hudson's Bay blankets in which I rolled my three guns. The guns and blankets were my prized possessions. I

166

packed my clothes in an old suitcase. There were two boxes of odds and ends that I wanted to take. Everything was loaded in that two-wheeled cart. I left a note on the table under a dirty porridge bowl. It read: 'Dad, your cow is at the Price's place. The chickens I fed and let out. I am leaving you forever. Your son, Oliver.'

"It was eight miles to the Vesuvius wharf. I started out just after one o'clock and it took me till well after four to push that load up and down all those hills. I transferred everything to my dugout canoe, leaving the cart at Mrs. Bennett's house. I paddled the four miles across to Crofton and arrived at brother Joe's house about 7:30 p.m. He helped me unload; then we went for a beer at the Crofton Hotel. This was my first time in a beer parlour. I was just past sixteen, but looked twenty-one. The beer was great. We celebrated my leaving Dad and our reunion. It was a great day for me. the start of my adult life.

"Jack Bennett had been our nearest neighbour for years and was also a very close friend. He had been more like a father to me than my own Dad. We worked and hunted together. He taught me how to file crosscut saws and how to make a canoe out of a cedar log with an adze. One winter we carved two canoes, complete with oars, from cedar logs. These we kept at Vesuvius and used for fishing and hunting. One fall we rowed across to Crofton to hunt deer with my brothers. It was the first weekend of the season. We brought back four nice bucks.

"Bennett hailed from Australia and wanted to go back for a visit, so we made a contract. There were sixty cords of wood to be delivered to the creamery that fall. Jack agreed to give me his three guns for helping to deliver the wood. The agreement was ten days work for the double-barrelled 12-gauge, fifteen for the .30-30 and two boxes of shells, and another five days for his .22 and 200 rounds of ammunition. When the wood was delivered, Jack had enough money for a return ticket to Australia and I had all his guns. It was a good deal for both of us. I've still got the guns hanging on my den wall. Jack Bennett is now ninety-two, still travelling and going strong.

* * *

After Ollie settled in at Crofton, he took a job as long-shoreman, worked hard and made good money. He married, bought a house and had three children, two sons and a daughter.

Some four years later he moved to Galiano Island and started his own logging operation. Here he built a nice home, complete with swimming pool. When the logging was finished on Galiano, he rented his home and moved up the coast to log. He was caught in the log slump of the 1950's and lost a fortune. This was the way with logging in those days. Logs that now sell for $200 per thousand were going for $27.50 per thousand, delivered, in Vancouver.

Ollie came down for a visit. We discussed his situation and then flew up to have a look at my camp on Redonda Island. He liked it. I told him to go up and get what he wanted to salvage from his northern camp and move it to the show on Redonda. He agreed to buy my camp for a quarter of a million dollars and take over a company with a substantial loss showing on the books.

After six years, he had recouped his losses and had money in the bank. Someone offered to buy him out, so he sold for enough to keep him comfortably for the rest of his life.

Ollie still lives in his home on Galiano Island. It is a beautiful place to retire. There is good fishing and hunting close by and the view and climate are terrific. His home sits on the beach looking east to Active Pass, where there is a continuous boat show throughout the daylight hours. Ollie is very happy.

He keeps an old caterpillar tractor and a welding outfit on his little beef farm. If things get boring, he goes out and breaks down the cat so he can weld it and clear a bit more land for pasture.

The Team Of Tom And Joe

At a young age I realized the bond between Tom and myself was much stronger than that between most brothers. It didn't matter what we did or planned; we did it as a team. All through our lives this bond existed.

This teamwork started when I was seven. Tom was almost ten when he shot his first grouse with our old 12-gauge shotgun. Uncle Frank had taught us how to handle guns. Tom had been allowed to fire the shotgun a few times, but only at cans or bottles. Though the kick of the gun would knock him several feet backwards, he was still game. I begged to try but was told, "You are two small and too young yet."

Dad and Uncle Frank were away working when Mother called us in one day.

"Y'all think you are big enough to shoot me a few grouse?"

"Sure are," was Tom's excited reply.

He was handed two shells and the gun. We were still in sight of the house when we flushed a covey of blue grouse. They flew a short distance and landed on some logs among small trees. We followed quietly and came upon four of them sitting on a log. Tom put the shells in the gun and promptly got "buck fever." Buck fever is an acute attack of excitement and nervousness that makes one's body shake all over to such an extent that it is impossible to hold or aim a gun with any accuracy. His legs were shaking so violently that he had to sit down. The longer he looked at the grouse, the more he shook.

"Come hold my legs tight together, then maybe I can shoot them," he ordered in a tense whisper. "It's no good like this, I've got to have something to steady the gun barrel on."

I went around in front of him and, putting my head between his knees, with an arm around each leg, I squeezed with all my might. This kept his legs steady enough. He rested an elbow on my rear end and BANG! The recoil knocked him over backwards with me on top.

There was a great tangle of two small boys and one old scattergun. Getting to our feet, we ran over to where the grouse had sat. Three were dead and the fourth flew up into a nearby tree. Tom had now recovered from his buck fever and promptly shot that one. We retrieved the four birds, then sat on a log to examine them. It seemed most of the pellets were in the necks and heads. Four grouse with two shots! We agreed we were indeed great hunters.

This was our first bit of teamwork and, probably because of the success, it affected both of us for the rest of our lives.

The following year Dad took an order for telephone poles from Jim Horel who was responsible for all the phone lines on Saltspring. We were shown how to select and fall cedar trees that would produce twenty-five or thirty foot poles with at least a five-inch top. By working long hours three or four poles were produced in a day.

We had a six-foot falling saw and a sharp axe. Tom did the trimming with the axe while I peeled with a drawknife. About every third day we harnessed that horrible horse, Dan Patch, and skidded the poles to a rollway built on the high side of our road. Tom would handle the cable and chains while I did the driving.

By the end of the summer we had managed to get over fifty poles ready on the landing. We later helped Dad roll them onto our light wagon and deliver them along the roads. To drop a pole at the markers Jim Horel had put along the new lines, we just chained one end to a stump or tree and drove off.

This was our first experience at logging. The delivered price for a pole was $1.50.

World War One ended in the fall of the next year. Dad had arranged for Tom and me to do the logging for Captain Justice's small lumber mill, which was capable of producing some 2,000 board feet of lumber per day. Being so young, we were kept hustling to get enough logs cut to keep the mill supplied. We fell the trees together. When we had enough on the ground, Tom would cut them into specified lengths, using a six-foot bucking saw. Justice sharpened our saws each evening and eventually taught us the art. It was my job to drive their team and haul the logs to the mill. This was a great learning experience for both of us.

The pay was twenty-five cents an hour. To keep track of our earnings, we devised an unusual system. We each chose a big stump near our road. On the way home each evening we put a small rock on the stump for every dollar we had earned that day. For eight hours, two stones went on each stump. If something happened that allowed only six hours of work, we would put one rock in the tight little pile and place another a few inches away until the full dollar was earned.

We were paid in cash twice a month. On paydays we placed the money on the stump and put the required number of rocks on each bill. A one-dollar bill got one rock, a five-dollar bill would get five rocks. If bills and rocks didn't balance, we would go back and let Captain Justice know about it. Finding we were short one month-end, we walked back the half mile to tell our boss. He asked us how

171

we kept track of our wages and, when we explained our system, he was so impressed he made up the difference without going up to check our count.

We worked there for two summers. Clive was the eldest of the Justice family and taught Tom the basics of cutting logs into lumber. I learned about the woods.

In the summer of 1920, we were kept busy cutting cedar poles for export and skidding them out to the public road. In mid-December it turned very cold. The ground froze and we had six inches of snow. Dad now owned two horses, a big Clydesdale and Dan Patch. With this lopsided team, working from daylight till dark, some two hundred poles were skidded from the top of the hill to the landing at Ganges. If we met any traffic on the way down, passing was a problem. One of us always walked well ahead of the team to advise cars or buggies to pull off the road to let us by.

We bored a hole through the top of each pole before it was put into the water. A cable was then threaded through some fifty poles to produce a raft. These rafts were chained together and towed to Montague Harbour. Here they were loaded on a ship and exported to Japan. Montague, at that time, was the only exporting port in the Gulf Islands. There was one lone building in the habour, a combined house and store operated by the Grey family.

Dad, Tom and I camped on the beach to help load our poles. This was Easter holidays of 1921. I remember Tom working as a boom man, in his bare feet for the full two weeks, putting the poles into slings to be hoisted aboard. Dad was on deck as tallyman. I stayed in camp, washed dishes and hunted crows.

There was a bounty of ten cents for every crow head delivered to the game warden at Ganges. I made just over seven dollars for the two weeks. Dan Lumley had towed our poles from Saltspring to Galiano Island and stayed there, using his boat as ship's tender. When we were to go home, he refused to allow the smelly crow heads on his boat. I must have looked so sad, he weakened and said, ''Put those damned things as far back on the stern as you can and get aboard.''

It was during this loading that Dad accepted an order to cut and export logs to Japan.

When summer holidays started that year, Tom and I were given a tent and a beat-up cookstove, along with other equipment and supplies to last for two months. All this was piled on our solid-tired T-model logging truck. We drove to the top of the hill between St. Mary's Lake and Vesuvius Bay and set up camp. We proceeded to fall and buck timber on the top side of the road.

This was the first truck-logging done on Saltspring. Our 1918 T-model truck was equipped with wooden log bunks and a trailer that Tom and I had built on an old axle which had two solid rubber-tired wheels. We fashioned a trailer hitch to pull this contraption.

This was when we started to appreciate the skills of blacksmithing. We helped Bill McAfee shoe our horses. We learned to thread and make bolts and irons necessary for equipping the truck and trailer. Gas came in 45-gallon barrels and was put in the truck tank by bucket and funnel.

The logs were cut in multiples of six feet six inches. We loaded the logs using peaveys to roll them along stout poles from the high bank to the truck bunks.

The haul to the beach at Vesuvius Bay was a little more than a mile and downhill all the way except for one short uphill stretch. This hill was hard on low-gear bands. On many occasions the team would have to be taken down to the beach to pull the truck back to camp where we would work on it far into the night, making the necessary repairs. It was during this summer that we devised a quick-change set of bands for this T-model. The Ford factory adopted our method. All later models came out with a similar system.

When the logs were boomed, they were towed to Vancouver harbour to be loaded on a Japanese ship. Tom travelled on the tug that towed the boom while Dad and I went via steamship, the old *Otter* from Ganges.

In the 1920's, Hastings Street ended at Hastings Park.

173

There was nothing but a burned-over logging slash beyond. We walked up a foot trail and over Capitol Hill, then down to the bay where the ship was anchored.

We again slept on the beach but had our meals with the crew of the tug that was acting as tender for the loading. It took ten days to get the logs aboard and stowed in the ship's holds.

Dad was paid in cash, over $4,000. I remember his telling Tom to keep well ahead of him in case of robbers lurking along the trail. I was instructed to be rearguard and was to whistle three times if anyone tried to come up past me. This was all very exciting, but the money got to the bank without incident.

Before we left Vancouver, Dad bought another used T-model, one-ton Ford truck, plus one new and one used Wee MacGregor dragsaw. This equipment cost just over $400.

Tom and I were thrilled by the idea of operating the trucks and a dragsaw apiece. After we had asked all the questions about the dragsaws the salesman would answer, we had to satisfy ourselves with the operator's manual.

During the boat trip home we ignored Dad. We were planning the start of our contracting careers. We had now become the most mechanized suppliers of wood on Saltspring.

We solicited contracts from the creamery, the hospital, Mouat's store, the Trading Company and others. We were so far ahead of competitors with team and wagon deliveries we were able to cut the price by ten cents per cord. We were quickly booked for a full year's operation.

In the 1920's, wood was the main source of fuel for steam power and domestic heat. We did so well that Dad refused to let us go back to school. Tom had completed Grade Eight and never got more education. Mother somehow got me back later to finish Grade Ten.

We made our own contracts and did the collecting. The money was turned over to Dad, who explained that most of it went to pay for the trucks and dragsaws. One day he

174

realized that saw logs sold for twice as much as wood. The dragsaws were sold. He then bought the timber on the old Cotsford property at the north end of the Island. The family moved up and logging was started the summer of 1924.

A one-drum donkey, powered by a ten-horsepower, single cylinder White engine was used for yarding. Above the carburetor was a reservoir that held about a quart of water. By means of a valve, this water could be let into the hot intake manifold. The water could be used only when the engine was hot or lugging hard. Somehow this cushioned the shock of the kerosene combustion.

The young Garners would try to get the engine overheated so the water could be used. Steam would pour out with every exhaust. Occasionally, great steam rings would float out on the still air and grow in size until their shapes became distorted. On a quiet day there could be as many as six or seven rings floating around, in sizes varying from six inches to six feet in diameter. As our experience increased, rings floated about most of the day. This was great fun.

Here again, Tom and I worked as a team, first in falling and bucking, then as donkey-puncher and hook tender and finally in booming up the logs.

After scaling, the booms were towed to Victoria by an old steam tug owned by Captain Cotsford. Charlie Olmstead did the engine-room work. The boiler was fired with four-foot split wood mixed with some thick bark. This tug was known as the *New Era*. She was some forty feet long and although stacked high with fuel, she had to stop to pick up more wood and water at least once on the way to Victoria. The towing distance was not much over thirty miles but took three or four days to complete. It would take hours to load wood and water at some pre-arranged cove.

Coal-fired tugs were available, and would have been much more practical to do this work, but part of the timber purchase agreement was contingent on the Cotsfords' doing the towing at one dollar per thousand.

Captain Cotsford was quite famous. He had held the Pacific Coast single rowing championship for several years

175

around the turn of the century. His racing boat was locked in a shed near our booming grounds. We found a way to open the boathouse door with a piece of haywire. When he was away on these towing trips Tom and I would get out his racer and try our skills. It was so light and unstable we couldn't get any great speed up without upsetting. After a couple of cold swims we put the little boat away exactly as we found it.

"We might as well stay with logging," was Tom's remark. "We can at least stay dry doing that."

There were some bad times for our family during these two years of logging. Mother and the girls did all the cooking and washing. There were three hired men to be boarded. Usually, fourteen people sat down for breakfast and supper every day. Hot lunches were packed and brought out to the woods each noon.

Clams from the beach were a major item at all meals. In winter the tide is generally high during the day, so we had to dig the clams by lantern light when the tide was low. Four of us could fill five or six sacks in a couple of hours, with sixty or seventy pounds in each sack. These would last for several days. Mother served them steamed or fried. Sometimes we had clamburgers made from the clams minced through the meat grinder. She made about six different kinds of chowder. This, with milk and butter from our cow, and eggs from the chickens, along with home made bread, made for a very economical cookhouse.

The work day at the house began at five a.m., and finished sometime after nine in the evening. This was very hard on Mother, who was now pregnant with her tenth and last child. Though there were neighbours who were anxious to help Mother with her cooking chores, Dad insisted that he could not afford the twenty dollars per month. The three hired loggers were paid sixty dollars per month each. This included their board and laundry. The out-of-pocket expense for the logging operation was less than $400 a month. That's about two days wages for one faller at today's prices.

Log prices were good and Dad wound up with just over $40,000 in his bank account. This was a sizeable fortune in those days.

The last Garner child was born two months after the logging finished and we had moved back to the big house at Ganges.

In 1926, after Mother left Dad, Tom and I agreed to become partners for life, operating independently, but always ready to help each other whenever necessary. Tom wanted to stay with logging and lumbering until he made enough money to retire. My goal was to own an apartment block with a hardware store and contracting business. The agreement was concluded by a handshake.

Our first adult venture together came in the fall of 1926. The Canadian Pacific Railway ran what was known as the "Harvest Specials," carrying hundreds of men from Vancouver to various parts of Alberta and Saskatchewan to help harvest the grain crops.

Jobs were scarce at the coast so there was little problem in filling the trains.

Tom and I boarded one of these along with some 300 others. We had been booked for a little town called Bow Island in southern Alberta. Arrangements had been co-ordinated so the farmer we were to work for met us at the station.

We were taken in his grain truck out to the farm and billeted in a big, horse-drawn, portable bunkhouse. Ten other men shared these quarters and we all ate in a cook trailer. The farmer's wife and daughter did the cooking.

We were each allotted a team and wagon. We fed the horses at about five each morning, and threw the harness on them before breakfast. We always had the rig out in the field and loaded with bundles by six a.m. We drove our loads to the straw-fired steam threshing machine.

An extra man known as a "spike pitcher" always helped to unload and pitch the bundles onto a big conveyor. Grain trucks hauled the threshed grain either to the elevators by the railroad or to a shed on the farm for storage.

We worked a minimum of twelve hours a day and put in seven days a week, weather permitting. The pay was forty cents an hour less one dollar per day for board. We landed back in Vancouver a couple of months later with just over $150 each. This was a lot of money in those days.

We gave Mother $200, and bought some clothes. The rest of that year we cut lumber and ties on Saltspring. We did not stay near Dad. Both of us boarded with Charlie Parman for the next few months.

Our friend, Vern Douglas, had been gillnetting for a cannery known as the Tallheo near the head of North Bentinck Arm at the mouth of the Bella Coola river. He gave such glowing reports of the thousands of fish to be taken, and all the money we could make, that Tom and I agreed to try it.

We signed on in Vancouver and got passage on the old *Camosun*. The trip up on the steamship was pleasant enough though the smells were something we were not accustomed to. Most of the passengers were Coast Indians travelling up to the various fishing areas. I asked a young chap who was the mate on the ship: "What in hell makes your ship smell so bad?"

He gave me a look that let me know he recognized a greenhorn.

"Maybe its skunk oil some of the Indians use," he explained. "It's supposed to be the sexiest perfume they know about."

"Yuck," was my reply, "I'll just stay upwind and forget the social life."

When we checked in at the cannery, we were assigned a room in the bunkhouse and a twenty-six foot sailboat, complete with a 200-foot-long gillnet. This outfit was to catch sockeye, humpies, and small spring salmon. We received twenty cents for a sockeye, five cents for a humpie, fifteen cents each for white springs no matter how big or small, and ten cents per pound for red springs.

As I pulled in the net one morning, I was surprised to find a huge salmon tangled in some loose webbing. This spring salmon tipped the scales on the packer boat at exactly 106 pounds. The scales were checked for accuracy each week. When "Hard Hat Bill" made the usual cut to see if it was a red or a white spring, I was disappointed to be told it was white and that I would receive only fifteen cents for this monster. If it had been red, it would have brought just over ten dollars. At today's prices the same salmon would be worth over three hundred dollars.

Hard Hat Bill is now a legend among the old-timers of the fishing industry. He used to wear the same clothes for months on end. I don't believe he ever washed them. His attire consisted of a black bowler hat, a suit of long grey Stanfield's underwear, socks and knee-high gumboots. Over this he tied a yellow oilcloth apron that covered his front from chin to ankles.

He was a fish buyer and packer. His boat was all red and powered by a big Vivian gas engine. He kept neither boat nor clothes clean by any standards. With dried blood, fish scales and grease over everything, it was really quite a problem to recognize original colours.

He was pleasant enough though he rarely spoke to anyone. He would hold out his hand for the tally book, make the correct entries and hand it back. He always let you have time to check his figures before casting off your lines to chug along to the next fisherman. Hard Hat Bill was past middle age when we were there. He had started his career before the turn of the century.

The fishing was closed each week for two days to allow enough spawning salmon to go up the river. This closure and the fishing boundaries of the Bella Coola river were enforced and patrolled by federal officers throughout the season. The brief lull gave us some time to relax and explore the valley.

A favourite pastime was to watch the grizzly bears as they cavorted and fished. We witnessed many real bear fights. One evening just before dark we counted fourteen of

179

these huge animals along the half mile of beach near the river mouth. God knows how many more were along the river out of sight in the thick bushes. When we got to within fifty yards of them in our borrowed canoe, it was not unusual to see a big bear stand on his hind legs to challenge our approach with a snarl.

There were several young men from Hagensborg fishing for the Tallheo. This was a little settlement almost ten miles up the valley from the wharf. Tom and Vern Douglas had challenged them to a basketball game. There was a narrow gravel road of sorts, leading as far as their community hall. This hall was used for dances and other social events, as well as basketball. Its ceiling wasn't much more than twelve feet high. There was a raised stage at one end and a lean-to for a catering kitchen. The floor area was so small there were no side lines. The walls were the boundaries of the playing area. Spectators watched from the stage.

Tom, Vern, two young chaps from Vancouver and I used my boat to sail across the inlet. From the wharf a local pick-up truck took us the rest of the way.

It was late July and hot. We were invited to sample some home made beer and apple cider. This local brew was good and strong.

"Save some of that stuff for after the game," Tom advised.

Their players were a rugged bunch. Most of them were of Scandinavian ancestry, born in the valley. We had only five players. It was one of the roughest games of basketball imaginable. The referee was a local who didn't seem to know when to call a foul unless a player was knocked unconscious.

We were all young, in good shape, and a bit faster than our opponents. What they lacked in speed they made up in body checks. At half-time they were ahead by three points. We had a huddle and Vern suggested a plan he thought would win the game. He always called me "Little Joe."

"Little Joe has the speed to get away from those big

guards, so we will just feed him the ball. You just get in the clear and we will get the ball to you," Vern said, looking straight at me.

The second half started more like a rugby match than a basketball game. Tom, Vern and the boys from Vancouver were concentrating on the ball while I stayed up under their basket. We scored ten points in less than ten minutes. The locals seemed baffled by our new strategy, so the game got rougher as our lead increased. We won by a score of 46 to 34. We shook hands and congratulated their team on a good game. They did not take their loss lightly!

There was a dance to follow the game. The girls were there and dressed in their best. It was obvious the girls were quite excited to have five young strangers at one of their dances. They were much more anxious to dance with us than the boys from the valley. We had time for a few drinks of that good cider before the music got going. Gertie. a pretty young blonde, took a special shine to me so we let the older people dance while we made our way to a big apple tree at the back of the hall.

Vern and Tom were apparently making too much time with a wife and girlfriend of two of their players. I'm told this ended in a fight and the losers left to get their guns.

We were doing some good old country-style smooching when Gertie's older sister found us. She told us excitedly, "It's better to get moving down the road than get shot. Those men are mad. If they find you fellows here when they get back, there will be shooting for sure."

The five of us took off and ran the eight miles down the gravel road, jumped into the boat, and were almost across to the other side of the inlet before we saw lights back at the wharf.

Gertie and I corresponded for almost five years before our romance ended. She finally married another fisherman.

In the late 1920's, Tom was living at Westholme, Vancouver Island. He had courted and married Marie Sondergaard. Just previous to this we had been batching together.

181

A few months after the wedding, living with the two of them got to me. A nineteen-year old was the last thing needed in a two-room shack with newlyweds. Packing my bags I left for Vancouver to live with Mother and help support the four youngest children. I worked in logging camps and did construction work, using most of my earnings just to make ends meet.

The Ruskin Dam was started in 1928. Ethel had married Isaac Anderson. Isaac was an experienced heavy construction carpenter and offered to take me along as his partner. That put me into the category of a full-fledged carpenter with relatively no training and little experience, at the age of nineteen. We were given some of the most meticulous jobs. The first was to build the huge bell-shaped foundations for the big turbines. The anchor bolts were three inches in diameter and had to be set in the wet concrete with great accuracy. We made no mistakes.

Not being fully qualified, I learned to say little and bluff a lot. Within three months I was promoted to night shift foreman on the main dam. This meant working twelve hours, seven nights a week. We belonged to the Industrial Woodworkers of America, which was then exclusively a carpenters' union. Our rates were one dollar per hour, $1.50 for overtime and two dollars per hour for Sundays and holidays. I was making over $350 per month after board. We were charged a dollar a day for three good meals. We supplied our own blankets.

The work was rough and dangerous. Concrete was poured twenty-four hours a day from two skylines across the canyon of the Stave River.

One evening I climbed to the top of a sixty-foot tower to get the lodged concrete moving down the chute. We were pouring the footings on the east side of the river. I hooked one leg over a two by six which had been fastened to the outside of the tower. As I leaned way out to give a pull to get the concrete moving, the two by six tore free. I found myself falling head down, towards a mass of jagged rocks. Just as in my encounter with the cougar, my subconscious

182

took over. While I fell towards certain death, instantly everything seemed to go into slow motion.

Three sets of cable guylines held the tower upright. These were some sixteen feet apart. As the first cable came within reach I grabbed it with both hands and hung on until my feet were down instead of my head. As the cable swung downward under my weight, I released my hands and dropped to grab the next cable. It seemed that I was not falling but floating, having plenty of time to reach out and grab each cable as I fell. I remember holding onto the lowest guyline until the cable surged downward a second time before letting go. I landed on my feet among the jagged rocks, some twenty feet below.

I snapped out of this strange trance to realize my hands were torn and bleeding. I was shaking violently and felt weak all over. It was some minutes before I was steady enough to stand and start walking towards the first aid shack.

Halfway there, I met men running with a stretcher towards the tower.

"Where are you fellows going in such a hurry?" I asked.

"Saw someone fall out of that tower and we are going down to carry him out," was their excited reply. They started moving on.

"Hold it! You are looking at the guy who fell!"

"You wouldn't be walking if it was you. Whoever took that plunge will either be dead or smashed to hell."

I opened my hands and asked, "Which of you is the first-aid man? I need some bandages and disinfectant."

They looked at each other in disbelief. The first-aid man came back and did a great job of dressing the wounds. Wearing a pair of new gloves, I went back to finish the shift. The following morning I went into shock and had to be rushed to a doctor. He gave me some pills that made me sleep all that day.

The Ruskin Dam was completed in the fall of 1929. The

stock market had just crashed, triggering the Great Depression. I left the job feeling pretty rich.

I first paid off the balance on Mother's house and lot, then I bought a convertible Oakland roadster. This had to be one of the classiest and fastest cars in the Vancouver district: robin's-egg blue with a wide cherry-coloured stripe down each side and a roof of light-brown canvas. It had five wire-spoked wheels that shone like silver. The spare wheel was mounted just back of the rumble seat. With a straight-eight engine, her top speed was over 100 m.p.h. When chased by the police, we just left them behind and parked in some side road until the coast was clear.

In the 1930's, if you had any kind of car, the girls flocked around. With that damned Oakland one could be mobbed. Things were great for the next few months. I stayed around Vancouver to play some senior baseball and have a fling with the girls.

There was no work available that paid the kind of money I wanted. After turning down an offer to go to South America on a hydro project, I realized with a jolt just how bad things were. There were twenty qualified men for every job. Some of the married carpenters who had been at Ruskin took work for as low as one dollar per day. This would barely buy groceries enough to feed their families. Others stood in queues for hours to receive a bowl of soup.

In the fall I went to Westholme for a visit. Tom and I shot several deer for our winter's meat. He and Marie were living in a small two-room shack on a hill above the shingle mill. They were planning on building a bigger house on the two acres Marie's dad had given them.

"Why don't you take a couple of deer to Mother and the kids, pack your duds, and move over here? You can build the house for us," Tom suggested.

"The meals are good and we have all the homemade wine and beer you can drink," Marie added, with a laugh.

"I can't pay you any wages right now," Tom explained, "but we can settle up sometime after our house is finished."

"Okay by me, Tom, you don't have to do any more coaxing."

I was back in three days with carpenter's tools, work clothes, guns, fishing rods and roadster. We had a party to celebrate the occasion. Marie invited most of the young people from Westholme. My favourite girl, Hazel, had insisted on coming along from Vancouver. There was plenty of home brew and good food. The party lasted into the wee hours of the morning. The last to leave were the Holman boys, rugged young men. That wine Marie dished out was really powerful stuff.

"We are going to dig the basement tomorrow. If any of you fellows are tough enough to come out, we'd sure appreciate the help." Tom challenged.

Big Henry Holman threw out his chest and pounded it with both fists.

"Tough enough, eh? I'll damn well be here at daylight, dig all day, then pack both the Garner boys home. They'll never be able to walk if they keep up to me."

Everyone laughed. Five others volunteered to help.

"Bring picks and shovels and a wheelbarrow. There won't be much pay. Lots of beer and sandwiches though. See you fellows at daylight, down by Nimo's Creek. Good night, gang," Tom laughed, and headed for bed.

When morning came everything was white with frost. We were finishing breakfast when a wolf howl came from the direction of the new house site.

"My God! They're here already! Better get down and show them where to start."

I pulled on coat and gloves on the way out the door.

The basement was dug and ready for the forms by four o'clock that afternoon. I've never seen better workers. Big Henry was like a machine. All one had to do was point him in the right direction.

We ordered a truckload of reject lumber from Clark and Son, out of the Chemainus mill. They delivered a load of over 5,000 board feet, at a cost of $7.50 for the works. The concrete forms were ready within a week. We bartered for

185

nails and cement with a Mr. Corbishly of Duncan, one rick of split fir wood for two bags of cement. Corbishly operated a fuel business. He had only recently taken on the cement agency. He was anxious to make sales so he let us have the cement and trusted us to deliver the wood later.

We organized another bee to mix and pour the concrete. A dozen men turned up the morning we began this task. Two hauled gravel from the Chemainus River while the rest hand-mixed the concrete on an eight by eight foot platform known as a "sweat board." It took twelve yards of gravel and sixty bags of cement. Water was packed from the creek in buckets. Despite the cold, every man was soaked with sweat. The concrete was in the forms by three in the afternoon. It was so cold we covered everything with dirt to keep the frost out. This was December 22, 1930.

It began snowing that evening and didn't stop until there were over two feet on the ground. I was concerned we might lose all our hard work to the weather. We didn't strip off the forms until the snow melted a month later. To my surprise, the concrete was smooth and hard. In the interval we cut and delivered the barter wood as agreed.

With the arrival of spring, we began building the five-room house with full basement. There was a kitchen, bedroom, living-room and dinette on the main floor and two more good-sized bedrooms upstairs.

We built a wood-fired furnace from an old oil barrel with door and smoke pipe welded to it. This we walled in with old bricks. These were free; all we had to do was dig them up and haul them from the abandoned smelter at Crofton. Wiring and electrical material cost just over twenty-eight dollars. We did all the labour. A friend did the plumbing. Pipe and labour came to forty-two dollars. This did not include the bathtub or hand basin. We washed in the kitchen sink and showered in a home-made shower.

Shingles were obtained on a barter basis from the Sondergaard mill. Windows and doors were swapped for furnace wood at the Cowichan joinery. The paint was a mixture of white lead and linseed oil from England. Tom traded a gallon of Marie's best wine for a 25-pound can of white lead and two gallons of linseed oil with the sailors on a British ship.

"How does your wife make that wine? Sure has a wallop to it," one old salt confided to Tom the day following the first swap.

"Uses mostly cougar piss and old boxing gloves," Tom explained.

"You need more oil and lead, just say so. That's got to be the best brew I ever tasted."

That evening Tom carried another gallon of dandelion wine to the ship and came back with enough paint to finish the job.

By the spring of 1931 most families were on direct relief. The government issued coupons for groceries. Tom and Marie were too proud for this so he worked on the road crew for nineteen dollars a month. Being a married man with no children, he was only allowed that much. There was no other work to be had.

When we started the house Tom had $146. When we finished, all bills had been paid except my wages. We had a housewarming party in May. All those who had helped were invited. After the celebration Tom counted what was left; it amounted to $3.80.

"You might as well have that for a bonus," he said, handing me the money. This bought a bottle of good Scotch.

Forty-nine years later I visited the house with Paul St. Pierre. It was for sale then for $46,000. The home is still in good condition and was considered a good buy at prices of the day. The fact is I almost bought the damned thing as an investment. A month's rent would be more than double the original cost.

Later in 1931, Tom started work for Empire Stevedoring and soon became a foreman. He stayed long-shoring until 1935, when he resigned to start logging. There was good money to be made in this business if one had the know-how. Tom certainly was successful.

187

I longshored for a couple of years. In our spare time Tom and I built several houses in Crofton. In 1933 there was a tax sale of vacant lots. We bought six lots, paying fifteen dollars each for four inside lots and $17.50 each for two corner lots. The houses we built were small but none cost more than $1,400 to build. We sold them for just under $10,000 each in the mid-1940's. Today, people are willing to pay over $40,000 for these same houses.

There was always time to help your neighbours during the 1930's. Barter was a common way of doing business. Half a deer could be swapped for a sack of spuds or carrots. A day's work would pay the milk bill for a month.

We walked the five miles to Crofton when the young salmon were there feeding on shrimp. Using a rowboat and spoon with something red on it, we often caught over fifty pounds of fish in a few hours. These young salmon weighed between two and five pounds and were great fun to catch. There were too many fish for three people, so the neighbours got a share. Marie fried some while it was fresh and then canned what was left. Nothing was wasted. She had her own smokehouse and knew how to use it.

Starting in late February and on through March, we hunted hooters, which are male blue grouse. These were considered a delicacy during the depression. On a quiet day their hooting could be heard as far as a quarter of a mile away. Once this sound was detected, it took only a short time to locate the bird. If the hunter created too much commotion and noise the grouse stopped hooting. After such a disruption the only hope of bagging him was to leave and return in a couple of hours. We always tried for a head shot with a .22 rifle. That way, no meat was wasted.

These birds made good stew if the meat was cooked for a couple of days. Roasting or frying made the meat dry and tough, but Marie devised a way to make them very tasty indeed. Stripping all the meat from the bones, she would put it through the meat grinder, using one piece of fat pork to the same quantity of grouse, and then add spices. We

188

called these "hooterburgers" and it made a nice change from fish and venison.

To keep the burgers fresh and away from flies, we bent a tall alder sapling down to where Marie could tie the bags of meat to the branches. When we let go of the tree it would swish upwards and the meat would be forty feet above the ground among the young leaves. We proved that blowflies never go this far above the ground. Incidentally, neither do game wardens. It was the only way to keep the meat from spoiling. Refrigerators were still some years in the future, but even if they had been available, there wouldn't have been money enough to buy them.

When Tom's house was completed, I was offered a contract to build two more places a mile north on the highway at the corner of Crofton Road. We agreed on a price of $150 each. This included a dug well, plumbing, wiring, brickwork and painting. The house had to be ready to live in before I received any money.

The building took the better part of three months. Mr. Pinson paid me in cash the same day both houses were finished, and rented for ten dollars per month. There were no taxes, compensation or other deductions. A hundred dollars for a month's pay was considered a lot in 1932. Our verbal contract was adequate. There has never been a complaint from renter, owner or contractor.

That was almost fifty years ago.

Marble Island

By August 1939 Tom and I were operating separately. He had a logging show and small sawmill. I was contracting in the house-building business and doing some roads and bridges.

In September, World War Two was declared. Within weeks all materials and men were needed for the war effort. Closing down the contracting business, I started with Marwell Construction on defence projects.

My first job was building a large seaplane hangar and docking facilities at the Patricia Bay airport near Sidney, Vancouver Island. Starting as a carpenter foreman, I was soon made general foreman of this phase of the construction.

When this was completed, the company asked if I would go to Vulcan, Alberta, as Assistant Superintendent on a training airport they had contracted to build. This meant leaving my wife and two young daughters alone in Victoria. There was neither time to take them along nor suitable accommodation to house them in.

We were separated two months when blackouts on the

Pacific coast came into effect. A phone call assured me that everyone was in a panic. I hitched a ride on an Air Force plane and arrived at Pat Bay the following morning.

In Victoria, the situation was chaotic. Everyone was talking about getting away from the coast and the potential dangers of being bombed. Driving after dark, except on authorized missions was prohibited. Hotels, houses and other buildings had to have their windows completely covered, or the lights kept off. At night, the west coast, including Vancouver Island, was in complete darkness. The next day, after helping my wife pack, I bought her and the children train tickets for Calgary. A plane was waiting to take me back to Vulcan. Luckily, a small house on the outskirts of town became vacant, and here we spent the next ten months. The alkali water tasted horrible. We missed the trees and mountains.

Worse were the periodic dust storms. The fine dust sifted in through even the tiniest cracks, and covered everything with layers of fine silt. "Travelling real estate" the locals called it. It took days to clean the house after a storm. One consolation was that we did not have to live with coastal blackout regulations.

When the job was completed, we packed and again headed west. We rented a house in Vancouver.

After a few days at Marwell's office to finalize the Vulcan project, I was invited to handle a very tough job. Doug Welch, one of the partners, called me into his office and asked if I would accept the task of building a radar station on Marble Island, off the west coast of the Queen Charlottes. He produced maps and explained that this was the most westerly piece of land in Canada, and was separated from Japan only by the waters of the Pacific Ocean. He explained the fear that the Japanese might invade the Queen Charlotte Islands and use them as a springboard for attacks on the mainland.

"Radar is the only means of detecting such an invasion in time to do something about it," he said.

Plans prepared by the R.C.A.F. were produced, along

with some engineering reports. I pointed out with some concern that the engineer's closing comment was written on some water-soiled pieces of notepaper, and stated, "Camp and tents blown off the island in a storm." No one was sure a station could ever be built out on this island, though it was indeed a strategic location.

"If you are willing to give it a try, I will guarantee you all possible support from this end," said Doug. "You will have a free hand to do the job as you see fit. Any reasonable expense is of no consequence if the job can be completed in a relatively short time. The C.O. at Alliford Bay Seaplane Base has guaranteed 24-hour a day radio communications and all the machine guns and ammunition you think necessary, plus air patrols when weather permits."

Doug left his desk and walked to where I stood.

"Well, Joe, there is a war on, so what do you say?" he asked with a smile.

"Sounds like this could be a bit of a challenge. I'll give it a try. When do we start?" I asked.

"This afternoon if you like."

He went on to explain that men could be called from any industry or even out of the armed forces, if they could contribute to getting this top priority radar project operational in the shortest possible time.

"I'll have a crew hired by tomorrow noon and will want air transportation to Alliford Bay by two p.m. if you can arrange it," I replied.

"I have an accountant who is also a timekeeper," said Doug. "He can go along with you and set up a temporary office at Queen Charlotte City. He's familiar with all the procedures of progress draws and the bookwork required by the Treasury Department."

"It would be a big help to get things started and under control. Have him packed and ready to leave tomorrow," I replied.

I spent the rest of the afternoon calling a crew. I hired fourteen of the best, including brothers Tom, Oliver and Lloyd. Fred Robson, Margaret's husband, was hired as a master mechanic. When I asked him if he thought he could handle the job, he replied, "Hell, yes! I fix anything from alarm clocks to 1000 horsepower diesel engines, and keep them going."

"You'll do. Be ready to leave one week from today. You'll be up there for at least four months, so make a list of equipment you want to take and pack everything you'll need, except a girl."

Fred laughed. "I'll be there, you can count on it."

The accountant and I left Vancouver airport next afternoon and landed at Alliford Bay just before dark. Harry Winnie, the Commanding Officer, welcomed us with great enthusiasm. He was pleased and relieved that we were going to build the station. We discussed the pros and cons of the job with his engineers, and talked till well past midnight. Harry agreed to have a Stranraer aircraft at my disposal at daylight. He would do the flying.

It was dawn when we put a sleepy-eyed accountant on the dock at Queen Charlotte City, with instructions to establish an office and charter a boat. We headed out to look over the situation from the skies. The little island was no more than a quarter of a mile long and about 200 yards wide. It was pointed at both ends and looked much like a large ship in a rough sea. We flew over and around it for half an hour. We checked all sheltered bays and inlets on Graham Island, a mile to the east, which might be useful for storing materials until they could somehow be put on Marble. It was a reasonably quiet day for the west coast, yet the seas were running and breaking some fifty feet up on the rocky beach. Any attempt to land near the island was out of the question.

We could see it would be impossible to put a scow near enough to the island to unload without having it smashed to bits. Landing people and food from the supply boat would also be a perilous manoeuvre. This would have to be done by using a strong boat that could be manhandled up on the beach when not in use. Any type of power boat would be useless. We decided to try a riverboat, with seating for two

193

sets of oars and four passengers, or equivalent cargo. Just how the heavy equipment might be put ashore safely was much more of a problem than either of us had anticipated.

Flying low through the passage that separates the two main islands of the Charlottes, we could assess the shallow channel and its jagged reefs. Farther east we could see several A-frame camps. Big spruce timber was being yarded to the water, then lashed into "Davis" rafts. Noting the size of these huge logs gave me an idea.

"Harry, do you know the boss of the outfit we're looking at down there?"

"Sure do."

"Where can he be contacted?" I asked, with enthusiasm.

"He should be in the cookhouse about now, there on the big float just ahead and to our left."

"Let's land and have a chat with him," I suggested.

Harry banked the flying boat, made a perfect landing, and taxied up to the float. The man we wanted to see was there to help us tie up. I was introduced to Jim Carstairs, the "Bull of the Woods" in logger's lingo. Jim invited us to stay for lunch and chat awhile.

Harry and I explained what we were going to try and do on Marble Island. Jim's opening remark was direct.

"On the west coast of these islands, it is rough and dangerous at any time of the year. Right now I wouldn't want to face it in a battleship."

"It sure looked bad from the air, but I believe if you could put together about a dozen of these big spruce logs, and lash them with double headsticks and heavy cable, such a raft might hang together long enough to put the equipment ashore out there," was my suggestion.

Carstairs said nothing for a minute or so, then looked at each of us in turn and gave his opinion.

"I think your project out there will be impossible to complete. If we build you this raft twice as strong as anything we've ever built, it might just hang together long

194

enough to put your machines and supplies off on that surf-bound piece of real estate.''

We discussed size and construction details. It was agreed the raft should be about forty feet wide and eighty feet long, with logs not less than three feet in diameter at the small ends.

"I'll have my men double-lash everything. It will be ready one week from today if that's okay with you," Jim stated.

I considered this briefly. "Jim, let's make it ten days from today and instead of double lashings, make it quadruple.''

"Okay, but who's going to tow it out to the island?'' Jim asked.

"Jack Hann has a big seiner called the *Bertha G,* and knows the passage as well as anyone around here,'' Harry suggested.

Jim concurred. "Couldn't get a better man for the job.''

"Okay then, ten days from now we head out just ahead of the morning high tide.'' I thanked him for his help and for the great lunch.

"Anytime we can do anything to help you, let us know,'' Jim shouted as we taxied out for takeoff.

Jack Hann was contacted that evening, and he agreed to be ready in ten days. The *Bertha G* would carry all the necessary towing gear. Hann's comments were also brief and to the point.

"You fellows must be more than a little crazy to try to build on that damned island. Only thing it's good for is eagles and seals. The winds will probably blow the build-ings into the ocean if you do manage to put them up.''

Next morning shortly after daybreak, I was airborne for Vancouver to supervise the loading on scows of all the equipment and prefabricated buildings. We planned to take them through the narrows and then transfer everything to the log raft.

The cargo consisted of cookstoves, dishes, beds and

bedding, diesel lighting plants, prefab buildings, plywood, barrels of gas and diesel fuel, one complete water system, three 10,000 gallon storage tanks, food for thirty men for four months, first aid supplies, two machine guns and thousands of rounds of ammunition, a logging donkey, a small sawmill and a bulldozer. There was a complete four-bed hospital unit, including drugs and supplies. All this had to be loaded in such a way that the items loaded last would be off first, and used in that order. To feed and shelter thirty men out in the Pacific was going to be a major undertaking, until some buildings and cooking facilities could be established.

On the little island, we found a big cave for shelter. Here we slept and cooked for ten days. If a bad storm had come up during the first week, the seas would have washed our entire camp off the island. During this period we were blessed with good weather and managed to land more than half the equipment and buildings.

We were lucky enough to get the cookhouse and one bunkhouse roofed in before the first storm hit. All hands were busy moving stoves, beds and groceries under cover, when suddenly everyone stopped and stood listening to a strange roar.

"What the hell is that noise?" Fred Robson shouted.

"It's the start of a storm. All hands hurry and get things tied down or into those buildings." Running up to the lookout, I sent the men from there to help.

From this point, I could see the storm in the distance. About ten miles out to the southwest there was a black line of low clouds swirling and moving towards us. The roar got even louder as this front approached. It struck the beaches with a roar like thunder, driven by 60-mile an hour winds. Within minutes, our wind-gauge was registering gusts well over 100 knots. Hailstones and rain hit in a cloudburst.

The noise created by the waves and wind became so great that voice communication was impossible. Rocks as big as a man's fist were being blown through the air. It was so dangerous the crew had to take shelter either in the buildings, or behind rocks and logs. From a small cave, I watched all our bags of precious cement disintegrate. The seas roared up the rocky beach like tidal waves. Some were twenty feet higher than any we had seen up to this time. So strong was the storm, it actually blew wet three by ten joists right out of the tight piles, into the air, and scattered them onto the frothing sea. Some of these heavy planks would be blown off the tops of the waves and carried as much as a hundred yards through the air before falling back in the water, to disappear in foam and spray.

The worst of the storm lasted about an hour. Then the wind abated to a steady 60. It was possible to come out of hiding and go down to the beach to assess the damage. Over half the lumber was gone and all the cement destroyed. Nails and hardware soaked in sea water had already begun to rust. The pile of bricks, over 2,000 of them, had been washed around in the waves and rocks until there was nothing left larger than a good-sized marble. Luckily, most of the plumbing and electrical supplies had been carried off the beach and into the buildings the previous day.

We had lost almost all our groceries. Sacks of vegetables and cases of canned goods had been swept off our storage ledge, which was over twenty feet above normal high water. Suddenly, everyone realized that we were critically short of food.

Next morning when the *Quallace* came out to stand by, we hoisted our pre-arranged signal, a red flag, to show the Gale brothers we considered it too dangerous to attempt any unloading. The arrangement was that they go back to shelter and try again the next morning. If a green flag was up, they were to stand by until the big skiff could be launched.

In our crew were six men from Alberta. Though they were a rugged group, this storm had scared the hell out of them. They had packed their bags during the night and announced next morning that they would rather leave now than stay to starve or drown at some later date. It was four

197

days before the sea quieted down enough to get these men out to the packer, and bring some supplies ashore.

Jim and Frank Gale owned and operated our supply boat, the *Quallace*. She was a 45-foot west coast fishing boat. Fred Robson and I were acting as "boatmen" when we took the six terrified men out to put them aboard. It was always dangerous transferring anything from one boat to the other. This day the waves were such that one minute the big skiff was ten feet above the decks of the packer and the next we could see the propeller and keel level with our eyes.

We took the men out, two at a time, and somehow made the transfer without drowning anyone. It was imperative to keep the boats close without allowing any actual contact. This was done with poles and ropes handled by men whose lives depended on every move. Any bump would smash and swamp the skiff. The prairie boys were so anxious to leave, they needed no coaxing to leap from the skiff to the deck of the bigger boat. Their bags and suitcases could be tossed to them from a safer distance.

When all six were safely aboard, I scrambled from the skiff onto the packer. I had with me a grocery list that looked sufficient to feed an army for a year. The cook had taken stock and ordered what was required to replace our food losses. Coffee, tea, sugar, and meat had been rationed by the government and were available only with coupons. This was indeed a problem from our standpoint. The storm had taken four months rations in a single day.

When we were out of the rough waters, the Gale brothers gave notice; they would not carry on unless a second boat was chartered to give them some measure of safety should their boat have trouble. The storm made everyone realize the dangers of operating out in the wide-open Pacific. It was suggested I try to charter the *Burnaby M*, a 50-foot seiner owned by the Haida Indians of Skidegate Village.

"If you can get that boat with a good crew, maybe you

could hire some of the Haida men to help out there," was Jim Gale's suggestion.

Arriving at Queen Charlotte City, both Gale brothers and I headed for the Skidegate reserve. I was formally introduced to Ed Collison, the Chief, and also to his half-brother, Jim McKay, the skipper of the *Burnaby M*. Their big boat was up on the beach being caulked and copper-painted. The fishing season had just ended so most of the Haidas were at home. The *Burnaby M* was formally chartered. Jim McKay agreed to be skipper and Fred Russ accepted the job of engineer. Because we were able to pay good wages, a dozen more young men were hired in less than an hour. The big boat was launched at high tide that evening.

It was arranged that all hands would leave early next morning for Marble. Gales' store provided groceries. We purchased almost everything they had in stock and stowed it aboard the *Quallace* in readiness for the early departure. But when Frank Gale Sr. learned we had no ration coupons, he refused to let the goods go.

"I can't replace those rationed things without coupons," he stated. I got on the phone to Harry Winnie to explain our predicament.

"Hang tough! I'll be over in our crash boat in less than half an hour."

Twenty minutes later there was a great roar down by the dock and Harry stepped ashore. He had brought with him the purchasing officer from the base. Papers were produced and signed by the two officers and myself, stating that we had received the groceries as emergency rations for west coast radio detachments. We all knew this might have repercussions if the Ration Board got sticky. The C.O.'s parting words were: "If there is a court-martial for this, I'll come out and get you so we can face the charges together."

"Thanks for everything, old boy." We laughed.

In minutes the crash boat was out of sight in its own spray as it raced back across the channel. It was powered by two big straight-eight Rolls-Royce engines and capable of doing over 40 knots.

Our arrival back at Marble Island with the two packers, replacements for the crew, plus enough food to see us through, shot morale from low to high.

What amazed Robson and my three brothers most was the way the Haidas took over the big skiff and hauled all the supplies and men ashore in a way that was a pleasure to watch. They took the boat through the waves and breakers as naturally as young ducklings take to a pond. The crew of the *Burnaby M* was also great. There were few words spoken. They worked as one big human machine. Each seemed to know exactly what was needed, and anticipated every move.

When the Haida boys had all their gear safely in the new bunkhouse, Lloyd, Fred and I went in to introduce ourselves. We wanted to find out what each could do best. They proved to be fine young men. Their average height was a little over six feet. We learned that most had attended outside schools and had studied the arts and music.

George Brown started the introductions. He told us he was Captain of the Rangers on the Queen Charlotte Islands, that all the men here were members with combat training, and each had brought his ranger rifle with 500 rounds of ammunition per gun. They had also brought along some hand grenades and emergency food rations.

"Might be pretty handy stuff if those damned Japs try to come ashore," was Robson's observation.

As we were introduced, George explained the skills of each man. When Fred Williams shook hands, he informed us, "I am the leader of our orchestra. We are known as "The Harmony Boys." He was apologetic because they had brought along some of their instruments, and asked if it would be okay if they practiced and played some music. He introduced the members of the band. They had brought drums, saxophone, trumpet, violin, a couple of guitars and one banjo. Brother Lloyd suggested they tune up and give us a demonstration.

The last man introduced was six-foot three inches, weighed over two hundred pounds and was put together much like Jack Dempsey.

"This is Phil Watson. I suggest you make him your labour boss. He knows how to handle the boys if they get out of line," said George. Shaking hands with Phil was like putting your hand in a steel vise.

"You are now the official boss of the Marble Island Haidas and will be paid accordingly," I said, rubbing my right hand to get the circulation going again.

"You can count on me to look after the boys," Phil grinned.

It was easy to sense the respect everyone had for him.

The Harmony Boys were tuning up their instruments and getting ready for a song. Lloyd left to get the rest of our crew to come up and meet the new gang. Fred and I headed for the office. It was now early January and cold. We were about to open our door when the music started. The strains of *White Christmas* drifted out over the little camp. A full moon was just rising out of the ocean. Somehow, the combination froze both of us in our tracks. We stood perfectly still for a full fifteen minutes. Fred broke the spell by announcing, "That's some good crew you hired today. Might get this bloody job done with men like that around. Sure wish we had something to celebrate the occasion."

"It's a good feeling to have those men out here," I said. "Makes me think it will be a lot safer getting things on and off this damned island from now on. If you dig deep enough in the bottom drawer of my desk, you can come up with some pretty good snakebite medicine. It should lift the boys out of their doldrums from that bloody storm."

I had bought four bottles of good Scotch at Alliford Bay the previous week. We took this up to the bunkhouse and proceeded to cheer up the crew a bit. It proved to be a great evening with all hands getting aquainted. Phil was the one who called the party to a halt. At eleven o'clock he blinked the lights three times and commanded; "Okay gang!

201

Party's over! We've got a war on and plenty of work to do tomorrow, so let's hit the sack for an early rise and shine."

The diesel generators were now in operation, replacing the coal-oil lamps and gas lanterns we had been using. The music and Scotch had done a great deal to bolster the sagging spirits of everyone in camp, especially the Air Force boys who manned the wireless and lookouts, around the clock.

Next day everyone tied into his job with vigour and enthusiasm. In only a week, we had the main cookhouse completed. A gravity water system was operating. We had hot water and a stove with an oven, for the first time since landing. We had to get a second cook to help with the extra work for the larger crew. A scow was on its way from Vancouver with cement, bricks and lumber to replace what the storm had destroyed. Bread and pastry could now be baked. Everyone was tired of living on rye crisp and hardtack. Art Christison had been sent up as head cook. He was jet-black and hailed from Georgia. Forty years later, when we visited the Charlottes, Fred Russ told the story about the time Art was on his way to Marble Island.

"Hell! We could have got that man ashore two days earlier. He was making such good pastry and meals, we did't want to let him go. When our boat would hit the big seas outside the inlet, Art would turn sort of green and lose all his breakfast. He begged to be taken to the inside so he could go back home. We wouldn't do that. When we finally did get him in the big skiff to go ashore at Marble Island, he was so scared he turned white. We actually had to lift him over the side and drop him in that skiff."

The *Burnaby M* had come out three days in a row, but the waves were so high it was too dangerous to attempt to put groceries or men ashore. Things went smoothly for the next while, then another storm struck.

We had beached the big log raft with a full load of supplies. It was partially unloaded when heavy seas started to pound the island and push the raft far up on the rocks. The tides were at their highest cycle, so our raft was high and dry. The noise of the waves and the big raft pounding on beach was like thunder.

Three days later we got a long cable out to the *Burnaby M* and with the boat pulling and the bulldozer pushing, we were able to move the damaged raft only about ten feet at one end. Then she stuck tightly again. The cable broke near the boat when the raft stopped moving. This loose end tangled in the propeller. It looked as though the *Burnaby M* was headed for a watery grave.

Again, the crew did the impossible. Fred Russ cut the cable with a fire axe, then launched their dory. He and the deckhand cleared the cable from the propeller shaft, using a pikepole and gaff hook. The skipper was able to apply power barely in time to pull out to safety. One more minute and the packer would have been a goner.

Next day, at low tide, Ollie and his helper drilled holes in the rocks seaward from the raft; then they rigged the main line from the donkey through a block fastened to the eye-bolt anchors they had put in.

"I don't think the donkey will have enough power to move that raft one inch," was Ollie's emphatic declaration, as we looked over the situation.

"What do you suggest then?" I queried.

"Hell, we got lots of dynamite in the shed. Why don't we blast her loose?"

"If you know how to load the powder under it, we can give it a try," was my suggestion.

"Sure as hell no good to anyone where she is," was Ollie's remark as he spat on the headstick.

He and his crew carried a dozen boxes of dynamite to a big crevice under the high side of the raft. They piled boulders on the boxes to keep the charge in place. They ran a fuse through a long piece of water pipe. After coating the pipe with grease, the cap end was put in one of the full boxes of dynamite and tied securely. Just before the tide was high, Ollie stretched the main line singing tight. Everybody, except the donkey puncher and Ollie, was cleared from the area.

203

Five minutes before high tide, Ollie lit the fuse, then took over the donkey driving himself. The dynamite was now under several feet of water. There was a deafening bang, a huge spray went up, and the raft seemed to heave ten feet into the air. The donkey roared. Through the smoke and spray we could see the big raft lunge towards the open ocean. Everyone let out a great cheer.

The boatmen again took the cable out to the *Burnaby M* and this time she was able to haul the raft free and back into the inlet for the final load of goods.

"All she needed was a bit of a jolt to get her going," was Ollie's laughing remark.

"She sure as hell got a jolt all right." I had to laugh too.

We had built a steep railroad leading from the beach on the east side up 300 feet to the radar building. The little rail cars were pulled up this incline by a single-drum gas winch. There was some 200 feet of track along the level from the top to the radar site. This level portion was operated completely by manpower. It was dangerous when a car was heavily loaded, yet the boys managed with only one sprained ankle and some badly barked shins.

A team of three experts from the Air Force came to install the special tubes and wiring. Our crews were not allowed inside the building once this secret radar equipment was being put in place.

There was a recess left in the main concrete foundation about fifteen inches deep and twelve inches square.

"What in hell is that square hole for?" I asked the officer in charge.

"That is to be filled with high-test dynamite and wired to a secret switch that only the operators know about. If the Japs land, the orders are to throw the switch."

"Won't that kill the men on shift?" I queried.

"It will kill the operator, but the Japs will never be able to copy our radar tubes. The charge we put in there is enough to blow the building and contents to Kingdom

Come. It's really not such a big deal. The Japs would kill everyone anyway."

"Nice war we're having," was my parting comment.

To get the secret equipment from the war supply depot in Vancouver to Alliford Bay, a destroyer was used. The cargo was then transferred to a small scow. Harry and I agreed to beach this scow on Marble rather than risk a transfer to the log raft.

On each corner of the scow, a machine-gun was mounted and manned during the trip out through Skidegate Channel. Two planes, with bombs, acted as escort. Harry Winnie explained to me in confidence that two Japanese submarines had been sighted in the area and it was suspected they would try either to destroy the equipment or pirate it from the scow.

Jack Hann, with the *Bertha G*, did the towing through the narrow and treacherous Skidegate passage and on to Marble. He asked me to be on his boat to help co-ordinate and supervise during this risky manoeuvre. As we approached the narrowest turn in the passage, Jack handed me a razor-sharp fire axe. It was a tense Hann who gave the instructions.

"Now listen carefully, Joe! Our lives may depend on what I have to say. This tide is travelling out towards the ocean at over ten miles an hour. The front end of that scow will strike the rock shoulder as we go through the turn ahead. It should bounce clear and follow, but if it hangs up and swings on us, you will have to cut the towline. If I swing my left hand down, you chop that rope instantly. If you miss, we will be jammed onto the jagged reefs. This could sink both scow and boat at the speed we will be moving. I'll need full power on to keep the boat under control."

I took my position near the big hemp rope where it passed over the stern. After taking a couple of practice swings with the axe, to make sure there would be no mistakes, I glued my eyes on Jack and waited.

We flew past the shores as we travelled with the riptide. It was swirling and boiling like rapids in a river canyon at flood time. It seemed only minutes until we were into the turn. The port front corner of the scow struck the rocks with a crash. I watched Jack's left hand as the towline came up so tight, water actually squirted out of it where it passed over the hardwood rail. The scow groaned and bounced, then cleared the rock shoulder to follow like a trained seal. I wiped the cold sweat off my face and walked to the wheelhouse where Jack stood with a tight-lipped grin.

"Was ready to give the signal when she broke free," he said.

"Wouldn't want many like that in a day!" was my hoarse reply.

The cook brought hot coffee.

The big ocean swells were only a mile ahead. It was here the four machine-guns were taken from the scow and mounted on the two Air Force boats that were also escorting the convoy. You can be sure the gunners needed no coaxing to leave that scow and get aboard the boats.

Brother Tom and I left the *Bertha G* to ride the scow and handle the line changes and signals that would be necessary when we neared Marble Island. Weeks of advance preparation had gone into this important manoeuvre. The tides and wind were the major factors to contend with. We planned to beach the scow on the east side of Marble, about an hour after high water. On this particular day, this would be at three o'clock in the afternoon. We hoped the scow would settle on the beach before its bottom was pounded out.

The *Burnaby M* was to have the strawline, from the donkey on shore, stretched out some 800 feet off the east side and held tightly so it wouldn't sink to snag in the big boulders on the ocean floor. As we came nearer we could see the boat standing off, and knew she had the cable ready for hooking to the scow.

As pre-arranged, the scow passed as close to the *Burnaby M* as conditions would allow. Jim McKay threw a light line to me as we passed. This was tied to the end of the strawline which was pulled over and shackled to a bridle at the back end of the scow. The boat then cleared the strawline from her tow bits and the donkey was signalled to go ahead. This caused the scow to swap ends and start backing towards the narrow entrance to the beach. The *Bertha G* had been instructed to hold the scow in position by pulling on the towline as needed. Thanks to the skill and good judgement of Jack Hann, the scow and cargo were manipulated to within feet of the prepared landing spot. When the shore lines were secure and tight, the *Bertha G* was cut free. With a wave of his hand, Jack turned his boat and headed for quieter waters. The Air Force boats circled the island until well after dark. The Japanese subs were not seen on this day.

By daybreak, the lethal big tubes and acid-filled crates were off the scow safely and on their way to the radar building. All hands had worked through the night to accomplish the seemingly impossible. For some there had been no sleep for over thirty-six hours.

With high tide the next afternoon, the *Burnaby M* pulled the scow off the beach only to find the bottom smashed out of it. They were able to tow it slowly away from the island, but when the scow hit the big ocean swells the towline parted. The battered little wreck drifted out towards the open ocean, never to be seen again. All felt the loss sad, but justified. The completion of the radar station was now assured.

An end to the hazards and isolation seemed only a few weeks away. Little did we know that the worst was yet to come.

It happened a few days after the scow left, but on the opposite side of the island. A fairly big sea was running with waves averaging fifteen feet high. The *Burnaby M* was standing by to unload. They had several barrels of diesel to be taken ashore. Charlie Williams and Don Moody were doing the boat duties that day. Phil Watson had sent them out to bring in the barrels on a towline. Don neglected to remove his gumboots. He and Charlie were rushing the job and before they knew what happened, the big skiff fouled the towline and instantly capsized. The boatmen found themselves in the heavy surf, in grave danger of drowning. The undertow was so strong a seal would have trouble moving among the rocks.

The alarm went out and all hands came on the run. Big Phil never hesitated. Throwing off his heavy clothes and shoes, he dove into this foaming surf to pull one of the men from under the water, then tie him to the swamped boat. George Brown threw Phil a rope. Don had gone to the bottom because of his boots and heavy rain clothes. Phil dove and was able to tie the line around the drowning man's waist. Unconscious, he was hauled onto the rocks and revived with mouth-to-mouth resusitation.

If you don't know what is meant when a west-coaster warns, "Look out for the three big ones!" I'll try to explain what can happen.

I was running along the top of a reef some fifteen feet above normal breakers, headed out to help Phil. The swells were breaking some fifty feet away. There was no thought of danger coming from that direction. Without warning, the first of the three big ones knocked me off the reef into a pothole of foaming water, on the shore side. The first big wave came over the top of the reef in a solid wall some ten feet high. I was sucked down into a hole so deep all daylight from the surface disappeared. The second wave shot me up from the depths and I was able to gulp one breath of air. The third wave came over the reef like a small Niagara Falls and I went down again into the darkness. A passage went under the reef and out to the ocean.

It seemed eons before I saw daylight again. Pulling off my heavy gloves, I clawed frantically for the surface and some air. I neither blacked out nor panicked, but when I crawled out onto the rocks and lay with my head down, it seemed as though quarts of water ran out of my nose and mouth. Unable to stand, I crawled some distance towards shore and safer ground. Twenty minutes later I staggered up the beach to where brother Ollie and Fred Robson were talking very seriously about something. Fred was the only one who had seen me disappear in that wall of water. He was telling Ollie there was no chance of ever seeing me again when I surprised them, looking like a drowned rat. Fred must have thought he was seeing a ghost. He jumped sideways and shouted, "How the hell did you get here? We were sure you were a goner!"

"Wasn't easy, Fred. How are the other boys? Did they make it?"

"Yeah, they got out okay, a bit shaky and waterlogged though. All the Haida boys are up in the bunkhouse having a meeting right now."

Ollie had talked with Big Phil after he got ashore. Phil said, "Bad spirits are here and we're all going to leave for our village to have a potlatch."

"When?" I asked

"Now," Ollie replied.

"They can't leave now, it's too bloody rough and dangerous. Half of them will be drowned the way that sea is pounding onto those rocks."

In less than ten minutes, Ollie, Fred and I were surrounded by some twenty young Indians and old Mr. Moody, who had taken charge to explain the Haida custom. It was his son Don who had come nearest to a watery death. The old man explained how the good spirits had saved the men and had to be honoured by a potlatch.

"We go home now to lose the bad spirits of this island. We must honour the spirits now, or somebody will die for sure," he explained.

It was easy to feel the fear and sense their desperate need. They all seemed to be expecting something bad to happen at any moment.

"Phil." I said, "you must not try to leave in a storm like this, someone will drown for sure."

His reply was blunt.

"It's okay, we must go now."

"No," was my firm refusal.

With a single voice all the Haidas shouted.

209

"We go now! It is an old custom of our people."

"If you use the skiff, each of you must sign a paper relieving us of any responsibility if you don't make it," was my stipulation.

They held a short conference and agreed to sign.

"They are going to go no matter what," was Fred's observation. He had been trying to persuade his helper to influence them to wait for better weather.

"We must go now!" George insisted.

I suggested we could use the machine-guns to stop them committing suicide in the big waves.

"You get your machine-guns, but we must go anyway!" was George's quiet but definite reply.

With that, one of the Haida boys climbed the cliff to watch the ocean, as an eagle would, from the branches of a big spruce tree. This lookout man gave the boat crew signals when it looked safe to start out for the *Burnaby M.* It was better than any movie, to watch the show these men put on in the ensuing hour. Their strongest and best boatmen manned the oars.

The lightest man on each trip was in the bow. Four were at the stern, and at a given signal of the one in the tree, the boat seemed to be pushed or carried into an incoming wave, slide down with it, and somehow was far enough out to prevent it from swamping in the next breaker. Always, two of the four men handling the stern wound up on the back seat, and safely boarded the *Burnaby M.*

When only two Haida men were left, Jim McKay came ashore for a discussion with Fred and me. Jim looked at his watch. It was almost four p.m.

"It'll be dark soon, so we go. In two days at four o'clock we'll be back! Fred, you come and bring the skiff in on the last trip."

Jim offered me his hand and without another word headed for the waiting boat. Fred had never learned to swim, though most of his life was spent on boats.

Our skiff came ashore on the crest of a big wave. The

boys were there to carry it on up to safety. That was our worst day! It had to be some kind of miracle that saved four of us from drowning.

"Spirits," the Haidas say. Maybe they are more in tune with things like that than we are. I'm sure there was something that helped me out of that deep hole.

Two days later, at a quarter to four, the *Burnaby M* was standing off the west shore waiting for the skiff to come out for the crew. Fred Robson and Ollie made the first trip, bringing three of the Haidas. These then took over the landing duties. Within an hour, all were safely back on the island and ready to go to work. They were confident that their potlatch had rid Marble Island of all its bad spirits.

Shortly after this near-tragedy, a letter was sent to our Lieutenant-Governor, explaining the courage and bravery displayed by Phil in saving the lives of the two boatmen. Some days later we recieved a reply, commending Watson for his actions. There was also the appropriate British Empire Medal. Instructions as to how it should be presented were clearly explained in the letter. A meeting of the band was convened at an early date. Included were the Senior Officer of the Royal Canadian Mounted Police, the Commanding Officers of the Armed Forces, the Chief and all his Council, plus other dignitaries wishing to attend. My role was to represent the Lieutenant-Governor and present the medal with all the pomp and dignity such an occasion demanded. A two-day holiday was proclaimed. One day was spent travelling and one day recuperating.

We proceeded to the big Skidegate hall. The hall had been decorated for the occasion. A large crowd was in attendance. Phil, Chief Ed Collison, Harry Winnie, Jim McKay, the Senior Officer of the R.C.M.P. and myself were all up on the stage. Two young Princesses saw to it that tea and drinks were served, whatever the preference.

Following the welcome by Chief Collison, I was introduced, and asked to present the medal to big Phil. I spoke of the near-tragedy and the courage displayed by our hero. After a few more drinks, Phil and I decided to become

211

blood brothers. Chief Collison agreed to solemnize the occasion. I was given the name which, translated, means "Stormy Waters." Some Haidas believe it is spelled "Guiwa." Others say it cannot be spelled, only spoken.

Next morning we were on our way back to Marble Island. Jim McKay was at the helm. The rest of us nursed hangovers and drank coffee.

The Haidas have historic legends that are passed down from one generation to the next. It might be interesting to relate some of them here. Jim McKay told me this one: "The Haidas lived on the west coast of the island many years ago. We had a bigger town out west than we now have at Skidegate. Several hundred years ago, the bad spirits came to our town. Nearly everyone died. Many people, maybe a thousand died in that springtime. All the houses were full of the dead. Those who lived hiked through the woods across the island to the east coast. Only a handful made it all the way to Skidegate. There they started a new village where we live now.

"If you go where the old town was, the streets are still there. When I was a small boy, I came with my grandfather to one old town opposite Marble Island, on the big island. We pulled our canoe up in the bushes and went to this old town place. We shot a deer and camped. On a moonlit night we walked along one old street to a big cave and rested.

"Then we heard it; first, the sound of drum music and next a strong voice chanting a war song. My grandfather told me it was the spirits of the old warriors who still walked the streets to sing and dance.

"Two nights we stayed and listened to the drums and chanting. Grandpa warned, "Never go close to the music or the spirits will take you away forever."

"Are you sure you heard songs and drums?" I asked.

"Many times I hear it. Now I have taken my grandson so he can hear it as I did. Only by moonlight and in the springtime do the spirits of the old people come back to play and chant."

"What made your people die?" I asked.

"Devils with big sores and scars came," he replied.

He seemed to be describing a sickness similar to smallpox.

I know where the old town is supposed to be. Maybe one spring, with the help of a helicopter and a grandson, we will visit and listen.

The Japanese Current flows by the west coast of the Charlottes. It then veers north to go up towards the Aleutian Islands and Alaska. This current keeps the water temperatures warmer than that of most of our coast. It was not unusual to find glass fishing balls or other Japanese wooden things on the beaches.

Big seal-like creatures known as sea elephants were often seen near Marble Island. These monsters weigh several tons and have a nose similar to that of a bull moose, only longer. The nose looks much like an elephant trunk cut short. These rare and strange creatures are usually found only in tropical waters. They were extremely curious and followed our boats on several occasions. The Haidas believed they were bad and did many things to discourage them from following. They often shot close to their heads to scare them off.

Sharks up to twelve feet long sometimes followed the big skiff toward shore when the cargo was meat. We never knew if these were the man-eating type. No one jumped in to prove that point.

Another unusual incident occurred. Three of us towed a half-sunken scow from Van Harbour to the entance of Skidegate Channel. Two sea elephants had followed us the last few miles. It was getting dark. We beached the scow then anchored the *Burnaby M* where we thought it would be safe for the night.

About two a.m., we were awakened by the crashing of waves and wind in the rigging. We leaped out of bed to find the boat dragging anchor and drifting dangerously close to the beach. Snow was blowing so thickly, visibility was reduced to a few yards.

We started the engine and steered out into the center

of the channel. We just idled her into the wind until the storm abated. Jim McKay was sure the bad spirits from the sea elephants had caused the storm to wreck the big scow.

During the last month we moved the sawmill, donkey and bulldozer off Marble and shipped them south. We cleaned up the job which included the painting of all the buildings with that horrible yellowish-green camouflage paint. We planted some spruce trees to the seaward side of the camp so it could not be spotted easily by a passing boat or submarine. After handing the keys to a young Lieutenant, we left for home.

It was understandable that there would be problems getting men and supplies on or off the island. Though we left the big skiff, three of the Air Force men were drowned within a month.

In the summer of 1978, Gloria Hobson, George and Berta Brown and I chartered a helicopter to fly from Queen Charlotte City out to Marble for some pictures and a look-see. Storms had completely demolished all the buildings at the beach area. At the foot of the cliffs, piles of splintered lumber and bits of plywood were strewn in disarray. The wood was white and worn smooth from the constant pounding of the storms. That was all that was left of the hospital, cookhouse and four bunkhouses.

The inclined railway was there but the timbers were moss-covered and rotting. The diesel engines had been plundered at some earlier date. The radar building was barely visible among the trees on top of the hill. Its roof sagging in the middle, it stood among stunted spruce trees, looking like an old sway-back horse in a field of tall grass.

As we walked the beach, past memories returned in a flood. When I went out to the big pothole for a look at my near watery grave, it was exactly as I remembered it. I stood for a few minutes staring down into its depths. I was shocked back to reality when two young seals popped up a few yards from my feet. They had come through the cave passage that led to the ocean.

Up in the trees along the ridge, dozens of eagles

perched. Some were Golden Eagles with huge wing spans. The rest were Bald Eagles. Nests could be seen in the trees with young birds poking their heads up. Hair seals stared at us with big saucer eyes. Jack Hann's words came back from the past.

"You fellows must be more than a little crazy to try to build on that damned island. Only thing it's good for is eagles and seals."

After an easy takeoff in the chopper, we cruised home through the Skidegate Channel. During the half hour flight, George Brown and I chatted about things that had happened during the construction. We agreed that, had helicopters been available in the early 1940's, the radar project would have been completed in less than half the time, with most of the dangers eliminated.

In the fall of 1979, Phil Watson visited me. We reminisced for an hour or two about Marble Island and the west coast of the Queen Charlottes and found time to enjoy a couple of good Scotch and sodas. Phil told me how he had hunted seals with his grandfather and uncle.

"I was about nine or ten. We would land in the bay on the east side of Marble Island, pull the big canoe up on the shore, then climb up the rocks and sneak through the trees and long grass until we got within shooting distance of the seal rookery. There would be several hundred in and around the bay. The smell was so high it made me gag.

"Both men had two rifles each and it was my job to carry the extra guns and pass the ammunition. They were crack shots and would sometimes kill up to fifty before they all took to the deeper water.

"The government paid five dollars for a hair seal nose. At that time it was the way to keep down the seal population and conserve salmon and other fish. I remember the water being red with blood and waiting for it to clear so the dead seals could be brought up from the bottom with long gaffs and spears. Then the noses were cut off. The seal bodies were released to sink back to the bottom. This was when the big sharks came in.

215

"We made our cooking fire on the rocks nearest Van Harbour. From here we could see the high bluffs and watch the big waves breaking against them. There were strange marks along the face of the bluffs, that looked like scratches made by some huge hand. When I asked Grandfather about them, he told me the legend of the 'Wosco,' the big sea wolf.

"Long ago, some of our people lived over there on top. There was an old lady who was kind, very big, and also very fat. One day she found some puppies on the beach in the bay. The pups were wet, cold and hungry. This old lady carried them home and cared for them. They grew big and loved to swim out in the ocean. When the lady wanted fish she got the message to the 'Woscos.' Off they would go and soon return with a killer whale in their mouths. Then there would be great feasting. There was another lady living nearby and she became jealous of the fat one. One day when the Woscos went out to fish, this wicked woman, who had strong powers, created a terrible storm. So big were the waves that when the Woscos returned to climb up on the bluffs, they were washed back into the ocean. The marks on the bluffs were made by their claws before they drowned. The wicked one then turned them into stone. You remember those two big humps behind the bluffs? Those are supposed to be the big sea wolves which look after Marble Island.

"I had to believe Grandfather's story. It all seemed so possible to a 9-year old."

Later, as he was about to leave, I asked him if he still had his British Empire Medal.

"It's a miracle I still have it," he replied. "A few years after the war ended, my house burned down. All my belongings were destroyed in the fire. A few months later, when I was rummaging through the ashes, I found my old jewel-case. It had become so hot it was distorted almost beyond recognition, but when I pried open the lid, my medal was inside, looking as good as the day I received it.

I'm sure some of the Spirits from Marble Island stay with the medal to protect it for my descendants.''

Albert And The Bears

"My first memories of being part of the family start when we went to the Cotsfords' place at the north end of Saltspring. I was almost five years old and was given the job of riding our big Clydesdale horse from the house out to where the men were working in the woods. I was helped up on his back and given a big basket of lunches. I was usually able to hold the basket and steer the big animal in the right direction. I arrived about noon to join the loggers for lunch. There was a Swiss chap in the crew who taught me to count up to ten in German. He must have been very patient. I can still remember how to do it.

"When the donkey was yarding logs, I stayed for the afternoons, learning from Ollie to be a signal man or whistle punk. I would ride home with my older brothers after quitting time. There would be as many as five of us on old 'Punch's' broad back. This saved the boys the mile walk after a hard day's work.

"I was about six when we moved back to Ganges. I went to school there for one year. Dad was building onto our big house and I remember almost falling off while helping him put shakes on the roof.

"The memory of going on the boat to Vancouver is not too clear. I started Grade Two at the Matthew Begbie school that fall. It was shortly after this that Dorothy's bottle got lost. She learned to drink out of a cup in short order. There was no money to buy another. Dorothy must have been almost seven months old when Mother explained that she should be learning to drink and eat a bit at that age. After all, this was number ten for her.

"In the spring of 1928, I was selling papers on the corner of Hastings and Main Streets. On good days I made as much as fifty cents to help pay expenses at home.

"In the summer of 1929, brother Oliver came for a week's visit. During this time the bigger and tougher paper boys were trying to chase me off my corner. I warned them about my older brother but they were still giving me a rough time. I had many fights and lost some to the older boys. I asked Ollie to come down and help. The first day he came we got our papers on the corner just after lunch. I had moved the stand from Main Street to just west of the old B.C. Electric Building.

"There was a vacant lot and some railway tracks to the back of this building. One of the bigger boys wanted my new location and started pushing me around. Ollie had been leaning against the brick wall some yards away. He walked over slowly, grabbed the bully by the scruff of the neck and marched him to the vacant lot. In less than ten minutes this fellow left with a couple of black eyes and some sore ribs.

"Half an hour later he came back with his older brother. The bigger boy challenged Ollie to a fight. It lasted half an hour or more. Ollie gave him a terrible beating. The losers again left to return with what they considered the 'toughie' of the neighbourhood. I was nine years old then and Ollie was eleven. The 'toughie' was almost four years older than Ollie but not too much heavier. Theirs was a terrible fight that lasted over two hours. Neither gave in.

219

The fight ended when one of the many onlookers called the police.

"I had no further problems after that day and continued to sell papers there for the rest of the year.

"Ollie confided in me as we walked home that evening, 'I could have beaten that tough one easily if we had stopped for lunch. I was getting pretty hungry.'

"Mother doctored our cuts and bruises. We didn't tell her all that had happened; we didn't have to. She insisted I take a paper route in our neighbourhood and deliver the papers after school. This was more profitable. I made almost three dollars every week and kept that route for two years.

"We added a big kitchen-livingroom to our house in 1928. Joe was home to do most of the work. We got fruit trees and planted a garden in our back yard. Things were pleasant and comfortable until we moved out to the Fraser valley to live on the Shields' farm. There we had a bigger garden, a cow, some honeybees and chickens. We stayed there during the worst year of the Depression. We raised a pig, which ran loose and followed us around like a dog. He was such a friendly little fellow. We fed and kept him until Mother decided he was big enough for pork. She arranged for a butcher to slaughter him, then wrap the meat in paper packages. When she brought the meat home, none of us would eat a bite of it. No way were we going to eat our pet. The meat went to the neighbours at bargain prices.

"Pearl was now married to Gordon and working up at the Reno Gold Mines. She wrote Mother, suggesting I come up during the summer holidays and try for a job as flunkey in the big cookhouse. When summer holidays started, I went up by train. Though I was twelve, the cook said I was too small for flunkey duties. He gave me a contract to pick blueberries. In a long day I could make about two dollars. I made over $80 in two months.

"The hills were steep and there were a lot of black bears where the best berry patches were. The bears kept their distance if I banged a stick against the pails. This was quite an experience for me. Sometimes there would be up to six bears within 200 yards of where I was picking. They made strange grunting noises and usually left if the wind blew my scent in their direction.

"Some snow fell in early September, so I went home in time for school.

"The next year, we moved to Westholme. I worked with Tom during that summer. He was longshoring and building a donkey in his spare time. I learned to babbitt and fit the bearings to the big shafts. We built a sleigh and bolted the winch to it. When it was finished, we loaded it on a logging truck and moved it to Crofton. There I worked as a whistle punk and chaser for the rest of the summer. We took out two booms of logs.

"I bought a car from Ollie for five dollars. It was a 1924 Chevrolet. I learned to keep it running after a fashion. It was eight miles to Duncan. It took two five-gallon cream cans full of water to make it one way. When we went to a show or shopping, we started with both cans full of water in the back seat. We had to fill both at a gas station before starting home. When we finally took the radiator off, we found a six-inch long split in the bottom of the core. When we soldered this, we were able to leave the cans at home. It was transportation and we learned a lot.

"Next year I quit school to get a steady job in a tie mill on Mount Prevost. The pay was fifty cents per hour. I bought another car. I was missing too many days trying to get there in the old 'Chevvie.'

"When the mill closed, Joe offered me a job blasting stumps. He and Tom had started a subdivision in Chemainus. I was shown where the roads were to be built. Joe dropped me off with ten boxes of powder and some fuse with blasting caps. He gave me ten minutes of instruction, left a bar and shovel, then drove off.

" 'Pick you up after five,' he shouted as he drove away.

"I had never used powder before. I blasted stumps for ten days without getting blown up. It now takes over two years to get a blasting ticket. Ollie came up to help and

221

taught me how to bite the caps onto the fuses. We didn't have crimpers. That's how it was in the 1930's.

"On weekends there was work to be done, repairing the fireboxes of the big steam boilers of the Chemainus mill. This was hot and dirty work. Jobs were still scarce and men plentiful. Unless you knew the foreman, there was little chance of being hired. The pay was 55 cents an hour. Brother Joe was the foreman.

"When World War Two was only six days old, I enlisted. Soon I was in the 57th Anti-tank Regiment and on my way to Halifax to board the Queen Mary for overseas.

"Our regiment was made responsible for signals and seeing that the various detachments were billeted in the proper places. Loading took just over two weeks.

"My buddy had a Crown and Anchor gambling board. He made me half owner and partner. I had four dollars and borrowed that much more. By the time we reached England, we had won just over five hundred dollars each. This was almost equal to a year's army pay.

"I was now a full-blown Sergeant and was one of the electricians of our outfit.

"We spent almost a year southwest of London, handling search-lights for the anti-aircraft gunners. We had been given orders to waterproof all trucks and jeeps in readiness for D-day. I had attended a crash course on this particular waterproofing. Everything had to be coated with a heavy, waterproof jelly. Orders were out to prepare for the channel crossing at midnight.

"Those bloody 'buzz bombs' had been going over all that day. Four of us had been working late to finish our truck, and were just getting ready for supper when we heard a bomb cut out almost over our heads. When you heard the motor stop on one of those babies, there was perhaps a half minute before it blew up. We dove into a slit trench under a big oak tree. Next thing I remember was clawing the dirt away to get some air. The damned thing had exploded in the tree and buried all four of us. I had six pieces of shrapnel in my back, five of which were taken out

222

in a hospital just north of London. I still have to explain the sixth piece every time an X-ray is necessary. Also, those damned gadgets they use to detect metal before boarding an aircraft pick it up every time.

"When my truck hit the beach the next day, it struck a mine. All seven occupants were blown to bits. A good spirit must have been looking after me the previous night.

"Months later, on leaving the hospital, I was assigned to shop duty in Scotland, to repair electric motors. All in all, I spent six years and one month in the army. My extra pay was sent home to Mother.

"Getting back to the Pacific coast, I looked around for a couple of months, then decided to go logging on Galiano Island for brother Tom. Lloyd and I went partners and did well until we ran out of timber.

"In the early 1950's, we moved our outfit to Knight Inlet and logged for Evans Products. We were caught in the bad log slump of 1952. Log prices dropped out of sight and we were forced into bankruptcy. The logs we expected to sell for $50 per thousand, dropped to below $25 in less than a week. We had to sell our camp and all the equipment for much less than half its actual value. After paying our bills we were strapped.

"Ernie Butler, an old friend, was trucking lumber at Hundred Mile House in the Cariboo country. He offered me a partnership in his contract. He had a couple of big trucks and wanted me to take one over. I arrived there on January 2, 1953. The mercury outside Ernie's tarpaper shack was registering -40 degrees Fahrenheit. This cold snap lasted over three weeks. At that temperature, diesel fuel goes solid and can't be poured out of a can. It's like heavy grease and will not flow through fuel lines, unless heated. I spent the three weeks stoking our big airtight heater night and day, to keep from freezing to death. By the time it warmed up, we were fully acclimatized and ready to go to work.

"The sawmills started cutting again when the weather warmed up to about -10 degrees. That's still pretty cold.

You toss the wash water out the back door and it's ice before it hits the ground.

"I was now married, had one child and another on the way. After our son Stuart was born that spring, my wife Barb moved up and we rented a house at Lac La Hache for the summer. Until 1954, when more paving was done towards Williams Lake and on north, the blacktop roads ended there.

"In the fall of 1954, we pulled stakes to move farther north. I bought a second-hand logging truck and started hauling logs for Garner Brothers Cariboo Limited. This was a good contract, so we bought a house on the west side of the Fraser River. I hauled logs for the next two years over the old wooden bridge that crossed the Fraser at the south end of the town of Quesnel.

"Garner Brothers were the first major mechanized loggers in the Quesnel forest district. They had cats for skidding and power shovels equipped with automatic tongs for loading. The loaders were so efficient that most loads were overheight.

"I remember a very embarrassing day for brother Joe. I had on an especially big load and, as the truck started across this bridge, I could hear noises like gun shots, just back of the cab. This old bridge was only wide enough for one vehicle at a time, single lane traffic. The six by six cross-timbers were eighteen feet above the bridge deck, and that's what caused all the noise; they snapped when the logs struck them.

"I knew if I lost momentum the truck would be stuck tight and block the bridge for God only knew how long. I shifted down a couple of notches and pushed the accelerator to the floor. The truck ground to a stop when the trailer cleared the far side. As the smoke and slivers settled, there was not a cross-tie to be seen that wasn't broken. The foreman of the Department of Highways arrived about the same time as Joe.

"There just happened to be a couple of power saws in the back of Joe's pickup. He put two fallers on the cab roof.

When the roaring stopped a half hour later, the bridge was clear and the traffic rolling again. The R.C.M.P. took a dim view of things. A survey for a private road started the next morning.

"Some miles below this old bridge, a skyline was rigged over the river to carry the logs across. Things went much better once we got off the public roads. We used bigger trucks and hauled loads of 100 tons and over.

"It seems there were always bears around the camps to contend with. The last year we logged at Knight Inlet, there was an incident with a big 'rogue' bear, as Stanton called him. This animal was mangy and mean. He chased other bears and almost killed both our Labrador dogs the night he wrecked the cookhouse. He packed away a full side of beef before we could get out of bed to get a gun on him. Either we or that bear had to go.

"Putting some high-smelling beef in a box, we took it down to the garbage dump and placed it where a regular bear trail came out of the woods. We put six sticks of dynamite in with the meat. We attached an electric cap, complete with 200 feet of blasting wire and battery. I loaded up my .306 rifle with 220 grain, Silvertip shells and coaxed Ole, the bull cook, to come along to work the plunger should Mr. 'Rogue' Bear come out for his evening meal.

"We didn't have to wait long. Half an hour before dark, he came out, sniffed the wind, and headed for the box. For some strange reason, he stopped with the box between his legs, and almost centred under his stomach.

" 'Push, Ole,' I whispered.

"As the plunger went down, the bear went up. The big animal sailed high into the air with all four legs flailing in a running motion. The blast didn't even knock him out. When he hit the ground, his nose was pointed straight at the stump we were hiding behind. My first shot struck him in the ear. He fell dead not more than ten feet from where we stood. Mr. Stanton came over next morning to inspect this ornery old bear.

" 'That's only the second 'rogue' I've known to come

into this valley in the last 20 years.' He went on to explain that only a sick animal will act so belligerently.

"The grizzlies from this area are some of the largest in the world. Stanton had guided a party four years earlier. At the head of Knight Inlet, they shot a bear which scored second largest ever taken, according to Boone and Crockett ratings.

"My next interesting encounter with bears came when two of us were surveying a road some miles south of Quesnel near Narcoslie Creek.

"My Lab, instead of sleeping by the pickup, had followed us this day. We were busy marking a new truck road when a big black bear roared out of some thick brush only fifty feet ahead of us. The Lab gave chase and both disappeared over a ridge about a quarter mile away. My helper this day was a local rancher.

" 'Al,' he said, 'we had better find a couple of trees to climb! That bear will turn and chase your dog back this way, as soon as she gets near her cubs. Saw her yesterday with three young ones travelling with her.'

"In less than five minutes we could see and hear them coming. That old bear wasn't more than three feet behind the dog's tail and charging straight for us at great speed. We both flashed up two nearby trees. The dog used the trees to hide behind. The bear must have smelled us and reared up on its hind legs, snarling and snapping its teeth, not more than twenty feet away. She made several runs at the dog in the next couple of hours, but would not leave.

"I tried to climb down a couple of times, but the disturbance brought her, growling and grunting, to the bottom of the trees. We encouraged the dog to chase this riled-up critter. She would retreat no further than a hundred yards, then chase our dog back to the trees.

"As the sun went down, she sauntered up the ridge towards where we figured her cubs must be. My partner took courage to climb down and head for the pickup, while I stayed put to keep the dog quiet. He made it, then drove the vehicle to the trees where I was waiting.

226

"After getting the Labrador into the cab, I glanced back. The trees we had climbed had no limbs for at least twenty feet up. The sight of that bear coming for us had somehow helped us overcome any normal climbing problems we might have had; we made it up out of her reach in a flash. Our first stop when we reached Quesnel was Hoy's store. We each bought a .45 calibre six-gun and carried these on all future cruising or road expeditions.

"We logged in the Quesnel area for the next ten years. We developed and used some of the biggest and most modern equipment of the times. In the late 1950's, we designed and built the first pre-loading logging trailers. This method of hauling was so successful, it spread to almost all the logging operations in western Canada and the United States.

"Eventually, selling my shares in the Cariboo operation, I retired to a cattle ranch just north of the Quesnel airport. Here we raised some pretty good registered Hereford cattle.

"As we got older, the cold winters got to be something to dread more than enjoy. We sold the ranch in 1978 and moved back to the coast to retire. Even after some 27 years of living in the Cariboo, I never did get acclimatized to those mornings when the mercury hung at 40 degrees below zero.

Lloyd

"I stood leaning on the railing of a B.C. ferry, staring down at the water. I was headed for the town of Ganges on Saltspring Island. Memories of my past were rushing in. Like the waves, they were trying to tell me something. I was deep in thought as the ship turned into Active Pass. Some of these recollections were funny, some serious, and a few quite sad. I was just up on a visit from my home in Los Angeles, and was realizing how much our old family habits still governed my present way of life.

"I had wound up my political campaign against Barry Goldwater Jr., for senator of Los Angeles, and had lost. I needed a change and I wanted to see some of my remaining relations again and romp around the country where I had grown up.

"Ganges was my birthplace. I was the ninth child of a family of ten, and the youngest of five sons. Our family occupied the biggest house on Saltspring Island. It had been built by Dad and my older brothers.

"In 1926, my Mother and most of the family moved to Vancouver. Tom and Joe had gone ahead to build the house. When we moved to our home on Second Avenue, we didn't know that the big Depression was just around the corner.

"I can remember walking down Hastings Street to the Woodward's store, a distance of some five miles, to buy rolled oats that were on special. The purchase of a 50-pound bag would result in a saving of just over one dollar. As I was under twelve years of age, my fare home via streetcar was four cents. Mother would explain all this and let me know how proud she was to have a son helping with the family needs. My other duties included walking to the Canadian Pacific Railway freight yards to sweep the leftover wheat from the boxcars, which I packed home to feed our chickens. Albert and I sometimes walked three miles to the fish docks at the foot of Gore Avenue to buy a bucket of herring for 25 cents.

"I was a paper boy at nine and made five dollars a month, which I gave to Mother. My first summer job was near the town of Langley, some 25 miles up the Fraser Valley, east of Vancouver. I worked on a chicken farm, feeding 1200 chickens. At the age of ten, I made ten dollars for the summer's work, from which Mother gave me two dollars for my own.

"We finally moved to a house near Langley. It was on North Bluff Road and was owned by Charlie Shields. Here we had a cow, pigs, bees for honey, and a larger area in which to grow fruit and vegetables. This country living was sure better than city life.

"Mother influenced us greatly. Her advice was, 'Don't work for somebody else, get out on your own!' We must have remembered, for in later years we were all determined enough to become quite independent.

"In 1937, we moved to the village of Westholme on Vancouver Island, where my older brothers, Tom and Joe, lived and worked. I got a job as a bolter in a shingle mill owned by Mr. Sondergaard. Brother Tom had married Sondergaard's daughter, Marie.

"I had turned fourteen, and it was now time for me to

229

learn to drive. Albert had somehow aquired a 1924 Chevrolet touring car. This 'tin lizzie,' as we called it, was the automobile used to teach me the basics of mechanics and driving. Al was my teacher. We were always taking the damned engine apart and putting it back together. We would tear down the grass field at full throttle, slam on the brakes, make a wild U turn and come screaming back to our yard. Mother also tried her hand at driving but with little or no success.

"We built a stump puller from miscellaneous parts and pieces. We used this crude piece of machinery to clear the roads for a subdivision Tom and Joe had started in Chemainus. Here we built a new home for the family. I was named foreman of the shingling department. All summer long, I nailed shingles to the sides of that damned house and still wasn't finished when school started. Being just fourteen, I had been fool enough to volunteer for the job.

"While I was attending high school in Ladysmith, my hip problem first developed. One day, after some heavy contact sports, I walked into the classroom and collapsed. My hip had come out of joint. This was to affect all my activities for the rest of my life. An immediate operation was impossible. We didn't have the money. Through the kind efforts of R.C.M.P. Constable Sam Service, brother of poet Robert Service, I was later taken to St. Joseph's Hospital in Victoria. The operation was not one hundred percent successful. Later, in Vancouver, another operation was performed, with more success. I was in bed for fourteen weeks at home in Chemainus. Mother looked after me and gave me a lot of advice. I had to listen, I couldn't walk!

"In 1939, with my hip considerably better, I apprenticed to a cabinét-maker named Sid Andrew, who had his shop in Chemainus. I was now sixteen. The walk to work helped strengthen my leg and hip muscles. I was unable to join the army when World War Two broke out, but I went to work on defence projects.

"I worked with brother Joe, who was a superintendent for Marwell Construction Company. They were building

230

military installations throughout British Columbia. My first job was at Mission, B.C., where a long-range radio-rombic station was built for the Navy. My next construction project was a radar station on Marble Island, a small, totally isolated island off the west coast of the Queen Charlottes. During this period, we had a close association with the Haida Indians. They worked on the construction and were a great help in preventing our crews from drowning.

"My first wife was a petite, 5-foot, 4-inch gal. I was twenty-one and she twenty-four when we were married. We lived together for only six weeks when we agreed to divorce. This was the fall of 1945.

"When Albert came home from overseas, he and I decided to go into the logging business on Galiano Island. Brother Tom had purchased a boat, which was known far and wide as the fastest in the islands. He called it the *Dragon Lady*. I decided to go him one better. I had one built called the *Circle It*, which could do about 50 miles an hour. A week after it was launched, a piece of driftwood went through the hull and it sank. I managed to swim ashore, but the boat stayed at the bottom.

"A float plane school had started on Quamichan Lake, near Duncan, B.C. I was anxious to get into the air. After twenty hours of training, I bought my first float-equipped aircraft, a Cessna 140. About a month later, I hit a sandbar at the mouth of the Fraser River and flipped the damned thing over on its back. No one was hurt and there was little damage.

"Helen Harrison taught me to fly. When she came to instruct at Duncan, in 1946, she had put in over 1,700 hours teaching flying. She was made a member of the Canadian Aviation Hall of Fame during the 1970's, having logged over 15,000 hours of flying in aircraft of all sizes and makes. Aviation is still the number one love of her life.

"On Galiano Island, I had been in a logging partnership with brother Al. One day I decided to sell out to him for thirty thousand dollars. I went through this small fortune in six weeks. I had bought another airplane, a tugboat and a brand new Studebaker car. It was sure nice to be a playboy at twenty-one, even if it only lasted such a short time. It was necessary for me to get back to logging to recoup my losses.

"In 1946, Albert and I agreed to go into partnership again. Things were booming up the coast. We called our company Kent-Timber Limited, and logged at the head of Knight Inlet. Kent-Timber, along with most of the coast operations, was practically forced into bankruptcy when the price of logs plunged to less than half their regular value in a period of a few days. This was in 1952. We later sold our company to Earl Laughlin.

"During this period, I married Mary Langton and started raising four children: Richard, Mark, Lyle and Mary Lynn. We built a large home, complete with swimming pool, in West Vancouver. Disgruntled, though, after a short stint in the city, I sold the house and moved the family to Cultus Lake in the Fraser Valley. From there I could commute by air and go back to the work I loved, the timber business. At Cultus Lake, the floats of my plane could be tied to a tree in our front yard. My marriage was slowly but surely breaking up. Mary and I agreed to disagree, which lead to divorce number two. I decided I belonged in aviation.

"I went to work for Finning Tractor Limited. They sold and serviced logging tractors throughout all of British Columbia and the Yukon. I became their flying salesman and pilot. I met hundreds of interesting people on this job.

"Two years later, I left Finning to join Dietrich-Collins Equipment Limited as their chief pilot and sales engineer. Again I retraced air paths along the entire B.C. coast and part of Alaska. During the five years I worked for this firm, there were many close calls, either from bad weather or mechanical problems. I decided to call a halt to my commercial flying activities.

"By 1947, the Garner brothers owned four float-equipped aircraft between them. This was a substantial part of all the privately-owned float planes in British Columbia. We considered ourselves pioneers because of our extensive use of light, float-equipped aircraft both in business and big-game guiding. Thirty years later there are several hundred planes and helicopters servicing the same industries.

"My general interest was still with the outdoors. I managed to obtain one of the rare Guide Licences, covering all of our Province. Brother Tom had a lodge at Chilco Lake. This is a big lake in high, rugged country just east of the Coast Range of central British Columbia. We flew hunting and fishing parties there and to many other places. At one time, Tom and I included uranium prospecting in our flying activities.

"After leaving Dietrich-Collins, I moved to Redding, California, where I sold heavy equipment. My present wife, Pamela, was with me when this move was made. We settled in Los Angeles and tried our hand at real estate, construction and politics. I still go north on occasion, to fish, hunt and relive the past.

Never Fly Over An Eagle's Nest

We used aircraft for most of our trips. Tom had a Cessna 195 and I flew a Piper Pacer. Both were equipped with floats, radios and all available navigational instruments. We prided ourselves on having a full panel for the times.

One of our more memorable trips started from Duncan, August 15, 1951. We both left Quamichan Lake at the crack of dawn, agreeing to meet at Quesnel where the bridge crosses the Fraser River. We had arranged for two 45-gallon barrels of 80-octane to be delivered by a local dealer. This was pumped into the wing tanks using a hand pump. We always carried our own funnels with chamois strainers to ensure clean fuel.

Leaving Quesnel, we agreed to meet again at Alta Lake to take on more gas. That noon we were at Finlay Forks, where the Crooked River joins the Peace. We had arranged to have gas delivered there by riverboat. This was our last stop before going on through Sifton's Pass and into the country where the rivers flow north to the Arctic Ocean. After topping all tanks, we took off downriver, then turned to head further north. We had agreed to meet and camp that night at Dahl Lake, some 150 miles farther on. There was no habitation along this last leg of our journey.

Ted Robson was my passenger and Bill Auchanachie was travelling with Tom. We were going to try for a trophy Stone sheep. Ted was doing the map reading and helping with the navigation. We were out of Finlay Forks about half an hour when he pointed to the map and said to me with great concern, "Joe, do you realize that the lakes shown on these maps sure don't look much like the ones we're flying over?"

After looking at the map and then down at the lakes, I had to agree. The country this far north had not been properly mapped or surveyed. However, we had no problem recognizing Dahl Lake with a pack trail passing along its south side. Tom and Bill were there waiting. We had travelled just over 900 miles since daylight that morning.

An old grub box supported by four topped trees sat twenty feet above this campsite. Around the trunks of the four trees, dozens of big fish hooks were secured by long nails through the eyes to hold the barbed end out. This was the way to discourage wolverine and bears from climbing up to rob the cache. A pole ladder leaned against a big pine tree fifty feet away. I used it to climb up for a look. The box was watertight and covered with a heavy metal lid. There were cans of meat, vegetables, sugar, salt, canned cream and two pressure cans of insect repellant.

As evening progressed, the numbers of mosquitoes and black flies increased. The area became almost solid with buzzing insects. Our campfire did little to repel the hordes. By dark they were so voracious we were forced to retreat into our sleeping bags. Tom retrieved the cans of repellant from the cache. Before the night was over I took one of the cans to bed with me. Covering my head with the sleeping bag, and leaving only a small hole to breathe through, I tried to get some sleep. It was hopeless. Within minutes, the opening was filled with the pests. When it was no longer possible to breathe, I used the repellant. This would give temporary relief. I passed the night between catnaps and mosquito bites. Never before or since have I seen such masses of bloodthirsty insects.

When daylight came we headed up the mountain to where we had spotted a number of rams. The mosquitoes were so thick we had to keep moving. We kept going for several hours and climbed to over 7,000 feet. There was a breeze up there that gave us some relief. While eating our lunch, we decided to fly out as soon as we could get back to camp and load up.

The only game we got close to on the mountain was a couple of curious grizzly bears, a colony of whistling marmots and a cow moose with her half-grown calf. The moose were in an alpine lake with only their noses above water. They knew how to get away from the flies. The rams we had spotted had moved across the valley to a higher mountain some four miles away. By twelve o'clock, thunderclouds had formed and were building up in all directions.

"It's going to be rough flying with all those thunderheads around," Tom stated, in his quiet way.

We were airborne by mid-afternoon. We had agreed to meet at Finlay Forks for gas and to stay overnight at the forestry camp there which served meals and had a bunkhouse with pole bunks. Travelling south, we encountered extreme turbulence. We had almost reached the Divide when we heard thunder, and lightning started flashing on all sides. The ceiling pushed us down to tree-top level. About then, all hell broke loose.

We were trapped in the center of a cloudburst. Rain came down in sheets. The turbulence got worse. The windshield was a solid sheet of water. I opened the side window to fly for a small lake that could be dimly seen half a mile ahead. Without hesitation, I put the plane in a steep sideslip and dropped onto the surface with the least possible forward motion. It was sure good to be down after the beating we had been taking.

I looked over at Ted, who was pale in spite of his tan. He gave me a grin and asked, "Now what?"

"Well, we're safe for now. I'm not at all sure this crate will fly out of a lake this size though!"

We were on Fox Lake. The altimeter was recording 3,300 feet as we taxied in to tie up. A pack trail used during the Klondike Gold Rush passed through this area. This had been a stopping place. We found the rotted remains of two fair-sized log cabins and in the stunted spruce trees nearby was a third. Half the roof was in fair condition and the log walls were still sound. The door and windows were just openings. Some grim messages were carved in the logs on the inside. I copied a couple of them in my log book. The one which impressed me most read: *SNOW WAIST DEEP. ABOUT 45 BELOW. FINISHED EATING LAST DOG YESTERDAY. HEADING S.E. AT DAYLIGHT. FEB 11,1897. B.COLLISON.*

Most of the other messages were almost as grim. Any one of them could have been the last contact left in this world by the writer.

We stayed under the half-roof until the rain stopped. We were getting hungry; most of our food was in Tom's plane. It was after eight p.m.

"Ted," I said, "you make a fire and I'll see what there is for supper. We'll spend the night here. If Tom and Bill are okay, they will have to fly through this pass to get to our meeting place. Too late to do anything tonight. If they don't show up by ten o'clock in the morning, we'll go looking for them."

I picked up my rifle and started out to explore. My clothes were soaked through before I got out of sight of the lake. There were caribou signs everywhere. I found a large beaver colony in the creek that flowed out of the lake at its north end. I flushed a covey of fool-hens and shot the heads off three. These ended up in our frying-pan with some crisp bacon. From the emergency supply kit, we took some tea and powdered milk. We were now ready for some much-needed sleep.

Except for the gnawing of the beavers, the silence was complete. I curled up in the plane. Ted spent the night in the old log shack. There were no mosquitoes. At daylight we had tea, bacon and rye crisp.

"I'm going to try a takeoff. I'll do it alone to see how tight it is."

I untied the plane and climbed in. There was no wind. I headed to the north end, made a short turn to ripple up the surface of the lake, then gunned the engine. At full throttle, she bounced once, took to the air and cleared the trees with some feet to spare.

I took a short cruise, looking for Tom and Bill. They were nowhere to be seen. My gas gauges were registering less than a quarter full so I landed to load up and get ready to leave. Everything was aboard when we heard a plane motor in the distance.

"Listen!" Ted whispered.

It was one of the most welcome sounds I had ever heard. Loud and clear now, we could hear the familiar whine of the Cessna. It was headed straight for our little lake. Tom circled twice, then turned her on edge and dropped in. When he taxied up and got out, his first words were, "What the hell are you doing in a place like this?"

"Waiting for you," Ted and I answered together.

"You can't get that fool plane out of a lake this size and at this altitude."

"Got news for you, brother, I've already been out looking for you. Where in hell did you two spend the night?" I asked.

"We tried to outrun that bloody thunderstorm. Headed southwest and set down on a big lake about twenty miles from here," Bill shouted. He also had a few more choice remarks as he read the carved messages on the old log walls.

"Tom, if you take our extra gear in your plane, I'm sure I can get out with just Ted. We'll head for Finlay Forks and gas up. We're both getting too damned low for comfort."

The takeoff was close. One of my pontoons took the top

238

off a slim spruce tree. Landing at Finlay Forks, Bill cut loose with a string of unprintable cuss words, ending with, "Give her back to the Indians if they still want it. Too many blood-loving mosquitoes and no-seeums for my liking."

We all had a good laugh.

We came home via Chilco Lake, stopping there long enough to catch an apple-box full of big rainbows. We had been away just four days. What a trip! That northern part of British Columbia has fewer people per square mile than any other place in the world. It also has some of the most rugged and spectacular scenery, but only from the air can its magnificence be fully appreciated.

The next fall we planned a caribou hunt. That year the Game Department decided to open the season for Woodland caribou in the Rainbow Range and the top portion of the Itcha Mountains. For several years, both areas had been closed to hunting this particular species.

On September 16, 1954, we again left Quamichan Lake at the crack of dawn. We flew up Bute Inlet, then followed the Homathko River over the south end of Tatlayoko Lake and on to Chilco where we gassed up at the Lodge. We had breakfast while Tom unloaded some mail and groceries. Tom owned the Lodge and guided, while sister Ethel and her two daughters, Leora and Dorothy, did the cooking and catering for the guests. We visited and fished for a couple of hours, then flew on to Tsacha Lake.

This small lake is located near the northeast side of the Itcha mountain range. The pack trail going from Pan Phillips' Ranch, the "Home Ranch," through the Blackwater country and on into Quesnel, passes along its south shore. The top of the Itchas are over 7,000 feet above sea level and were in the clouds this day.

We made camp to wait for the weather to clear. We intended to land on the lake near the top of the Itchas. Our maps gave the elevation of the lake at just over 6,000 feet. I had never landed at such a height. We made two tries to get into it. On the third attempt we wound up in a hailstorm at 7,000 feet and were forced to land. Visibility was less than 200 feet when I put the Pacer down on Itcha Lake.

We set up our silk tents, then hunted till dark. There were lots of caribou tracks but we did not locate the herd. Moose were everywhere. Not more than twenty yards away, big bulls stood and stared as we passed. I'm sure these huge animals did not even know what a hunter was. Two trophy bulls on a low ridge actually walked to within ten paces, sniffing and grunting as they approached. I stood behind some trees until they decided to move on.

There was no point in shooting a moose even though the season was open. In order to take off at that elevation the payload would have to be less than 100 pounds, plus the pilot.

In one gully, amongst stunted trees, I found moose horns stacked seven and eight deep. The big animals must have stood there, out of the winds, and rubbed off their loose antlers against the scrubby trees. Moose shed their horns each winter and grow a new and usually heavier set for the next rutting season. The rut starts in late August or early September, depending on altitude and conditions.

Although we did not get a shot at a caribou, we learned a lot about high mountain flying. Around noon the second day it was warm and muggy. I tried several times to take off down the longest part of the lake. Although the lake was almost a mile long, I could not get the Pacer to come up on the step of the pontoons. At that altitude the 125-horse-power Lycoming engine could not exceed 2300 r.p.m. At sea level and full throttle she would rev up to 2550 or 2600 r.p.m. Tom's Cessna had enough power to handle the altitude with some revs to spare. Although concerned, he gave me a ribbing when I taxied in to tie up.

"That damned thing will never get out of here unless we get a good wind," he said with a laugh.

"By the look of the trees it must blow well over a hundred miles per hour a lot of the time. All the limbs are swept back in the same direction, and the trunks all lean the same way," I answered.

We were hunting again early the next morning. When we got back to the lake at noon, the wind was blowing a steady fifty miles per hour with gusts well over seventy miles per hour.

"I'm going to try a takeoff as soon as I load the gear and guns," I told Tom.

"Hell, this bloody wind is not in the right direction for that," Tom answered.

"I'm going to try it dead into the wind," I explained. "She should jump into the air from a standing start if one of those gusts hits her right."

"Maybe," Tom shrugged.

I put the guns and gear aboard, then climbed into the pilot's seat.

"Put your flaps down halfway and leave them on until you get some altitude," Tom advised.

"Better get your seatbelt good and tight. It's going to be plenty rough up there," George Syrotuck, one of our hunting-partners, suggested.

They were having all they could handle just to hold the plane into the wind once it was out of the sheltered bay.

"See you at Chilco Lake if she gets off," I shouted back.

I shoved the throttle to the wide open position. I hadn't moved forward more than one hundred feet when a gust lifted the little plane off the water and some fifty feet into the air. The Pacer could fly safely at sixty miles per hour. A slower speed would put it into a stall. I was lucky, the wind blew steadily for the next few minutes. She climbed out at 300 feet per minute. By the time I was across the narrow part of the lake, the plane had gained over 1,000 feet.

The air was so turbulent there wasn't time to be scared. It took considerable effort just to keep the thing from flipping over or taking a nosedive. For the next while the plane took a terrible pounding in the downdrafts and turbulence near the high peaks. An hour later we were all catching trout in the Chilco River some seventy miles southwest of the Itchas.

That same fall, I saw a sight from the air that I will never forget. It was a clear, sunny afternoon. We were cruising into the Blackwater country to visit George Turner and his wife, who were trapping and raising mink for the market. There was a long hay meadow at the opposite end of their lake. I was flying low over the tall grass. The pontoons were no more than fifteen feet above the meadow. Suddenly, in front of the plane, a huge grizzly reared up on its hind legs, with both front paws slapping up at the floats. We could see his huge mouth wide open in a snarl.

I climbed a bit to take a sharp turn and come back over the bear. He did the same thing again. When we tried for a third time, he bolted for the woods. We landed and taxied up to the crude wharf built of lodgepole pine logs. The house and mink sheds were as rough as the country they stood in.

George invited us to take a look at his prize breeding mink. There were several pairs in the pens along each wall. There was a rough path between the cages. This walkway was not more than three feet wide. We were halfway along when I happened to glance back over my shoulder. Following us was a family of skunks. It looked like a mother with three almost full grown young.

"George!" I said, "We have some company that doesn't smell too good!"

George stopped to take a look, then with a strange expression on his face, whispered, "Don't move fast or we're all in bad trouble! I was planning to nail their hides to a board last winter, but they left for a while."

"Is there a door at the far end?" I inquired.

"We have to go out the way we came in," George explained.

Those damned skunks were coming closer as we walked slowly towards a deadend. Even with both sides of the shed open, except for the heavy chicken wire, the smell was so strong it almost made me gag. At the end we turned to face the striped creatures. They also turned to put their dangerous end towards us.

242

"Keep still!" George ordered.

We stood for a full five minutes before the skunks started to slowly amble towards the open door. As we followed, the mother kept looking back over her shoulder to make sure we were not getting too close.

While we were having tea and sandwiches, Tom told about seeing the big grizzly.

"Hell! He's been hanging around here since spring," George stated.

"I'd rather face that bear in the open than those skunks in the shed," I observed.

In the spring of 1956, we bought Samuel Island and logged the timber off it. This is a small island between Mayne and Saturna, facing the Gulf of Georgia, about forty miles southwest of Vancouver. E.P.Taylor had owned it and used it to breed and train some of his race horses during the 1930's and 40's.

There were two nice homes and a big fancy barn, complete with over 50 acres of hay and pastureland. The improvements included a good water system and wharf. We paid $48,000 for the 328 acres. After the timber was logged, we sold it to Charles A. Lindbergh's daughter and son-in-law for the same price we paid for it.

I flew over to the island from Duncan two or three times each week. There was an active eagle's nest directly in my usual approach pattern. I had flown over this nest several times. I could see the two half-grown birds in the nest as I flew by. The parents were bigger than turkeys, with snow-white heads and wingspans of over eight feet.

It was the last day of the month. I had the pay cheques for our crew. The two young birds were standing on the nest made of sticks and limbs. They were flapping their wings in preparation for their first flight. I passed closer than usual for a better look. From below, the two parent birds attacked the plane. In a flash there were talons, open beaks and feathers flying in the wing struts. There was a sickening thud as the big male collided with the leading edge of my right wing. It left a six-inch dent in the metal

243

and its body stuck and jammed the elevators at the tail assembly.

I tried the controls to find that the direction could be changed by using the rudders, but the elevators were useless. I was about 300 feet above the bay and had to do something to land the plane. Pulling on half-flaps and using the throttle for elevation, I was able to make a long power approach. On the third try, I made a landing of sorts.

Getting some wooden wedges and a claw bar, I was able to bend the metal enough to clear the bent parts so the controls would work. It was quite something to find out how much a dent in the leading edge of a wing affects the air flow that lifts a plane and keeps it flying.

I took off and headed to Vancouver airport for repairs. It cost over $2,000 to get the Certificate of Airworthiness reinstated. Although the lesson was dangerous and costly, it was by no means the only such encounter experienced by pilots along the coast of British Columbia.

The Poker Game

The war had been going on for more than four years. Tom bought a big home with some acreage, just north of the city of Duncan. He and his friend, George Syrotuck, consumed a bottle of Old Angus Scotch the day they decided to buy the property. In addition to the main residence, there were a couple of caretaker's houses and a big barn. George agreed he and his wife could live there and help with things around the main house. Tom gave the realtor a cheque and promptly named the estate Old Angus. Within a week, they moved to the new premises and Tom gave a great housewarming party. This was the first of many lively social events at Old Angus.

One of the most memorable was a strange day and night of gambling in various forms. Things started at the Elks Club just before noon, when Jack and Mack, a couple of gambling loggers from Nanaimo, dropped in for drinks.

I was there with Tom, Ted Robson and George Syrotuck when the two arrived. Jack first tossed coins with Tom for drinks for the house. A few minutes later he did the same with Ted for doubles all round. Jack lost the toss with

245

Ted, and taking out his wallet, presumably to pay for the drinks, removed a bill, crumpled it in his hand, and challenged Ted to call odd or even for the amount of the bill.

"How much is the bill for?" Ted asked.

"Never mind, just call odd or even," Jack taunted.

"Is it a ten, twenty or what?" Ted asked again.

While Ted hesitated, Tom announced, "I'll call it odd for whatever it is." Jack opened his hand and Tom checked the serial number of the crumbled one thousand dollar note. The last digit of the serial number was a three.

Jack handed the money to Tom and challenged him to a game of pool for double the amount of the bill. Tom declined, giving as his reason the size and condition of the club's pool table. A couple of drinks later, Tom invited us all out to Old Angus.

"I've got a full size billiard table in the front room and a regulation trap set up in the backyard. If you care to come out I'll take your pool bet, then shoot you for twenty-five dollars a bird on the trap range."

"Hell of a good idea," Jack agreed.

All five of us went out in Jack's Cadillac.

Tom won the pool game and the two thousand dollars fairly handily. George got Crown Royal, glasses and some ice from the liquor cabinet. The bottle lasted long enough for two rounds of drinks, less than five minutes at the most.

"About this trap-shooting," Tom asked Jack, "have you got your gun here?"

"Just happen to have a single and a double in the trunk of the car," Jack replied.

"I've got lots of trap load and clay birds," Tom volunteered.

"Well, let's get the show on the road then." Jack was anxious to get even. They picked up their guns and four boxes of shells apiece.

Jack was one of the best shots in the province, having won Class 'A' a month earlier. Tom and Ted were aware of this and suggested another drink before the first round.

What they didn't know was that Jack shot better with some drinks under his belt than he did sober. Tom lost fifty dollars on the first twenty-five targets while Ted lost seventy-five dollars. On the second twenty-five, Jack broke them all and collected another one hundred and twenty-five dollars, seventy-five from Tom and fifty from Ted. By the time they had finished the one hundred targets, Jack had won almost five hundred dollars.

It was starting to get dark. They went back to the house and polished off another double rye, then concluded that a poker game was a good way to round out the evening.

While Tom and George set up the poker table in the den, I made a fire in the fireplace. Two new decks of Bicycle playing cards were laid on the poker table, one blue and one red.

George produced another bottle of Crown Royal while Ted, Tom and Jack agreed on the rules of the game and settled the value of the chips. One joker was to be left in and played as the "bug."

"By Hoyle's Rules," Jack explained, "the bug can only be used for aces, straights and flushes."

"That's the way we always play it at our club here in Duncan," Ted agreed.

"What value do you want the chips to be?" Tom asked, as he sipped his drink. Jack suggested that the whites be five dollars, the reds ten dollars and the blues fifty dollars.

"That's setting things pretty high! Somebody could get hurt," I reminded them.

George and I were the more sober of the group. Mack had passed out and was sleeping on a couch in the corner of the room.

"What's the buy-in?" George asked.

"A thousand," Jack suggested.

"Too rich for me!" George announced.

"Come on, Jack," said Tom, "let's have a reasonable game so everyone can play. Let's make it five hundred buy-in and table stakes."

"I still can't play, I haven't got five hundred on me,"
George explained.

"I'll be banker and stake you," Tom offered.

The chips were dished out and paid for, except for
George's. Tom gave him five hundred dollars worth and put
the money in the kitty. Ted wanted three thousand dollars
in chips and Jack asked for five grand. I took two thousand
dollars worth and wrote a cheque to cover.

There was less than a thousand worth of chips left for
Tom. He promptly took out his wallet, laid it on the table
beside his stack and announced, "I'm playing my chips on
the table and ten grand more."

Jack bolted upright in his chair. He looked across at
Mack on the couch. Mackenzie was Jack's bookkeeper.

"Mack, for Christ's sake, wake up and get my cheque
book from the car," he shouted. There was no reply or
movement from Mack, so he yelled again, and still no
response.

"He's out cold," Ted suggested.

"I'll go over and get the bloody book myself. Hold the
game until I get back. It'll only take a couple of minutes."

Jack was back in short order with his cheque book.
George had refilled the empty glasses. Jack picked up his
glass and downed the contents. He then laid his cheque
book by his stack of chips and announced he would call all
bets up to twenty grand.

"Let's get this ruddy game started instead of worrying
about the money so much," Ted urged. Ted was better
fixed than any of us. He had retired a couple of years earlier
as a young millionaire.

It was a pretty heavy game that followed. George won
the first pot with a pair of kings back to back. It was a stud
pot. He dealt the next hand of draw poker. Ted opened for
fifty and Jack raised two hundred. I called and Tom raised
four hundred dollars. George and I both discarded our
hands. Tom won over two thousand dollars with three
sevens. It was Ted's deal, and he dealt stud.

I got the joker face down and the ace of spades up. Jack

248

sat next to Ted and his hand showed a king. I bet ten dollars. Tom raised that to fifty and George dropped out. Ted called, while Jack raised another one hundred. I just called, as did Tom. Jack was feeling no pain by now, and was betting high. Ted dealt Jack a second king, giving him a pair showing. He bet five hundred, as he had the high hand showing on the table. I called, Tom called and Ted folded. Jack's next card was an ace. Mine was a king and Tom was dealt another ace. Jack opened that round of betting with a thousand. I called and raised thirteen hundred. That was all the money I had on the table. Tom called with his pair of tens backed up. Jack called and put his I.O.U. in the pot for another five grand. Tom folded and I won the pot when the fifth card helped neither hand. I took in just over eighty-six hundred dollars.

As the game progressed, it became a battle between Jack and Tom. They were betting so wildly that George and I decided to drop out of the play and just watch. By twelve o'clock, Tom was the big winner, while Jack had lost nearly everything he owned. He had been writing I.O.U's for various pieces of logging equipment. He had lost and won back his Beaver aircraft in a couple of big pots. The aircraft had a table value of twenty thousand dollars. Ted was playing along and winning the occasional pot.

It was nearly one a.m., when two good hands were dealt. Ted dealt this hand of draw poker. Jack picked up the joker and the ace, eight, six, and three of hearts. Needless to say, he bet plenty, five grand. Tom called and drew one card. He was dealt the ace, king, queen and nine of clubs and queen of spades. He threw away the spade and drew the four of clubs. This gave both players an ace high flush. Jack pushed his I.O.U. for the Beaver aircraft in the pot, to start the betting after the draw.

"I've got a Cessna 195 on floats that should equal your Beaver. Is that okay with you, Jack?" Tom queried.

"Near enough," Jack agreed.

Backed by his Cessna, Tom wrote his I.O.U. for twenty thousand dollars, put it in, and announced that he was going to raise the size of the pot. Ted counted the pot as George and I checked his counting on paper. There was just over fifty grand in the center of the table. Tom wrote his I.O.U. for the amount, which included his Stinson airplane on floats, plus one Jervis Inlet logging camp, as is, where is.

"Figure you can afford to lose all that?" Jack asked.

"Call the bet or I'll take the pot," Tom replied.

Jack shouted at Mack again, "Mack, for Christ's sake wake up and get over here to help calculate!"

If Mack was able to hear his boss, he certainly didn't move a muscle or show any signs of life.

Ted laughed as he spoke, "Guess you'll have to do your own bookkeeping for the rest of the night, Jack. It will take more than a loud voice to get Mack awake."

Jack grumbled, but announced he was calling the bet and raising. It was almost half an hour before the two players were agreed on the fifty thousand dollars in cheques and I.O.U.'s Jack was putting into the pot. When the call was placed in the centre of the table, Jack asked Tom if he could raise with the balance of cash and cheques he had in front of him.

"It's okay with me if you want to do it," Tom answered.

Jack counted and pushed his last seven thousand into the pot.

Tom called with a personal cheque made out to cash.

The pot now totalled just over one hundred and sixty-four thousand dollars.

Jack laid his cards face up on the table, announcing, "I have an ace high flush here."

Tom looked the hand over and announced, "I've got you beat Jack, mine is a club flush with ace, king, and queen high. Yours is only ace, king, and eight. My queen beats your eight-spot."

Tom reached out to pull in the pot.

"Just a minute," Jack demanded, "I can call my hand

a double-ace flush. That will beat your ace, king and queen.''

"There is no such thing as a double-ace flush in the book of Hoyle, and that's what we agreed to play by,'' Tom interjected.

"In Nanaimo, we play double-ace flushes and straights,'' was Jack's counter.

"Never heard of such a thing in any poker game I've ever played in,'' Tom argued.

"Leave the pot where it is. I know where there is a book of Hoyle not too far from here,'' George said. "That's the only way to settle this. Come on Joe, drive me over to Frank Ferries' house and we can bring it back.''

We drove to the house only to find a note on the door which read: "Gone to Victoria. Be back by ten o'clock tomorrow. F.F.''

When we got back to Old Angus, Ted, Jack and Tom were seated in front of the fireplace, having another drink and discussing the pros and cons of poker in general.

"Can't get that book until ten o'clock tomorrow. Frank is in Victoria,'' I said.

"Best thing is leave the pot as is until then,'' George suggested.

We all had another drink while we argued against the double-ace flush. None of us had ever played in a game where such a call had been made. Jack kept insisting that in Nanaimo he played in games where such a call was possible. It was about half an hour later when Jack stood up and announced he had to be getting back to Nanaimo for an early meeting next morning.

"Why in hell can't we settle this our own way, Tom? I'll be home before you can get that Hoyle book on rules. After all, it's only a friendly game.''

"What do you suggest?'' Tom asked.

"We could start by burning all those ruddy I.O.U's and cheques.''

"Then what?'' Tom asked.

251

"Well, you could take the cash and I'll take your Stinson aircraft."

Tom thought for a minute or two, then agreed. They shook hands and proceeded to burn all the I.O.U's and cheques that were still on the table. It took a while because the fire had burned down to only a few coals. We had a good-night drink, then carried Mack out to drop him in the back seat of Jack's Caddie. He did not wake up or show any real signs of life, other than breathing.

Jack's parting words were, "I'll pick up the Stinson after lunch tomorrow."

Tom, George, Ted and I were waiting at Frank Ferrie's house when he arrived about 9:30 next morning. He looked surprised as he got out of his car. He greeted us with, "What the hell are you orangutans up to now?"

Ted explained the poker game as briefly as possible.

"You have the latest book of Hoyle's Rules and we want to check the possibility of a double-ace flush, as Jack called his hand," George asked excitedly.

"Hell," Frank exploded, "there's no such goddamned thing as a double-ace flush! Jack's best hand could only be an ace-king flush! If he wanted to call the bug an ace, then he held a pair of aces. You boys have been taken. I've played a lot of big poker in the Yukon and I know what I'm talking about."

"Get the book, I want to see this in black and white," Tom said, with a crooked little smile playing at the corners of his mouth.

"Come on in and I'll get you boys a beer while we look in the book," Frank invited.

"Christ! A beer would sure taste good after last night!"

George spoke for all of us. Frank found the book on his den table. He handed it to Ted, then took five bottles of cold beer from the fridge.

"Best beer I ever tasted. Thanks," Tom said.

I was anxiously looking at Hoyle's book with Ted.

On the front cover, written in bold red letters was,

252

HOYLE'S RULES OF GAMES, and then, in smaller print, "As Webster is to Dictionaries, so Hoyle is to Games."

"Turn to page seventy-five, that's where you'll find out about poker," Frank advised.

Ted and I were busy reading. When we came to the top of page seventy-eight, Ted shouted, "Here it is boys!"

He read the paragraph aloud.

Wild cards: A Joker added to a pack, or any rank or group of cards [usually deuces], may be designated in advance to be 'wild'. The holder of a wild card may cause it to stand for any other card he wishes. Except by special house rules: [a] a wild card ranks the same as the natural card it replaces; and [b] a wild card cannot stand for a card the player already holds, so that there cannot be, for example, a 'double-Ace-high' flush. The bug as the Joker is given restricted wild-card use: It may represent an Ace and it may be used to fill a straight flush, flush or straight. Therefore, two Aces and the 'bug' are three Aces, but two Kings and the 'bug' are merely a pair of Kings with an Ace.*

"Now," Ted explained, as he read the passage over for the third time. "It proves we were right and Jack was wrong, according to this here book of Hoyle."

"It can't be any plainer than the way it's written," Frank said. "Read it once more Ted."

" 'A wild card CANNOT stand for a card the player already holds, so that there cannot be, for example, a double-ace high flush'."

"You should have claimed that pot, Tom! Yours was the best hand! You won it according to Hoyle."

Ted was very serious now.

"What about the Stinson you told Jack to pick up this afternoon? He'll be here in a couple of hours," I reminded Tom.

---

* HOYLE'S RULES OF GAMES, Albert H. Morehead and Geoffrey Mott-Smith eds., (New York: Signet, New American Library, 1959).

"Damned if I know," replied Tom, showing signs of the strain of last night's party.

"You made a deal and shook hands on it. All the cheques and I.O.U's were burned. That was about three o'clock this morning."

"Yeah, I remember," Tom said.

There was a long silence. It was up to Tom to decide. He finished his beer, then stood by the table looking at all of us.

"Hell, fellows, I gave my word," he said, with a broad smile. "We shook on it, so Jack takes that aircraft to Nanaimo with him as agreed. The damned thing never did perform too well since we put it on floats. Peace of mind is worth a hell of a lot more than any bloody aircraft."

When Jack arrived at Quamichan Lake to fly the plane home, Tom produced Hoyle's book and asked him to read about poker.

"Don't have to read the rules. I know how to play," was Jack's reply.

This made all of us mad. As Jack walked to get into the pilot's seat, Ted grabbed him by the arm. He was really upset at what was happening.

"Jack," he hissed, "there is one hell of a lot you have to learn yet. Mostly about people, but everything about poker."

"Yeah, maybe," Jack shrugged.

He climbed in and took off down the lake towards Nanaimo.

"Well, that's that," Tom exclaimed. He looked a bit sad as he watched his plane and friend disappearing in the distance.

It cost Tom a pretty penny to keep his agreement after learning the facts about both poker hands. His reward was peace of mind and some real friends who stayed loyal to him for the rest of his life.

To the best of my knowledge, none of our group ever gambled with Jack again. If he insisted on getting in on a game where we were playing, we would just cash in and leave the table.

I am the sole survivor of those who played in that unusual poker game. George Syrotuck took a violent heart attack while fishing with his wife at Cowichan Bay. He had a
twenty-pound spring salmon on his line when he died. Jack
passed away in Nanaimo in 1978.

Ted died of a heart attack in 1979. He was on a friend's
boat heading up to Rivers Inlet to catch some of the big
springs that run up in the fall.

Tom went to his "Happy Hunting Grounds" when his
plane crashed in Desolation Sound in 1958. The headline
from the *Cowichan Leader* read: TOM GARNER DIES IN
PLANE CRASH, September 6, 1958. He was in his 52nd
year.

Partners

Some thirty years after Tom and I made our "partners for life" agreement, we were on a fishing trip to Spruce Lake. This small lake lies high on the east side of the Coast Range, some miles to the north of the Fraser River.

Our new Cessna 180, on floats, was tied tail to the beach, about twenty feet away. I dished up fried trout for each of us while Tom poured hot tea from a billy can. After lunch we sat relaxing in the sun.

"You figure we got enough made to retire on?" Tom asked me, with a broad smile, and in such a quiet voice that unless I had been really listening, I could have missed the question.

I was silent for several minutes, my mind reaching back into the past.

"The way I see it, we have more than we set out to get," was my reply. "It's just over thirty years ago that we made our deal as partners. This is the first time we have mentioned retirement."

"Well, I've got all I will ever want. If you feel the same

256

way, we will split it all down the middle and then do some steady fishing and hunting," Tom suggested.

"Sounds good to me. I've got that apartment block with the hardware store underneath. That's what we set out to get. Been going short on fishing the last few years. Damned business is so big and spread out, it takes all my time just tending to it."

"Okay Joe, you get the lawyers and accountant together and we'll split it all down the middle next Tuesday morning. Let's start at nine so we can have lunch after."

The takeoff from Spruce Lake was smooth and routine. We had just cleared the treetops at the south end when the engine coughed, sputtered and almost stopped. Tom snapped on the carburetor heat. Some minutes later we were cruising normally on our way home. Tom looked over at me and remarked, "If that old motor hadn't caught and revved up back there, we would have settled all our affairs without any help from lawyers and bookkeepers."

"You could be right on that," I laughed. "Pass over the controls and I'll spell you on the flying for a while."

After tying the plane at the south end of Quamichan Lake, we went into Duncan and briefly discussed our proposal for dividing everything.

"It's a big break in our lives, but there do not seem to be any major problems or decisions to be made," was Tom's comment, as we separated to go home, each with a dozen nice trout.

We met in the main office at nine a.m. sharp. We advised the lawyers and accountants that all minor details would be worked out later and unless our wishes created major legal or tax problems, to let it go as we agreed between ourselves. By 11:30 that morning we had divided almost $2,000,000 worth of land, buildings, heavy logging and construction equipment, several boats, two hunting and fishing resorts and three aircraft.

Everything was calculated at book value. As the list of assets was read from the last income tax return, we agreed on ownership by a wave of the hand. When values were summed up near the end, Tom was about $70,000 ahead.

"You sure those figures are correct?" Tom asked.

"Well, they are pretty close," the accountants assured us.

"What's left to divide now?" I asked.

"As I see it, there are the two new bulldozers, the apartment block and the hardware business to deal with," we were advised.

"What's the book value?" Tom asked.

"The bulldozers are $50,000. The hardware business with building is around $200,000," was the answer.

Tom's solution was short and simple.

"Joe has been doing most of the work concerning the block and hardware business, so if I take the bulldozers and he takes the rest, it will be fair and settled as far as I'm concerned. I've been wondering how to square things for being away so much lately."

Tom stood up, looking at me with a smile, and stuck out his hand. "Okay with you, partner?"

"It's more than fair, but if that's how you see it, it's okay with me," I agreed, shaking hands. "Now let's all go and have a good lunch. It's on me today."

"Let's have a drink first," was Tom's suggestion, as he produced a bottle of Crown Royal in the familiar purple bag.

As we sipped a second drink, the accountant looked at Tom and asked, "Do you realize that your last decision cost you over fifty grand?"

"Things are settled as Joe and I see it and that's all there is to it. Let's go to lunch without any more talk." Tom turned and was on his way out the door.

After the business was split and everything was properly registered, Tom and I did a lot of hunting and fishing for the next few years and enjoyed every minute of it.

Epilogue

Lona Beatrice Garner (nee Edwards), born in North Carolina, August 13, 1884, married in Spartanburg, South Carolina in 1903, spent the best years of her life on Saltspring Island, British Columbia.

Mother left her husband, Oland, in 1926 to live in and around Vancouver, B.C. There she bought and sold several homes, making a fair profit on each. In her later years one or more of her daughters lived near or with her. This eased her loneliness.

Mother started to become forgetful during the nineteen fifties. Latterly, she went to live in an apartment with Ethel in South Vancouver. Some days were good, some bad. On bad days she would inform Ethel that she was to lunch with President Roosevelt, Mr. Diefenbaker or some other dignitary who would come to mind. She would get all dressed up for the occasion, slip out and go downtown, then forget where she lived. This usually resulted in a frantic search in which the police sometimes helped. She called herself either Mrs. Garner or Lona Beatrice Edwards, whichever she felt like on that particular day. Mother was usually found at one of the several houses which she had previously owned.

The Garner sons arranged that sufficient money was available for their mother's comfort. She received nothing from her estranged husband during the thirty-five years of their separation. Although there was no apparent animosity between my parents, there was never a reconciliation. At family gatherings, if one of them accidentally arrived uninvited, there would be an almost instant departure by the other, even in the middle of a meal.

When Mother's health had deteriorated to a point that demanded constant professional care, Ethel called a meeting of the family. Reluctantly, we decided to find a suitable nursing home for her. She could not adapt to these strange surroundings. In spite of professional care and daily visits by her children, she failed rapidly.

Mother died quietly November 4, 1961, at age seventy-seven. She was laid to rest in Rose Lawn Cemetery next to her eldest son, Tom. Many old-timers from Saltspring attended the funeral, including the Seymours.

*   *   *

Olander Joseph Garner was born in South Carolina, June 3, 1879. He lived in and around the towns of Whitney and Spartanburg until 1903. This was the year of a great flood that completely changed his life. During the period of unrest following this disaster, he got into a shooting fracas with a member of the Ku Klux Klan, forced Mother, at gunpoint, to marry him, then fled to Canada for safety. For many years, Dad slept with a loaded six-gun under his pillow and a rifle, ready for business, over both back and front doors.

Most of Dad's time was spent on Saltspring Island until the late 1930's. He then moved to Vancouver, built a house and lived as a bachelor until 1962. He also kept a place on Saltspring where he spent considerable time. Throughout the 1950's, Dad apparently enjoyed himself golfing by day and going to dances at night. Twice weekly he called square dances for the old-timers, played banjo in the orchestra, and enjoyed an occasional waltz. He also found time for a couple of modern dances each week. His lady friends were many and varied.

Dad and Edie had become quite friendly during the early '60's. Because of failing health, the last months of his life were spent with this daughter at 3835 Main Street. Here he was nursed and properly cared for. Although he had lived his life as a staunch Catholic, Dad nevertheless changed to a Christian Apostolic Church in the neighbourhood.

As old age gradually won its battle, the family came to visit. Dorothy, the youngest, tells me that she spent enough time at the bedside for him to let her know that he wanted her forgiveness for his neglect. They both said things that cleared any animosity that might have existed between them.

On my last visit, Dad looked much smaller and more wrinkled than I had remembered him, yet his mind was alert and his eyes still had that piercing sharpness. As I entered the room, he greeted me with a faint smile and his usual, "Sure good to see you, son."

"Hear you are not feeling well. What seems to be the problem?" I asked, taking his extended hand.

Dad was propped to an almost sitting position by some large pillows. He touched his chin with a forefinger. There was a slight swelling. "Guess I've got a bit of your old tooth trouble. Sure makes a feller feel poorly." There was a pause. "You remember when we travelled to Victoria and Doctor Hall gave you laughing gas so he could pull that abscessed tooth of yours?"

"Sure do," was my reply, "I can even remember the train ride from Sidney to Victoria. I had just turned nine that spring."

"You were so sick from that gas we had to stay over in Victoria. We stayed at a house I had helped to build when you were a little boy. Can you remember the lady caring for you all that night?"

261

"I remember being scared into a panic. She had a monkey that jumped onto the bed and made weird noises."

"You were so scared the lady had to put the monkey in a box," Dad recalled.

"I remember being sick in a basin while she held my head and consoled me."

Dad smiled, closed his eyes and appeared to go into a fitful sleep. He awoke with a start, and surprised me with this question, "Son, what do you consider the most important thing in this life we are living?"

I thought before answering, "Well, I suppose health comes first, then respect and a possible third could be success."

"No, no," was his reply, "The only thing that really matters in this life is love. Mark my words. You will find this out as you grow older." He went on to ask me to help Edie carry out the affairs and requests as set out in his will. I agreed. He seemed satisfied and soon fell sound asleep. I left with a distinct feeling that he was reliving his past with clarity and some pleasure. This was our last chat.

Dad was buried beside Mother in the family plot at Rose Lawn Cemetery, February 9, 1963 at age 84. Again, many old-timers from Saltspring, Victoria and Vancouver were at the graveside.

* * *

Ethel, the eldest Garner child, was born July 12, 1905 in Victoria, B.C. and died September 20, 1964 in the Lionsgate Hospital, North Vancouver, B.C.

Ethel became a Saltspring Islander before she was a year old, growing up in the various cabins and shelters that Dad saw fit to move into. When she was twelve years old, she fractured her leg and was confined to bed for several months. Eventually she coaxed Mother to let her up to go outdoors. After hobbling about for a couple of weeks, she admitted to me that her injured leg had festered. "Joe," she appealed, "Mother doesn't know or she won't let me out, but I've got a swelling like a boil above my knee. It feels like there's a big sliver in there. Will you try to take it out with these sharp tweezers?" I probed .into the sore and pulled out two slivers of bone, one about one-half inch long and the other more than a full inch! The sore soon healed.

Five years later Ethel started nurses' training at St. Joseph's Hospital in Victoria. During her second year the same leg gave more trouble, confining her to a hospital bed for almost a year. The following is a letter to Tom which speaks for itself. He was then working on a ranch in Saskatchewan.

St. Joseph's Hospital
Victoria, B.C.
Oct. 3, 1927

Dearest Tommy:

Well how are you getting on — working hard I'll bet. We have noticed by the papers that they have quite a number of cases of Infantile paralysis out in Sask. Are there any near you?

Today is the 8th. I've been all this time writing this letter.

I had a letter from Mom the other day. She said Joe had gone back to Ganges to work. Hope he gets a good job. Do wish Maggie (Margaret) could get a good position so she could go to night school.

Last time you wrote you said to ask you for any money I needed 'if it wasn't too much', so I'm taking advantage of it. But I'm awfully afraid it is too much. You will probably think I have an awful lot of nerve but I don't know who else I can ask for what I want. I want a coat. My old one is just dreadful. It is so big for me now because I have got so thin I can almost wrap it about me twice. There are some real nice ones at Simpsons for $12 to $13. Mine is so old too. I have had it for over three years now. I don't know what you will think of me asking you for so much, but if you can't help me, do wish you would suggest something for me to do. My Goodness, it's the bunk not being able to do anything for yourself. Will be so glad when I can work again — which I hope won't be long now.

Dudley (Seymour) is out of the hospital now. He has gone to Vancouver to see a bone specialist because his leg didn't knit properly.

263

Enid Wakelin came to see us about two weeks ago. She had been up on S.S.I. for a holiday. It amused me so much when I heard her say that they had a story going around up there that I was going to have my leg off. Just imagine! Isn't that like the Island? She thought Dad was getting some artist lady from Victoria for the big house. Did you know that?

Just think — if I had gone on training I would be finished in December. My Goodness, when I came here I never thought that this is the way I would be at the end of three years!

It is raining here this P.M. Just wonder what kind of a day it is where you are. Will you come to see me when you come back? It seems years since I saw any of the family.

Well, Bye bye for now. Tons of love

Your sister Ethel

At Christmas that same year, Ethel came home to stay. Mother nursed her back to health and the very next spring she found work in a garment factory. That year she met and married Isaac Anderson. They had two daughters, Leora and Dorothy, presently living in Vancouver.

When her girls were in high school, (Isaac having passed on) Ethel worked for Tom at the Chilko Lake Lodge. There are many hunters and fishermen who will still remember the tasty meals served during those years. It was here that she had a stroke and collapsed in the yard. Under almost impossible weather conditions Tom flew her out to the Vancouver Hospital. She rallied again and was well enough to move to Victoria where she kept house for me. Here the physical demands were light and her daughters could come to visit.

She enjoyed the next few years until an undiagnosed bone disease forced her back to hospital during the summer of 1963. She kept on fighting until her youngest daughter brought her first grandson to the hospital. After that Ethel seemed to give up the battle for life and passed away quietly in September, 1964. A wonderful person always. Those who knew her were richer for it.

* * *

Edith was born on Saltspring Island February 29, 1916. She completed grade eight in Vancouver at age 13. Next year the Depression hit the family with a vengeance and Edie worked in a clothing factory to supplement the meagre family income. The following year Mother insisted she go back to school and finish grade nine.

Soon after this, Edie met and married Paul Adank, and raised two sons, David and John. She then had a fling at politics. W. A. C. Bennett asked her to be the Social Credit candidate for Little Mountain District in 1972. This was a federal election which she lost. Still active in politics and church affairs, Edie is a "going concern" and still lives in Vancouver.

*   *   *

Dorothy was born on Saltspring Island May 16, 1926. While still in diapers, she was carried to Vancouver. Being the baby of the family of ten, she was sometimes considered a bit spoiled. After having finished high school, she worked for awhile, then met and married Don Taylor. Of their four children, three were boys, Randy, Martin, and Dana. Noel, the only daughter, was second oldest.

While serving with the Royal Canadian Navy, Don had a terrible experience with polio. He was almost totally paralyzed for a time and remained seriously handicapped for many years.

It was evident that Mother was more successful in motivating her youngest daughter to obtain a higher education than she had been with any of the rest of us. While Dorothy's children were still young teenagers, she enrolled in a program at U.B.C. that soon gave her a Bachelor's degree. It was necessary for her to take in boarders to help pay tuition fees and meet the day to day expenses of running the home.

My daughter Dana boarded there while attending art classes. She tells of an incident that impressed her greatly. There was a young man named Gary Lauk boarding there while studying at U.B.C. It was spring and very warm. One evening Gary came to the table wearing nothing above the waist. This drew an instant reprimand from Dorothy, "Surely you could dress a bit more appropriately for dinner than you are. It is bad manners and sets a poor example for my children!" she exploded. Gary looked at each of the young family, got up from his chair, and practically ran up the stairs to his room. He was back in minutes and sat down again without a word. He had added a tie but nothing more. There were giggles from the younger ones. Dorothy just glared and commanded, "Everyone of you just eat quietly or go to your rooms without another bite." Dana tells me that the atmosphere in the dining room was so thick it could have been cut with a knife during the rest of that meal.

This same young man entered the political arena of B.C. a few years later, was elected and subsequently appointed to a Cabinet Post in the N.D.P.* government. Gary presently holds a seat in the opposition as M.L.A. representing Vancouver Centre.

Don and Dorothy 'agreed to disagree' soon after her graduation.

Subsequently our young sister moved to Los Angeles, Calif. Here she worked for the Department of Education and continued her studies. There, as a young grandmother, she received her doctorate in clinical psychology. Without a doubt, Mother would have been the proudest of our family had she been alive to see her baby so honoured.

---

* New Democratic Party, reported to lean heavily to the left, was born during the 1930's as the C.C.F. (Co-operative Commonwealth Federation). Dr. Lyle Telford, a close friend of Mother's and our family doctor for a time, was one of the party's founders. The New Democratic Party was a change of name in 1961.

Index

268

270

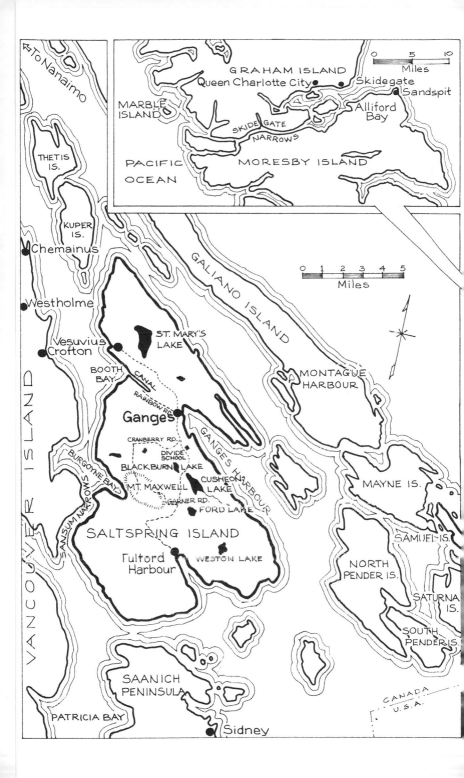

YUKON

NORTHWEST
TERRITORIES

0 50 100 150 200
Miles

ALASKA

• Dahl Lake

Sifton)(Fox Lake
Pass

FINLAY RIVER

Finlay Forks

PEACE RIVER

• Prince Rupert

QUEEN
CHARLOTTE
ISLANDS

BRITISH
COLUMBIA

• Alta Lake

• Prince George

• Itcha Lake

FRASER RIVER

ALBERTA

• Bella Coola

BLACKWATER
COUNTRY

• Quesnel

PACIFIC
OCEAN

Tatlayoka • Lake

Chilco (Lake

• Williams Lake

Knight Inlet

Bute Inlet

• 100 Mile House

Spruce Lake

Redonda Is.

Campbell River

Courtenay •

VANCOUVER
ISLAND

Nanaimo •

Vancouver

Langley

Victoria

• Cultus Lake

• Seattle

Calgary •

CANADA
U.S.A.

WASHINGTON

IDAHO MONTANA

R. ENGLISH